Frank A. Vanderlip

The Banker Who Changed America

By
Vicki A. Mack

P I N A L E P R E S S

P.O. Box 293
Palos Verdes Estates, CA 90274

www.vickimack.com

ISBN - 10: 1492704903
ISBN - 13: 978-1492704904

Cover design by Vicki Mack
Front cover photograph Courtesy Los Angeles Public Library
Back cover photograph Courtesy Aurora Historical Society

o o o

Table Of Contents

◯   ◯   ◯

Introduction

Even though I never met Frank Vanderlip, I lived with him for thirty-five years.

For a lot of that time, I knew him as the founder of the area of Palos Verdes, California where I lived in his old house. After my stepfather John Vanderlip's passing in 2001, when I started going through his files, I learned his father had a much larger place in history.

When Frank Vanderlip was active, there were a number of powerful men known as Titans, including J. P. Morgan, the Vanderbilts and the Rockefellers. In many ways, Frank Vanderlip was one of them. In other ways, he was a very different sort of person.

It was easy for a man like Frank Vanderlip, who started out in farmer's overalls, to be overlooked by historians. His affect on the history of this country, however, cannot be understated.

Among other things, Frank Vanderlip was president of the largest bank in the country, one of the designers of the Federal Reserve system, Assistant Secretary of the Treasury, and an accomplished writer and speaker. His son John, modest and humble man that he was, never bothered to go into much detail to me of his father's past.

Frank Vanderlip had six children, three boys and three girls. His youngest son, John, married my mother in 1972, when I was seventeen. In 1977, we all moved into Frank Vanderlip's California home in Palos Verdes, known as the Cottage.

John was excited about his purchase of the home where he spent childhood summers. When we first walked in, he was dismayed by how years with no one living there had taken a toll. He was amazed to see that, under the dust and cobwebs, it was almost exactly like his father left it. And, he was excited about bringing it back to life, as he remembered it.

Soon, John and my mother started entertaining, very much as his parents did in the house forty and fifty years before. We were all dining around the same long, narrow, antique table, sitting on the same old, wooden chairs, using some of the same china.

In the living room, hundreds of Frank Vanderlip's beloved books were still on the shelves, organized by topic. A portrait of him hung over the fireplace. I loved to point out to guests that his eyes would seem to follow them as they moved about the room. This separated the normal visitors from the paranoid.

Three of the living room walls held oil paintings of the countryside around Frank Vanderlip's New York home. His wife, Narcissa, had decorated the Cottage with an eclectic collection of furniture that all together made an inviting space. By the time we were finished refurbishing, if Frank Vanderlip had walked in the front door, he would have felt right at home.

It is now one hundred years since Frank Vanderlip purchased Palos Verdes. It occurred to me that his complete story has never been told, and I thought it was time for him to be recognized as a historically important person. After writing my book, *Up Around The Bend*, about the Portuguese Bend area of Palos Verdes, with co-author Vicki Mack, I turned to her. Neither of us realized what a big project it would be, and how much there was to tell.

This book is the result.

> Don Christy
> August 28, 2013
> Villa Narcissa
> Portuguese Bend,
>   California

○ ○ ○

Foreward

Frank Arthur Vanderlip was forty-nine years old when he rode to the top of the peninsula then known as Rancho de los Palos Verdes, California in a big Packard in 1914 for his first look at his new purchase.

President of the country's largest bank, National City Bank of New York, Frank was a distinguished man with carefully barbered graying hair and mustache, and wire rimmed glasses. He was usually attired in well-tailored suits and neatly adjusted ties. But it had not always been so.

He was born into a farming life, knew the childhood trauma of his father's death, watched as the family's farm was repossessed and their belongings auctioned off, and worked in a factory as a teenager to support his mother and sister.

The story of how he transformed himself into a leading financier of his time and a visionary with the plan to make Palos Verdes such a unique area is not only his story, but one of the development of America.

His view from the top of the hill, of his 16,004 acre acquisition, was magnificent. In his own words, taken from his 1935 autobiography, "From Farmboy to Financier," Frank says, "*I came to a mental halt: although I had become used to handling large projects I was overwhelmed by this possession.*

"*The road over which I drove as I filled my eyes with a first sight of Palos Verdes Ranch was the corridor of one of the most exciting experiences of my life. Before me lay a range of folded hills, miles and miles of tawny slopes patched with green, thrusting themselves abruptly from the Pacific. Above me were broad natural terraces with here and there a little farm, backed by a range of taller hills. Wherever the road passed over a hillcrest I could see the shore-line of the ranch as a series of bold headlands spaced off by gleaming crescent beaches. I found myself reminded vividly of the Sorrentine Peninsula and the Amalfi Drive: Yet the most exciting part of my vision was that this gorgeous scene was not a piece of Italy at all but was here in America, an unspoiled sheet of paper to be written on with loving care."*

What started out in his mind as an investment turned into a labor of love for the rest of his life.

Writing this book has been somewhat the same. At times, it seemed to be like the universe, continuing to expand in all directions. Beginning during the Civil War, the story stretches almost to World War II, as his life and the history of this country each affect the other. Whenever new sources of information came forward, there were new stories and photographs too interesting to leave out.

I began with the idea of looking for what made Frank Vanderlip the man he was when he first stood on the top of a Palos Verdes hill and decided to form this special community in which I am lucky enough to live. I came to realize that, 150 years after some of the choices and events in his life, there is much we can learn from them about our modern world and, more importantly, about ourselves.

————————————

At various times, Frank Vanderlip was a farmer, a reporter, a government official, a banker, a land developer, an educator, and, most famously, one of the founders of the Federal Reserve system. Each of these callings was formed by, and then influenced, the others, in the way any life is a series of interlocking circles rather than a straight line.

There were a series of people, both famous and unknown, who thought enough of him to give him the help he needed to move to the next level of success. Why each chose to do so says a lot about the man.

Frank Vanderlip was a man of great energy. He admits he used it for serious purposes, commenting rather wistfully that he never learned to "play." He believed that was the reason hardly anyone ever called him "Frank." Most of his associates, and even good friends, used "Vanderlip," or affectionately, "Mr. Van."

The world of the 21st century is much less formal. Some of the country's biggest CEOs wear jeans to press conferences, and are addressed by their first names by both employees and strangers.

In the spirit of the present time, and after being surrounded for the past eight months by all things "Frank," I have chosen to refer to him throughout this book by his first name. My hope is that the reader will become so familiar with this fascinating man that "Frank" will become a friend with whom it would be pleasant to share a Ramos Fizz and good conversation during a warm day on his Beechwood lawn or his Palos Verdes terrace.

Everyone else will be referred to by both their first and last names, with one exception. James J. Stillman, president of National City Bank of New York, was the figure who looms above all else in Frank's life. I do not believe Frank ever called him anything but Mr. Stillman. Possibly no one did. The tradition will remain unbroken in this book.

Frank was blessed with an extraordinary wife, Narcissa Cox Vanderlip. She matched his energy and intelligence, and certainly deserves a full biography of her own. On their 1920 trip to Japan, when Frank forgot to mention the women members of their group in his final speech, Narcissa followed with a talk of her own, *"in a way that properly put me in my place."* I apologize to Narcissa for being forced to leave her in the background.

The original basis for this book was Frank's autobiography, "From Farmboy To Financier," published in 1935. In it, his own voice, intelligence, and dry wit come through clearly. Unfortunately, he was not as clear on exact dates, or even timelines. He sometimes condensed several actions to make a better tale, or assumed the reader was familiar with then-current events that are now over one hundred years old.

A prolific writer, speaker, and promoter of publicity, Frank left many other original sources. Throughout this book, any quotations in italics are his own words. Often, no one could give a better description than he has already done.

Frank inspired great loyalty and friendship in a number of people, to whom he returned the same. One of them was his "right-hand man" in Palos Verdes, Harry Benedict. Much information for this book came from his patient and helpful son Stephen Benedict, to whom I am deeply indebted for original photographs and documents, including diaries of both the European and Japanese trips and his father's unpublished autobiography.

I am grateful to Frank's California based grandchildren, Narcissa and Kelvin, along with Kelvin's wife Michele, and Narcissa's husband Parmer Fuller, for their friendship, interest, input, and support. My hope is that they will enjoy this communication with the grandfather they were born too late to ever meet.

Another tremendous help with original material he has collected in Palos Verdes was a big man with a big heart, Mike Cooper, whose continual enthusiasm was contagious.

A wise person once told me never to apologize for something I did not do, that was beyond my control to fix. As a photographer, I do, however, feel compelled to offer a word about the hundreds of photographs included. Some are probably being seen by the general public for the first time. Each was included for whatever special ingredient it could add. A number of the originals, pulled from bottom drawers, old boxes, or stored archives, were not in good shape. In several cases, the originals, now missing, had luckily been scanned, but not in very high resolution. So, my apology to the reader for the uneven quality that may appear.

———

Archivists and librarians should be some of the world's most honored individuals. They spend years collecting and protecting assorted bits of information, waiting patiently for the day something they have guarded will be the lost key to unlock one of history's mysteries. A number of them in various parts of the country added much to this work. All of them cheerfully listened to my requests, energetically searched through their materials, and produced gems of information and photographs that bring this story to life.

It is a rather long list, but I would like to thank each of them, individually, in no particular order:

Monique and Haru Sugimoto, Palos Verdes Library; Christina Rice and Terri Garst, Los Angeles Public Library; Jaimie Murray and Meredith Pyle, Brazoria County History Museum, Texas; Susan Wilcox, Palos Verdes Peninsula Land Conservancy; Kent Kenney, Atascadero Archives, California; Diana McIntyre, Palos Verdes Interpretive Center; Dr. Francine Bradley, emeritus, University of California at Davis; Mitchell Hearns Bishop, Los Angeles County Arboretum; Yvonne Ng, Arcadia, California Public Library; Mike Gilroy, Palos Verdes; Lee Pierce, Washington State Archives; Hannah Cooney, Coos Bay Historical and Maritime Museum, Washington; Sandy Snider, California; Greg Probst, Freeport-McMoRan Copper and Gold, Inc., New Orleans, Louisiana; Marjean Blinn, Palos Verdes Library; Holly Starr, Palos Verdes Interpretive Center.

Mike Fightel and Jennifer Putzier, Aurora Illinois Historical Society, Illinois; Roger Matile, Little White School Museum, Oswego, Illinois; Linda Stahnke Stepp and Rory Grennan, University of Illinois at Urbana-Champaign Archives; Nicholas Clemens, Niagara Historical Society and Museum, Niagara-on-the-lake, Ontario, Canada; Anita Mechler, Union League Club of Chicago, Illinois; Gretchen Greminger, Jekyll Island Museum, Jekyll Island, Georgia; David Fisher, Jekyll Island, Georgia; Skip Marketti, The Nethercutt Collection, San Fernando Valley, California; Thomas P. O'Malley, Washington, D. C.; Sidney F. Huttner and Kathryn J. Hodson, University of Iowa Special Collections and Archives; Jim Detlefsen, Hoover Presidential Library, Iowa; Neil Harvey, Nevsky-Prospekt.com; Daniel Hartwig, Stanford University Special Collections and Archives, California; Cynthia Sternan, Japan Society, New York; Kathy Connor and Shannon Jowett, George Eastman House Museum, Rochester, New York; Megan McCrea, Sunset Publishing Corp.; Joyce Dopkeen, Doug and Rochelle Turshen, Florence Brennerman, and Steve Turner, Sparta, New York; Patrick Raftery, Westchester County Historical Society, New York; Brad Emerson, Downeast Dilettante; Randy Ryan Bigham, Texas; Nilda Rivera and Lindsay Turley, Museum of the City of New York; Kerri Anne Burke and Patricia Fann Bouteneff, Citibank, New York.

Palos Verdes residents are grateful to Frank for the community, and I am grateful to the following residents for sharing information, photographs, and access to photograph their historic homes: Lee Jester, Dan and Vicki Pinkham, Steve Shriver, Maureen and Bruce Megowan, Lisa Wolf, Suzanne Crouzier, and Mike Gilroy.

A special thank you also to three researchers who never gave up the hunt, no matter how obscure the target they were given - Pam Cress, Colorado; Maurine McLellan, Kansas; and Therese Anlauf, Palos Verdes. Thank you to Stefanie Rowland for her patient technical help.

———————

There would be no book if it were not for my friend, project instigator, chief motivator, and supplier of lunch, the author and historian Don Christy. It was his vision that propelled me to become acquainted with Frank, and to write his story. Many of the Palos Verdes contacts are through his large circle of wonderful friends. Any mistakes I have made in telling the facts are totally mine, not his.

———————

Don Christy "lived" with Frank for thirty-five years. I have done the same for the past eight months. So has my own David, David O. Kase. He deserves an extra portion of love for letting me fill an hour every evening with discussions on "Frank's" progress, and for contributing his encyclopedic knowledge of historical facts.

———————

I am not an economist, or an expert on banking. There are many writers more qualified to go into these subjects. I will not try to go into the complicated theories Frank loved of how money flows. My goal is to explain Frank's world and explore parts of it many of us have never known, as well as aspects of history many of us have never considered. I am not writing to take sides on the effectiveness, details, or morality of the Federal Reserve or other issues. I am trying to show the facts as Frank saw them at the time he took various actions. It is impossible for a biographer to totally eliminate conjecture or to avoid the use of the words "possibly" or "might have." Hopefully, I have managed to keep these to a minimum.

Frank Vanderlip valued first hand information. As a reporter, he searched for it diligently in company reports. As president of the bank, on his desk each morning, there was a stack of file cards with details on every important transaction and every other bank's business. On his fact-finding trips to Europe, he directly interviewed bankers, kings, farmers, and factory workers.

I have tried to do the same, using as many first hand sources as possible for the events of his life, and checking facts and dates as thoroughly as possible. I can only hope he would have forgiven any mistakes, and would have approved of this story.

Vicki Mack
September 2, 2013
Palos Verdes Estates,
California

○ ○ ○

From Farm To Factory

Birthplace of Frank A. Vanderlip, Aurora, Illinois photo circa 1910

○ ○ ○

From Farm To Factory

A sixteen year old boy stood in his front yard, dressed in farmer's overalls, and watched as auctioneer Dave Hall sold off his family's belongings. It was a sadly usual sight in rural Illinois at the time, but Frank A. Vanderlip was not a usual boy. Memories of that day would have a lasting impact on his entire life, and on the future of the entire country.

General Sherman was marching his troops through Georgia toward the Civil War burning of Atlanta when Charlotte Woodworth Vanderlip traveled to her parents' home on South Lake Street in Aurora, Illinois, about forty miles west of Chicago, to give birth to her son. Frank Arthur Vanderlip was born there on November 17, 1864.

Charlotte, a pretty girl of eighteen, was the wife of Charles Edmond Vanderlip, who was thirteen years older. Her family was made up of industrious people. Her grandfather owned a powder factory, her father a wagon factory, cousins owned a machine shop.

She raised her children, Frank and his sister Ruth, and younger son, Wynn, who died at a young age, with enough love that Frank had a happy childhood. He was close to his mother throughout her life.

Charlotte and Charles Vanderlip circa 1864

Charles, whose health was poor enough to be rejected from service in the Union Army, learned the blacksmith trade. He became superintendent of Charlotte's family's wagon works in Aurora, Illinois, and then purchased a farm in nearby Oswego when Frank was little.

Charles was more educated than many men of his day who ran small farms. He read *Harper's Weekly*, owned a set of Shakespeare's works, and helped his son learn algebra. Charles wore a long, dark beard typical of the times, and was handy at constructing anything from farm buildings to a two-seat sleigh. He had, Frank said, *"a great deal of that capacity for forming sound rules of conduct which we call common sense."*

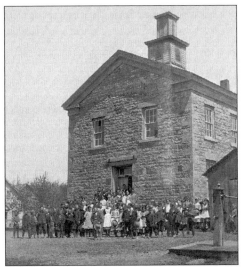

Frank Vanderlip's schoolhouse circa 1880
Water pump and outhouse on right
Oswego, Illinois

Frank inherited his father's work ethic and belief in duty, coupled with his father's own particular brand of common sense. While Charlotte would instruct Frank to select, from their food cellar, the apples with some brown spots so they would not rot further and contaminate the others, Charles told his young son, "If you do that, you will be eating bad apples the rest of your life. Pick out the best ones."

This advice stayed with Frank for life. He ignored the bad apples, and aimed for learned and influential friends, meaningful jobs, and substance over flash.

Life can be good for a young boy on a farm, far removed from the worries of post Civil War Reconstruction and its politics. There were cows to milk, a wonderful pony to ride, imaginary enemies to slay in a corn field with the remnants of an old sword and, for Frank, a constant supply of books to read. While he kept an eye on the livestock, he read constantly, tucking a serious book or a Jules Verne novel in the bib of his overalls until the cows were settled and he could pull it out and read in the saddle.

Even on the happiest of farms, death is part of the process. Hogs were butchered in the fall, for meat to sell and to feed the family through the winter. Frank knew it was necessary, but would, "*absent myself to avoid the sight, the scent of blood and the wretched cries of the animals I had known.*" Much later in life, Frank's sensitivity would reappear in Palos Verdes as a great love for birds of all types.

He was, however, a realist. Charles gave Frank his own calf to raise, and Frank took careful care of it until it was ready to be sold. His opinion of calves in general shows a sort of love-hate relationship. He spoke of their, "*perversity if you have a rope around their necks, and their seeming friendliness and even stupidity when they look you straight in the face, and then snort a quart of warm milk into your eyes and down the front of your Sunday clothes. There is a good deal of humanity in a calf, or a good deal of calf in humanity.*" He was quite proud of what he earned, twelve whole dollars. Later, he marveled at what he did with that money.

Instead of the air rifle most boys his age would have coveted, to use hunting gophers and small birds, Frank invested in a six year subscription to the New York *Weekly Tribune*. Included was a copy of Webster's "Unabridged Dictionary", a book he kept his entire life. He would explore the dictionary at random and commented, much later, "*I know I got my calf's worth.*"

Frank's grandfather Harmon Vanderlip's farm, near Madison, Ohio circa 1880
This is similar to the Oswego, Illinois farm where Frank grew up.

Frank never longed to join the western migration of covered wagons that passed by his farm, often with a cow trailing behind. But, when he was twelve, he decided to have his own adventure, and go off to see the first of many presidents he would encounter during his life. He ran away for the day, all by himself, to the nearby city of Aurora to see the recently retired president, Ulysses S. Grant.

Abraham Lincoln funeral car 1865
Used by U. S. Grant in Aurora, Ill 1877

The great man's train rolled into the station, with Frank crowded in close to the platform, beside a group of Civil War veterans, for a good look. Frank may have known this was President Grant's return to his home in Galen, Illinois at the end of his presidency. He probably did not know that President Grant was riding in the same, very special Pullman car that had carried the body of President Abraham Lincoln on his funeral trip to his burial in Springfield, Illinois in 1865. Frank's most lasting memory of the Civil War general was of someone shutting the railroad car door on President Grant's hand, which President Grant *"took rather simply."*

It says something about his mother Charlotte's sense of adventure that, when Frank returned home, instead of scolding him for missing school, she *"thought I had been very enterprising. It was a great thing to have seen General Grant."*

Disasters on the Farm - 1878

The world on the Vanderlip farm changed drastically when Frank was thirteen. It was winter, and Illinois was cold and snowbound. Charles sickened with what was then called a heavy cold. After one particularly hard coughing spell, the tall man left red stains of blood on the white snow. In the next months, he slowly wasted away with what was known as consumption, actually the slow deterioration of tuberculosis. The father Frank so admired died on May 6, 1878.

More disasters followed, without medications now taken for granted. Hopes for income from a flock of young turkeys were gone when turkey rheumatism destroyed them all. The Vanderlips' hogs sickened and died of cholera.

There was a $5,000 mortgage on the farm. Charlotte tried to meet the payments, with ten percent interest, out of the money she was able to make selling milk and cream and, in the spring, their male calves. They had no bank account, but, rather, kept careful track of what cash they could earn.

In spite of their efforts, the farm was finally sold at an auction, in 1880, and a second auction was held to sell the family belongings. Frank would never forget watching as the cattle were led away, and all the machinery, as well as dishes and furniture, were stacked in the yard and sold off.

SALE OF REAL ESTATE

BY virtue of an order and decree of the County Court of Kendall County, Illinois, made on the petition of the undersigned George C. Hoyt and Erasmus Woodworth as administrators of the estate of Charles E. Vanderlip, deceased, for leave to sell the interest in and to the Real Estate of the deceased at the February Term, A. D., 1881, of said Court, to wit: on the twenty-first day of February, A. D., 1881, we shall on Friday the twnety-fifth (25th) day of March A. D. 1881, between the hours of ten o'clock in the forenoon and four o'clock in the afternoon of said day, sell at public sale at the north door of the Court House in the village of Yorkville in said county, the interest of said deceased in and to the real estate describe as follows, to wit:

Newspaper auction notice Mar. 17, 1881
Kendall County Record, Yorkville, Illinois
For sale of Vanderlip farm land

"The nasal voice of Dave Hall, the auctioneer," Frank recalled much later, *"standing in a wagon so as to be above the heads of the crowd, grated on my ears when he began describing things that belonged to us; parts of us, really . . . Vividly I remember the gesture of parting with it all. From a pine tree my father had planted I cut some branches and carried those to Aurora."*

Apparently Frank had no lasting animosity toward the auctioneer. In the years ahead, Dave Hall's daughter, Helen, would become his lifelong friend and correspondent.

Along with his mother, his younger brother Hoyt, and sister Ruth, Frank moved into his grandmother's house in Aurora, where two maiden aunts already lived. At the age of sixteen, Frank became the man of the house, responsible, in his own mind, for five women.

Into Factory Overalls - 1880

To a casual observer, there may not be much difference between the overalls worn by a farmer and those on a factory worker. To a teenaged boy straight from the farm, coming to the *"great city of Aurora,"* those overalls and the nuances of style were something he never forgot.

On his first day as an apprentice at a factory lathe, Frank noticed that other workers were making fun of him. The legs of his farm overalls were tucked into his farm boots, a standard practice for anyone working daily with hogs and cattle.

The next day, even though he still wore his farm boots instead of factory shoes, Frank's pants hung appropriately straight, *"curtains around my boot tops."* He felt he had made social progress.

A young man, not Frank Vanderlip, at a factory lathe,
similar to Frank's working condition in Aurora, Illinois in 1880
photo circa 1911

A machine shop was far removed from the peace and quiet

Frank knew when he read his precious books in an open field with only cows for company. Grinding metal is noisy, dirty work, with shaving dust flying through the air and machinery oil everywhere. No factories or homes had electricity in 1880. Machines were run with steam flowing through overhead pipes and belts and gears, which would have heated the buildings, even in the sweaty Illinois summers.

Starting with a factory whistle at seven in the morning, Frank worked until six at night, with an hour for lunch. Saturday had an earlier quitting time of five o'clock. His pay was seventy-five cents a day, for a weekly paycheck of $4.43, after the seven cent reduction for only nine hours on Saturday, a fact he was careful to record.

Years later, after Frank became president of the largest bank in the country, an old friend recalled watching sixteen-year-old Frank walk to work. "I have a clear picture of him passing by on his way to work in the machine shop - a tall spindling boy in overalls, dinner pail swinging, with a look on his sober, young face which I did not then interpret - as if his thoughts were intent on a larger future."

Never one to be bored or unhappy for long, Frank discovered that there were times he could set the lathe to start a turning, and have a half an hour or so to read and study while the machine did its own work. Off-work hours were happily spent at the Aurora Public Library, and he even took himself to see a play, thrilled at the spectacle of the gas footlights coming on before the curtain went up. And, he traveled alone all the way to Cleveland for a grand event.

President Garfield is shot 1881

On July 2, 1881, when Frank was sixteen, President James Garfield had the grim distinction of becoming the second president to be assassinated, shot less then four months into his term. Telephone inventor Alexander Graham Bell even tried, unsuccessfully, to locate the bullet in the wound with a metal detector he specially designed. President Garfield finally died on September 19, and his body was taken home to Cleveland, Ohio for burial.

The funeral train arrived on Saturday, September 24, and the casket was set up for viewing in a grand pavilion, forty-five feet square. The angel atop a globe on the canvas roof reached ninety-six feet high.

On Sunday, a line of viewers stretched, six wide, over one mile in length to pass by the casket. The line of 250,000 people lasted all day and

Mourners viewing President Garfield's casket 1881

through the night. The entire population of Cleveland was only 150,000.

Frank was one of the people who came to pay their respects.
He prepared carefully for the trip, taking with him a *"substantial, pre-Civil War receptacle of black leather and heavy brass fastenings,"* filled with sandwiches lovingly stuffed in by his mother and grandmother.
He also carried his new purchase, a fashionable soft, black felt hat with a wide brim similar to the one worn by Garfield's assassin. The style had somehow become a tribute to the slain president.

After taking a train into Chicago and transferring to another bound for Cleveland, Frank decided to open his valise and have his dinner. He continues the story:

"Then began a struggle that lasted throughout the night. There was some kind of a trick catch on that hand-bag and I could not get the darn thing open. I was using fingers that had become strong extracting milk from cows and yet I had not the slightest success; the bag remained closed. With so much food in my custody I could not waste any of my sharply limited funds to buy a meal, consequently I went supperless. Ever and again during the long night I renewed my efforts to solve the puzzle of the bag's lock, but because it was borrowed I never dared attack the thing with the violence I sorely wanted to use upon it. Impishly it cheated me of breakfast, too, and only when I had at

last reached the comparative plenty of my relatives' home in Cleveland did the perverse metal fastenings of that bag unlatch."

Monday morning, September 26, was hot and sultry, with some rain. Frank stood respectfully on Euclid Avenue with thousands of others as the funeral cortege came through. He not only saw the dead president's coffin, but saw former President Rutherford B. Hays, and new President Chester Arthur. He saw marching bands and soldiers on parade carrying rifles with which, *"not so many years before, they had been killing men in grey."* He saw members of the cabinet, and a number of other dignitaries. *"These men were as deities to me,"* he reports. *"I came back to Aurora somewhat distinguished by my experience."*

A Year Of Higher Learning

There was no way an energetic mind like Frank's could ever be happy spending his days working at a factory lathe. Somehow, out of his salary, he managed to save up enough money for a year at the University of Illinois at Champaign, where he planned to study electricity, a rather visionary new field at the time.

Sadly, when the school year was over, Frank's savings were exhausted. He reluctantly went back to the machine shop and his overalls. When his boss commented that, in a few years, he would be able to advance to a higher job, Frank promised himself that there would be more to his life than a promotion to factory foreman.

Campus buildings   Men in library
University of Illinois at Champaign circa 1880

Sending for a mail order course in shorthand, known as tachygraphy, Frank practiced with chalk at his lathe. Never one to waste time, he would set up a piece to be cut on the machine, and then settle back for a half hour of writing on the tail stock while the lathe turned and ground out the part. Shorthand was a skill he would use throughout his various careers, even during a famous incident much later, when he was a bank president.

Into A Suit - City Editor In Aurora - 1885

Opportunity did not take long to knock. Or, more accurately, Frank saw a possibility for opportunity and seized it. In 1885, an article in the Aurora *Evening Post* mentioned that the city editor was leaving. With no experience on a newspaper, he applied for the job, and got it.

Suddenly, at the age of twenty-one, he was a man of importance, at least in his own eyes. He had business cards, and a free pass to anywhere on the Burlington Railroad.

He also had to collect delinquent accounts, set type, and even crank the hand press that printed each edition. But, he no longer wore overalls.

A Death

A note of sadness tempered Frank's joy in his new job. His ten-year-old brother, Wynn Hoyt Vanderlip, had been ill with tuberculosis ever since they lived on the farm. He died in April, 1885, and was buried in the same Aurora cemetery as Frank's beloved father.

A Friend

A lifelong trait that guided Frank along his path was his ability to find and befriend men he admired. They were not sports figures, or musicians or politicians. They were men of business, serious gentlemen with intelligence and success, who were pleased to mentor an eager student. An Aurora neighbor, describing Frank as an "ambitious young man," said, "He had that quality of character which finds and uses every honest, favoring chance."

The first of these men to recognize something special in Frank and to raise him to a new place in life was Joseph French Johnson. He was about thirty-two, a graduate of Harvard, with a year of study in Germany. He lived in Aurora with his wife, Caroline Stolp Johnson, and took the train into Chicago every day to work.

Mr. Johnson would go on to establish a newspaper in Spokane, Washington, become a professor at Wharton and NYU, lecture at Columbia, help revise New York State banking laws, work for the National Monetary Commission, and found the Alexander Hamilton Institute.

Joseph French Johnson .circa 1885

Determined to learn from him, Frank would visit Joseph Johnson and his wife at their home in the evenings. Their discussions were probably about news of the time, and about questions of monetary policy and finance.

Joseph Johnson's philosophy of life and success was so similar to Frank's own that, when he wrote an inspirational piece on the subject titled "The Price Of Success", it could be the story of Frank's life.

"I often wonder what it is that brings one man success in life, and what it is that brings mediocrity or failure to his brother . . . I have reached the conclusion that some men succeed because they cheerfully pay the price of success, and others, though they may claim ambition and a desire to succeed, are unwilling to pay that price."

He goes on to describe what must be done to succeed. Ambitious men and women before and since have had to decide if they were willing to pay the price when deciding on their path in life.

"To use all your courage to force yourself to concentrate on the problem in hand, to think of it deeply and constantly, to study it from all angles, and to plan.

"To have a high and sustained determination to put over what you plan to accomplish, not if circumstances be favorable to its accomplishment, but in spite of all adverse circumstances which may arise and nothing worthwhile has ever been accomplished without some obstacles having been overcome.

"To refuse to believe that there are any circumstances sufficiently strong to defeat you in the accomplishment of your purpose.

"Hard? I should say so. That's why so many men never attempt to acquire success, answer the siren call of the rut and remain on the beaten paths that are for beaten men. Nothing worthwhile has ever been achieved without constant endeavor, some pain and constant application of the lash of ambition. That's the price of success as I see it. And I believe every man should ask himself: Am I willing to endure the pain of this struggle for the comforts and the rewards and the glory that go with achievement? Or shall I accept the uneasy and inadequate contentment that comes with mediocrity? Am I willing to pay the Price of Success?"   *Joseph French Johnson*

Joseph French Johnson's job, when he met Frank Vanderlip in 1885, was in the newly developing field of investment counseling. Although Frank claimed that his first field of interest was physics and electricity, he was about to discover his true calling and his lifelong path.

In the words of the character Deep Throat in the movie "All The President's Men," Frank was literally about to "follow the money".

o o o

Chicago

State Street, Chicago photo circa 1890s

o o o

Chicago

A young man whose world was only twenty-one years removed from the Civil War can be forgiven for his nervous feelings when stepping into an elevator. He probably never rode in one in Aurora, Illinois.

The first elevators were installed in the 1850s, but ran on pulleys and counterweights, and sometimes on steam. The first one to run on electricity was installed in a New York department store in 1893, seven years after Frank Vanderlip cautiously rode a non-electric model to work at his new job on the ninth floor of an office building in Chicago, in 1886.

Chicago Board of Trade circa 1900
(at end of La Salle Street)
Grand Pacific Hotel at inner left
Frank's office was across from Hotel

His building was in the heart of the financial district, and across from the Chicago Board of Trade, where the Midwest Stock Exchange trading floor was located. This was an imposing edifice of commerce, *"with stained glass windows and imitation marble interiors stained at the base-boards with tobacco juice."*

The only employees of the company Frank went to work for, The Investor's Agency, were himself and his mentor, Joseph French Johnson, who had recommended Frank for the position. Mr. Johnson did so mainly for the potential he saw in the young man, and, possibly, partially because of his shorthand skill.

At first, Frank was a secretary. He took dictation from the firm's owner, and, laboriously at first, typed correspondence on a cumbersome typewriter known as a Caligraph, which had two sets of keys - one connected to lower case letters, the second set for upper case. It was an extremely frustrating piece of machinery to operate, even for someone skilled on a lathe.

Caligraph typewriter circa 1882

Once he had mastered the annoying machine which, he declared, *"assisted the commercial development of the United States by vanishing,"* Frank's active mind looked for more interesting assignments.

The Investor's Agency was basically a financial detective service for investors, mainly insurance companies. Frank took on the work of reading balance sheets and hunting out problems in companies that were putting out bond issues to raise capital. It was a brand new field, and Frank decided that his employer was going about the business backwards.

Instead of simply looking for companies with flaws, Frank believed that there was more money to be made in searching for those that were doing everything right. It was an extension of Frank's father's teaching to always look for the best apples in the cellar first, so that he would not be eating bad ones the rest of his life.

Chicago in 1886 - An Infamous Riot

When Frank took his first job in Chicago, it was a bustling place, filled with the special aroma of stock yards, where hogs and cattle were brought by rail to the one mile square Union Stock Yards for butchering and packaging, to then be sent back by rail to other parts of the East Coast.

It was also a new city, filled with the sounds of hammering and the nose-tickling dust of sawn wood, as construction still went on to rebuild after the devastating Chicago Fire of 1872.

All of this required a huge labor force, and immigrants were arriving from all over. The West Side housed workers and their families from Germany, Poland, and other European countries, in slum tenements of which reporter Theodore Dreiser wrote, only several years later, "the rancidity of dirt or the bony stark bleakness of poverty fairly shouted. . . they were decaying pools of misery, never still."

Just about the time Frank arrived, in May of 1886, workers at the McCormick Harvesting Machine Company went on strike for better conditions, including lowering the work week from the standard sixty to forty hours, as part of a national labor movement. They planned a peaceful rally at Haymarket Square on May 4. Police showed up to confront the 1,500 people who came to hear speeches.

Someone, never to be identified, threw a bomb. Witnesses described it as arching high over the crowd with a trail of smoke, landing and exploding, throwing out shrapnel. The police responded with gunfire. In the confusion, seven policemen and at least four civilians were killed by gunfire, with many more injured.

Haymarket Riot, Chicago 1886
Drawing shows speech, bomb exploding, and police opening fire,
events which did not all happen simultaneously

After a trial that drew international attention, seven men were sentenced to death, and one to fifteen years in prison, even though no evidence existed that any of them had ever made or thrown the bomb. Four of them were hanged, one committed suicide in prison, and the others were eventually pardoned by a sympathetic governor in 1893.

Newspapers blamed the incident on the labor movement, calling the demonstrators "anarchists", and used the riot to discredit unions in general. The Haymarket Riot is considered to be the start of the May Day celebrations still held by workers' organizations around the world.

Frank does not mention the riots in his autobiography, although he had been a worker himself at the machine shop in Aurora. Though he must have discussed the riots with his business associates, he was new to the town, struggling with his Caligraph, learning the brokerage business, and looking for ways to move up in the world. He does give his opinion of railroad labor unrest he witnessed as a reporter in 1894, saying, "*railroad officials who refused to deal with the representatives of organized employees were persuaded they were doing right. It was a revealing thing to discover that stubborn pride on both sides was the force that had tied up a railroad system for weeks, blocking commerce, blighting the lives of thousands who should not have been involved.*"

A Tribune Reporter - 1889

Three years later, in 1889, Frank was ready for a new challenge. He followed his mentor Joseph French Johnson, who became the financial editor of the Chicago *Tribune*. Frank became a reporter for the newspaper, at a salary of twenty dollars each week.

The Chicago Daily Tribune

There were constant challenges. He lived for scoops and news breaks, for getting the impossible story before a rival paper.

He loved his job, the characters he worked with, and those new ones he encountered daily, whether it was during a stock yard search for a killer or a hotel suite interview with a beautiful countess.

Chicago Tribune building 1893

For a man who, generally, kept his head on business, Frank wrote almost poetically about his time as a reporter, saying, *"The newspaper field is the greatest in the world to have been in,"* and, speaking of the news room, *" . . . the darkest shadows in the corners of that big room were really clouds of romance."*

A young man born on a farm and working first in a factory, with a strong sense of responsibility to support five women in his family, and with a determination to get ahead, has little time for the pleasures of a big city. By his own admission, Frank never "played." His only indulgence was going to the theater, rather than joining other reporters at McGarry's saloon, the newspapermen's watering hole of choice.

The first time Frank experienced the upper echelons of night life, it was at a grand hotel event with elegant men and women in evening clothes. His *Tribune* assignment was to write about the party and hand his story on, a piece at a time, to copy boys, who would rush each part to the newsroom to be type set for the morning paper. Frank took his job so seriously that he never even touched the champagne in the glass at his place, even though it was the first he had ever seen.

Moving Up To Financial Editor - 1892

Frank A. Vanderlip, Chicago Tribune circa 1890

Some part of Frank Vanderlip could have happily been a regular reporter forever. But, when Joseph French Johnson moved to Spokane, Washington, to help found the *Spokesman* newspaper, the position of financial editor became available. Frank eagerly jumped to take it. His salary jumped too, eventually totaling forty-five dollars each week.

With what he had learned at The Investors Agency about researching company reports, Frank was a natural for the job. He loved hunting through balance sheets and annual reports as much as other men loved stalking deer in the woods.

Feeling flush with his new salary and knowledge, Frank decided he was now wise enough to invest some of the $3,000 savings his mother had left from his father's estate. He chose bonds offered by First National Bank on a new development, the Central Market.

With pride and excitement, he then surprised his mother with another new concept of the time, a tour of Europe, with a boat fare of $79 for the crossing. Both mother and son were well read, and thoroughly enjoyed seeing historic landscapes from their books brought to life.

Charlotte Vanderlip was a young forty-six at the time, and Frank was a mature twenty-eight. They had a close relationship all their lives, and Frank found it amusing that, throughout the trip, they were often mistaken for husband and wife.

He was not so amused, when they returned, to learn that the Central Market Company had declared bankruptcy, and his mother's invested savings were gone. But the Central Market Company soon learned that they had lost the funds of the wrong man.

Frank's skills as a reporter and financial investigator took over. He found an Illinois law stating that all stocks must be purchased in full. And, he discovered that most of the stock had, instead, been given as bonuses to various insiders.

At a creditors' meeting, Frank politely but stubbornly insisted that he must be reimbursed. He successfully got his money returned but, more importantly for his future, came to the notice of Lyman J. Gage, president of the First National Bank. Mr. Gage would become the next mentor to move Frank along his life's path.

A Serious Man

Frank was determined to have a financial scoop for the *Tribune* at least once a week, but getting inside information wasn't easy. He decided he had to get into stockholders' meetings, where reporters were not allowed.

To do so, in Frank's mind, was simple. With a small amount of his own savings, he bought one share of each company he wanted to investigate, many of them owned by railroad magnate Charles T. Yerkes, who was not amused. There was nothing Mr. Yerkes could do when a stockholder attended a meeting, shorthand pad in hand, and took notes that turned into front page articles.

When other newspapermen gathered after work in a local tavern, Frank spent his time befriending businessmen and bankers. One of them invited him to join the prestigious Union League Club, the first of a number of such groups he would join as he moved up the social ladder. It was a way to meet and mingle with the city's important men. He never did so for frivolity, but as a way to make always better connections and keep up with business events.

Union League Club 1888

Dancing instruction booklet 1884

Always trying to improve himself, Frank decided to take dancing lessons. Elite society's place to do so was at Augustus Bournique's Dancing Academy on 23rd Street, which began as a series of dance lessons in the home of Mrs. George Pullman, wife of the railroad magnate, for her friends. Frank dutifully learned all the steps of the time, from the waltz to the polka. It was also training in etiquette. He was taught that, when dancing, if he was not wearing formal white gloves, he should have a clean, folded handkerchief to put between his hand and his partner's back, so he would not perspire on her dress. Frank later said that he never did put any of his lessons to use while he was in Chicago.

He also became one of the first students at the new University of Chicago, studying economics, constitutional law, and political economy for three years during the morning hours, before going in to work each day at the *Tribune.*

The business of finance was endlessly fascinating to a man who devoured company reports for pleasure reading. Frank was proud to say that he *"unearthed a great deal of the financial skullduggery of that period."* Working with the New York correspondent of the *Tribune*, he discovered and reported on large kickbacks secretly given by the railroads to favored shippers, an illegal practice under the Interstate Commerce law. The *Tribune* even arranged to print an edition in Washington, D.C., and put copy on the desk of every senator and congressman. Frank's methods for obtaining his evidence were, he admits, a little questionable, but he felt it was for the greater good and, he reasoned, *"Long ago I discovered that black is not black; never."*

The World Comes to Chicago - 1893

When the World Columbian Exposition opened in 1893, nominally to honor the four hundredth anniversary of Columbus' discovery of the New World, twelve million people came to Chicago to see it, out of a national population of sixty-three million. Before computers, television, or even radio, even before electricity was in general use, the fair was filled with technical marvels, including the newly invented Ferris wheel, with a diameter of 264 feet.

The fair must have been quite a sight - a park which was, in effect, its own city, filled entirely with white, neo-Classical buildings housing everything from machinery to artwork, livestock to restaurants. Buildings constructed for the fair were designed as temporary structures, made of wood frames covered with white plaster.

Court of Honor, World Columbian Exposition, Chicago 1893

There were buildings for displays by various states and by foreign countries, a mile long midway with sword swallowers and dancing girls, and a display village composed of native peoples from distant lands dwelling in their traditional ways.

By his own admission, Frank considered himself something of *"a grind . . . managing to work rather than play."* Even when attending the Exposition, he *"studied it as something designed for my special benefit,"* a way to educate himself and keep up with technology.

The magnificent grounds were designed and laid out by Frederick Law Olmsted, Sr., the most famous landscaper in the country, who also designed Central Park in New York City.

The visual impact of all the elegant, similarly styled buildings may have had some echoes thirty years later, when Frank chose Mr. Olmsted's sons, Frederick Law, Jr. and John Charles, to plan out his own land development in California, with all construction designed to follow one unifying style.

The Panic of 1893

While the Fair buildings glowed with excitement and clean white plaster, much of Chicago reeled from another, darker event. A financial panic had been spreading throughout Europe, and reached American soil. There was just not enough gold in the U.S. or any foreign treasury to cover all the outstanding business. As investors began to fear that their banks could not pay them on demand, they rushed to convert their holdings into gold.

Traders in 'The Pit', Chicago Board of Trade 1896

Banks, particularly in the South and West, called on other banks, mainly in New York, to pull the precious metal from their vaults and exchange it for paper. The system quickly broke down. Four thousand banks failed in 1893, taking down fourteen thousand businesses with them.

In Chicago, 30,000 men were out of work. Conditions in the working class parts of town were deplorable. Unemployed men slept in dank, smoke filled hotels, at a price of ten cents per night, on simple canvas hammocks hung four high, covered with "one thin blanket, which in several cases was reeking with vermin."

Unemployed workers in Chicago date unknown (probably between 1893 and 1909)

It was the worst depression the country had ever seen. It took a $65 million loan from J. P. Morgan to set things right, and started the movement to allow free and unlimited use of silver coinage, so there would be more money available. The *Bankers Magazine* of London commented, "The Americans are a people of magnificent achievements and of equally magnificent fiascos."

Frank was a financial editor at this time, not a reporter out on the beat witnessing the misery daily. Instead, he was busy reporting on the causes and repercussions of every financial action to stabilize the economy and the country. But he saw, first hand and up close, what the consequences were of a country so dependent on having enough gold in the vaults. It was a lesson he would not forget.

Editor, *The Economist* - 1894

Frank loved being a reporter. But, when he was offered an editorship at The *Economist*, a weekly paper, Frank jumped at the chance. It changed his position with the city's business and banking leaders, giving him a more respected role in presenting financial news.

And there was plenty to report. The Democratic convention was held in Chicago in 1896. One of the main political issues was the question of whether the U. S. should be on the gold standard, with all currency backed up by gold stored in the U. S. treasury, or if both gold and silver should be legal tender.

The reason for such a heated debate was that, as the country grew, more and more cash was needed. Railroads, in particular, were expanding their lines, financed by large stock sales. When the Philadelphia and Reading Railroad went bankrupt in 1893, it started a panic run on the banks. People wanted to take out their gold-backed cash before any more failures, or before there was not enough gold in the vaults and people would not be given their funds.

The convention pitted Democratic President Grover Cleveland, a strong supporter of the gold standard, against his rival for the nomination, William Jennings Bryan, who believed the country's financial health depended on allowing "bimetallism", or backing currency with both gold and silver, so more paper money could be printed.

Bryan's address, on July 8, 1896, is considered one of the greatest political speeches in American history. It ended with the famous line, "You shall not crucify mankind upon a cross of gold." He was nominated for president, but lost the election to Republican William McKinley, who guided the U.S. to officially adopt the gold standard in 1900.

Artist rendering of moments after 'Cross of Gold' speech published 1900

As editor of a financial publication, Frank would have been quite involved in this debate. He was most likely present at Bryan's fiery speech. The gold standard question, still hotly debated by some to this day, had great impact later in Frank's career, when he gave much thought to helping design the Federal Reserve System.

Somewhere along the line, as he became an editor, a change occurred in Frank. He stopped thinking first as a reporter, and became a man of finance. He recounted the change himself in his auto-biography, speaking about an incident in 1896, while he was at *The Economist*. *"I was called out of bed to the telephone and asked to come to the house of P. D. Armour* (head of the large meat packing operation, an extremely large part of the Chicago economy). *I got there just before midnight and found the presidents of most of the banks and the governors of the stock exchange."* It must have been a rather imposing group.

A large stock selling operation known as Moore Brothers was not able to cover its stock market speculations with the funds of a number of wealthy Chicagoans. The resulting fallout had the potential for a stock market collapse.

The men wanted Frank's help. Not with funds, but with words. They told him they were not opening the stock market the following day, and wanted this news reported in such a way that it would not cause a panic run on the banks.

This would have been quite a scoop for any reporter. But Frank now understood the ramifications of the story, and knew the lives that could be ruined in any panic sell off of stock.

So, he first made these influential men all promise not to see any reporters or let the story out that night. Then, he went to his former paper, the *Tribune*, and asked the city editor to contact all the other papers to say that he had a financial story he would share with them, but only if they would promise to print it exactly as he wrote it, and allow him to see their headline before going to press. All but one paper agreed.

His story was factual but calm, ending with the matter-of-fact phrase, "By the way, the Stock Exchange will not open today." It did not look like a great scoop, but staved off a financial crisis. Frank went home to bed a happy man. The Stock Exchange did not reopen for three months, until two days after William McKinley was elected president.

Another outcome of this nighttime adventure was that it showed the financiers that Frank was a man of intelligence, who could be trusted. One of the men who noticed was Lyman J. Gage. He first spotted Frank during the Central Market bankruptcy hearings, when Frank managed to retrieve his mother's $3,000 investment.

Lyman Gage was on his way to Washington, D. C., to become the Secretary of the Treasury under incoming President McKinley. He asked Frank to come along as his private secretary.

Lyman J. Gage circa 1897

How could someone who started on a small farm say no? Frank packed his bags, took leave of *The Economist*, and headed for the capital with Lyman Gage, even though neither of them had any idea exactly what Frank would do when they got there.

○ ○ ○

Washington
Part I

Inauguration of President McKinley, Washington, D.C. March 4, 1897
Frank Vanderlip and Lyman Gage somewhere on Capitol steps

o o o

Washington - Part I

William McKinley went to Washington as President in 1897, inaugurated on a wet, forty-degree day on March 4, in front of the Original Senate Wing at the Capitol.

One of the spectators that day was thirty-two year old Frank Vanderlip, who arrived in Washington the day before with his newest mentor, incoming Secretary of the Treasury Lyman J. Gage. Mr. Gage, formerly president of Chicago's First National Bank, had known Frank ever since the Central Market bankruptcy episode, and was impressed enough to ask Frank to come along as his private secretary.

It was an opportunity Frank could not turn down. He considered it to be a year or so of postgraduate study in the world of finance. Neither Frank nor Lyman Gage could have foreseen what was to come.

Into A New Office - 1897

There are only two buildings in Washington, D.C. that exude a stronger sense of power than the Treasury Building at 1500 Pennsylvania Avenue - the White House next door, and the U. S. Capitol.

Along Treasury's east front stand thirty granite columns, each thirty-six feet tall, and each carved from a single block of stone.

U.S. Treasury Building, Washington, D.C. circa 1898

43

Begun in 1836, the building housed troops during the Civil War, became the office for President Andrew Johnson just after President Lincoln's assassination, and was the site of President Grant's inaugural ball, on a cold night, when hundreds of partiers checked their coats with a staff who could not read and simply threw all of the garments into piles in one room. Some guests waited hours to retrieve their coats, other guests simply gave up, went home coatless, and came back to find them the following day.

Inside, the two-story marble hall known as the Cash Room is a Greek Revival styled extravaganza used for the daily financial business of the country, to supply local commercial banks with coins and currency, and to handle government accounts in the District of Columbia. Government checks were still cashed there until 1976.

Cash Room, U.S. Treasury date unknown

At the time Frank arrived, gold, silver, and paper currency were delivered in horse-drawn vans and unloaded at the Fifteenth Street sidewalk entrance, then brought through hallways on hand carts, put into a cargo elevator just recently installed, and taken up to the Cash Room vaults. Several million dollars were on deposit at any given time.

When Frank walked into the building on his first day, just after President McKinley's inauguration, two types of people worked there - political appointees, who came and went with each administration, and career government workers.

The career people, almost all men, were the ones who kept government offices running. They knew where papers were filed and who to see to get any particular task actually accomplished. When a new set of appointees arrived, it was the career men who explained to them what their jobs really were.

One of these men must have greeted Frank and showed him to the desk traditionally occupied by the Secretary's private secretary. It was in a small room just outside of the grand office where Secretary

Gage would do his work. Frank's job would be to greet visitors, politely inquire about their business, and decide which ones were important enough to see the Secretary. Frank immediately knew he had not come to Washington to wear out the carpet carrying calling cards to his boss.

On his second day at work, Frank changed the arrangements. Passing through the outer office, he set up his station on the other side of Secretary Gage's large table-desk. They worked companionably this way for several months. No source mentions what the career workers thought of the move, or who replaced Frank in the outer office.

Office of Secretary of the Treasury 1890
Desk in foreground was used by first Secretary of the Treasury, Alexander Hamilton.
It is still used by Treasury Secretaries today.
This may be the desk used by Frank, or it may have been a table to the right of this photo.

Lessons in Etiquette

Life in Washington has many layers. One is political, one is daily business, another is social. While he was in Chicago, Frank never found it necessary to pay much attention to the social part of life, in spite of his dancing lessons. Now he found himself in a bewildering whirl. He was expected to know an entire etiquette of calling cards and proper attire. He was invited to dinner parties, where he was expected to make light hearted conversation with female dining companions.

On his first Sunday night in town, Frank had his first embarrassing moments. Invited to an important home for dinner, Frank dressed carefully in what he mistakenly assumed was proper Sunday attire - what was known as a morning coat. His was probably a conservative, dark wool jacket with cutaway fronts, meaning that just below the second button, the front edges angled sharply toward the sides, allowing the gentleman's vest to be seen. It may have had a velvet collar and edges bound or stitched decoratively. His trousers would have been a quiet, dark stripe of some sort.

Morning suit circa 1890

Although Frank's family were not regular church goers, Frank knew this was the correct outfit for Sunday services in his social circle, and he assumed it was proper to wear all of Sunday.

"In that costume," Frank says, *"I was a figure suited to relieve from its stone pedestal any monument of a non-military statesman within the District of Columbia. I felt grand and not at all uncertain until I had passed the portals of the Brown residence."*

He immediately saw his mistake. The other guests, Washington professionals, were all in formal evening clothes. It was his farmer's boots in the Aurora machine shop all over again.

Three women came to his rescue. One was Secretary Gage's wife Cornelia, another was the wife of Senator Newlands. The third was an elderly Southern woman named Lucy Page, *"an elderly Southern woman of great distinction whose family was deeply rooted in the social life of Washington."* She made sure Frank received invitations to the important balls and parties.

Once invited, though, Frank's social problems only just began. There were elaborate rituals of card etiquette, rules for the proper thank-yous for each type of event, and countless other protocol pitfalls looming before an ambitious man. Help came from an unlikely source.

Chief Messenger Richard Green

Richard Green was a former slave who had, for many years, been the chief messenger at the Treasury Department. He was a master at the career workers' game, given his personality.

Frank describes Richard Green as, *"a man tall, black, handsome, wise and tenderly considerate."*

Richard Green circa 1920

Green started with the Treasury Department in 1871, and worked there for more than fifty years. He traveled throughout the U.S., in Europe, and in South America with various Secretaries. His post was outside the door of the Secretary's office, where, according to a complimentary article appearing in papers across the country at his death in 1925, "his height and bearing have attracted the admiration of visitors."

The two men formed what would be a lifelong friendship. *"In our relations,"* Frank remembered of that time, *"we were as two men encountering each other at a masquerade; our places in life, the color of our hides were but part of the scene in which we found ourselves."* No one was *"better informed about the social customs of Washington. My old affection for him fires up afresh as I think how tactfully Richard guided me in the way I should go."*

Green would stop by Frank's desk on some pretext, and casually ask if Frank had responded to an invitation or delivered a thank you, tactfully including in the conversation the proper way to do so.

He also officiated as majordomo for Secretary Gage's dinner parties, as well as those Frank was obliged to give. Frank could relax, knowing his events were in good hands. There are few people in Frank's autobiography about whom he speaks with so much personal admiration. *"When I see him now, in memory, clothed in evening dress, his finely modeled skull the very shape of sensitive intelligence, I know him for what he was, one of the greatest of gentlemen . . ."*

A Promotion

About six weeks after Frank moved his work station into Secretary Gage's office, Lyman Gage went to the White House to see President McKinley. He returned with news. Casually, he remarked that he asked McKinley for the only favor he would request while in office. It was to appoint Frank as Assistant Secretary of the Treasury.

Frank held his breath while Lyman Gage cleaned his glasses. Finally, Lyman Gage told Frank the President agreed. Frank would get a promotion, and the Secretary would get his desk back to himself.

Assistant Secretary of the Treasury Frank A. Vanderlip and Secretary of the Treasury Lyman J. Gage circa 1898

A Girl

With his new position, Frank got not only his own office, but also a carriage and two horses. He felt quite grand. He also found a young woman to escort to parties, and not just any one.

Several of President McKinley's nieces stayed in the White House at various times to help with his wife Ida, known for a number of ailments and a difficult way with the White House staff. Frank had the pleasure of escorting one of these young ladies.

"I tell you, that was a sensation for me, to go calling on a girl at the White House. In the darkness of my Government carriage with my thoughts cadenced to the clop, clopping of the horses' hoofs as I approached the iron gates and the graveled driveway of the place where our presidents live, often I experienced a Cinderella-like qualm. Suppose the spell were broken and I were to find myself grease-blackened and once more in the thralldom of overalls!"

Frank can be a serious-minded writer, but his imaginative side appears when he describes his visits to the White House. *"I never mounted the steps and crossed the stone porch to the front door of the White House without a feeling of awe; Lincoln's feet had trod those steps where mine were walking; beyond the door, possibly in corners, I liked to fancy, there still lingered atmosphere that he had breathed."*

White House North Portico entrance drive circa 1901

But he was still tongue-tied around women. Whenever he and the president's niece rode out in his carriage, they were accompanied by a White House military aide, in full uniform. *"If that convention now languishes be sure it was I who withered it with black thoughts,"* he reports. Frank felt drab in comparison, in his civilian suit, listening to his companion gaily conversing with her chaperone.

In Charge of Personnel

At the office, Frank was more comfortably in his element. Although there were three Assistant Secretaries, it was his office that adjoined Secretary Gage's.

Frank dealt with reporters when they came to report on Treasury business, a task for which he was well suited. He was also in charge of six thousand Department personnel, which gave him some power.

Whenever a new president takes office, so do many other people, as thousands of political appointees win or lose jobs. In 1897, there were still Civil War veterans who, under the law, were technically eligible for any civil service job. At Treasury, they all turned to Frank, some pleading, some demanding.

He quickly learned that if he granted a request merely on a whim, the decision might come back to haunt him. He tried, instead, to make choices based on whether or not each decision was right. That way, his authority stayed intact, and he could sleep well at night. It was a policy he would follow for life.

The Country Goes To War - 1898

If Frank came to Washington for lessons in finance, he was about to get a practical PhD. The country was going to war. War always needs money, and it was Treasury's job to provide it.

The Monroe Doctrine of 1823 set up a U.S. policy that said countries in Europe would not be allowed to further colonize or interfere with any country in North or South America, but Cuba and its existing Spanish rule were exempted. That was before the Panama Canal construction began in 1882.

Now the U.S. wanted naval protection for the planned canal, and the Spanish in Cuba were dangerously close. A number of Democrats, and some members of the government, like Assistant Secretary of the Navy Theodore Roosevelt, wanted to go to war. President McKinley and most business interests tried to keep the peace. Cubans revolting against Spain fanned the war with stories of Spanish atrocities.

Newspaper headline before war 1898

Newspaper sketch of reported atrocity 1898

Into this mix came two New York newspapers and their strong willed owners, each trying to outdo the other for readership and to be first to reach a daily circulation of one million. Joseph Pulitzer, of *The World*, and William Randolph Hearst, of *The Journal*, competed for the most lurid stories and headlines. When Hearst's illustrator, Frederick Remington, remarked that conditions in Cuba did not really seem bad enough for the U. S. to intervene, Hearst supposedly answered, "You furnish the pictures and I'll furnish the war."

When *The World* introduced comic strips printed in color, so did *The Journal*. Both used new printing methods that were not always perfect, and the ink tended to run, particularly the yellow, in a strip called "The Yellow Kid," whose clothing was that color. Readers joked that both papers were smearing not only the comics, but also

Cartoon of newspaper moguls arguing June 1898
Joseph Pulitzer and William Randolph Hearst
Dressed in bright outfits of "The Yellow Kids"

the news, and the phrase "yellow journalism" was born.

A new prime minister in Spain granted autonomy to Cuba, set to begin on January 1, 1898. Eleven days later, a small riot erupted in Havana. President McKinley, under pressure from Congress and worried about American business and citizens there, dispatched the U.S.S. Maine to Havana, and other naval ships into the Gulf of Mexico and off the coasts of Lisbon and Hong Kong. War was almost inevitable.

Infantry boarding ship for Cuba 1898

On February 15, a massive explosion tore the Maine apart, and she sank in Havana Harbor. The Navy investigation stated that it was caused by something outside the hull. A separate investigation by Spain claimed something inside the ship set if off.

U.S.S. Maine after explosion, Havana Harbor 1898

Investigations even into the 20th century have not agreed on whether it was caused by a shipboard accident, the Spanish, or even American or Cuban interests wanting to start a war.

The country was ready for arms. Headlines read, "Destruction of the War Ship *Maine* was the Work of an Enemy," and "The Spirit of War Pervades." The slogan "Remember the Maine! To Hell with Spain!" appeared everywhere.

New York Journal *headline February 16, 1898*

President McKinley and Congress had no choice. On April 25, 1898, the U.S. declared war on Spain.

Along the eastern seaboard, there were worries about an attack by the Spanish fleet. Congress voted $50 million for defense, but that was not enough. Coastal security had to be strengthened, harbors had to be mined against intruders, ships must be built, and armaments needed to be purchased.

Edward Walker Harden Scoops Admiral Dewey

In early spring, the new revenue cutter *Hugh M'Culloch* sailed for the coast of China. Aboard, at Frank's suggestion, were a newspaper cartoonist and the man who succeeded Frank as the financial editor of the *Chicago Tribune*, Frank's friend Edward Walker Harden.

At 4:30 a.m. on a May morning, a brave White House watchman knocked on President McKinley's door to tell him that Admiral Dewey had just won the Battle of Manila, destroying the Spanish fleet in the Pacific. By military etiquette of the time, this news should have been delivered through proper armed service channels. Instead, it was delivered by a *Tribune* reporter who had received the first cable off of the overseas wire, from Ed Harden.

Edward Walker Harden circa 1920

"*Back in Manila,*" as Franks tells the story, "*Harden learned that he had scooped the earth and also scooped the admiral, and other naval officers assured him that the old man would set him ashore, and to be ashore in Manila then was the equivalent of being marooned. Scared stiff, Harden then discovered what had happened and asked for permission to come aboard the flagship to explain.*"

After their defeat, the Spanish had cut the telegraph cable to Hong Kong. Admiral Dewey met with three reporters who witnessed the battle, including Ed Harden, allowing them to travel on the *Hugh M'Culloch,* the vessel chosen as the dispatch boat to take the news on its way. Dewey's instruction to them was that his cable should go out first on the wire when they arrived in Hong Kong. All three men agreed.

On arrival, Ed Harden, the youngest and most agile, jumped ashore, and a wild rickshaw race ensued to see who would reach the cable office first. After some minor scuffling and debating, Ed Harden's message, marked 'urgent' and paid for with $9.90 in gold, jumped to the front of the line. "Now, this does not go ahead of the admiral's dispatches. I promised him," Ed Harden instructed.

And, as the messages wended their way across the Pacific from one telegraph office to the next, Admiral Dewey's stayed in first place on the single cable line, until they reached an island with two lines. There, the Admiral's was held up because his had been ordered repeated and needed approval. Finally in the U. S., the official message was delayed again for another hour while its code was translated.

Still the newspaperman years later, Frank comments, *"For me, that struggle in the cable office at Hong Kong always has been the real battle of Manila Bay; there is suspense in it to a degree that there never was in the foregone conclusion of Dewey's smashing attack. My children, with the little Hardens, thrilled to it again and again, so that it is a family legend, but even if it were not I should lug it in here because in 1898 Harden's adventure made me know in every envious fiber that I was a reporter in my blood and being."*

War and Money

Cartoon for new war tax 1898
A cigar and a beer mug agree

In June, Congress passed the War Revenue Act of 1898. This was, as Frank said, *"a far-reaching tax bill so that the people began forthwith to pay something on account for their war."* It put taxes on beer, tobacco, some recreational facilities, even on chewing gum, and set up an inheritance tax with rates anywhere from .74 to fifteen percent.

Another provision that had peculiar repercussions was a three percent levy on long distance telephone calls, aimed at the wealthy, who were presumed to be the only people using such a service. The first telephone exchanges began just twenty years before this time, in 1878. Theoretically, this tax was just planned to fund the Spanish-American War but, as the first coast to coast long distance call was not until 1915, someone in Congress was thinking ahead.

The three percent tax was still in effect one hundred and eight years later, when someone apparently realized the Spanish-American War was over, and the tax was finally repealed in 2004.

The War Revenue Act had one further addition, which changed the course of Frank's life. There was to be a bond issue of $200 million. Frank was put in charge of sending out the loan and procuring the subscriptions.

Congress made a special requirement, on the theory, as Frank says, that *"where the treasure is, there the heart is."* If the general public were invested in the bonds, they would stand behind the war effort. All of the bonds must be offered to the smallest subscribers first. They would be issued at par, meaning there would be no commissions or premiums. Anyone who invested even twenty dollars would be certain they would get back their full twenty dollars plus a full three percent interest.

Magazine sketch, buying war bonds at Sub Treasury, New York 1898

Taking in $200 million is not a simple business, especially when it comes from investors in amounts as small as twenty dollars. Frank was given the newly built and still empty Post Office building on Pennsylvania Avenue, and six to seven hundred clerks and workers.

There were no computers, or even electric calculators, to do the work. As Congress had directed that the smallest purchasers be served first, the order of purchases had to be determined. Bond traders who tried to find ways to buy large lots had to be weeded out. And the provision that even a twenty dollar purchase could be paid in five installments kept hundreds of men busy just calculating the correct interest.

War bond activity in the Treasury Department 1898

All of this had to be done quickly. The War Revenue Act passed on June 10, and the bond drive was to close at three o'clock on an afternoon in July. It was arranged that the final subscriptions would be loaded onto a wagon at the post office and brought to the Treasury at exactly that time. No one could rephrase Frank's story better then the account given in his own words.

"Perhaps the chronology of my recollections is not accurate but in my memory, at least, . . . a Treasury wagon and its horses came down Pennsylvania Avenue at a gallop. I seem to remember now that we could hear the horses clattering as a man in the office who had picked up a ringing telephone instrument suddenly began to shout. He climbed up on a desk and at the very moment the messenger ran in with the mail which closed the

subscription the man on the desk repeated the news of victory in Cuba; Santiago had fallen. While most of the hundreds of clerks were cheering the announcement a few of us were checking the total of the subscription."

Newspapermen, even those who have gone on to become Assistant Secretaries of State, pride themselves on their accuracy. So, Frank can perhaps be guilty only of forgetfulness, or the desire to paint an exciting picture, when he wrote these words thirty-six years after the facts. Because the U.S. destroyed the Spanish fleet off of Santiago de Cuba on Sunday, July 3, 1898, and the bond subscription drive closed eleven days later, on Thursday, July 14, 1898.

Either way, the drive was a complete success. Americans sent in subscriptions to purchase over $1.4 billion dollars in bonds, seven times the amount being offered. Giving them out to the lowest amounts first, 230,000 *Twenty dollar Spanish American War bond 1898* people put in from $20 to $500 each. No one person got over $4,500.

It was a triumph for the country, for the President, and a special one for Frank. And it brought him to the notice of some very important men.

Frank A. Vanderlip 1898

○ ○

Into The Bank

National City Bank, 52 Wall Street, New York 1893

○ ○ ○

Into The Bank

James J. Stillman was a good judge of men, and he had his eye on Frank Vanderlip.

Born in Texas in 1850 to a father who invested in Rio Grande Valley land, he grew up in Connecticut, and became a partner in a New York City firm doing business in areas as varied as cotton commodities and railroad construction.

James J. Stillman circa 1901

When he was twenty-five, his father died, leaving him over one million dollars. Between his investments and his business skills, James Stillman came to the notice of National City Bank President Moses Taylor, who made the young man the next president. Two of his daughters married two sons of John D. Rockefeller, head of Standard Oil, the bank's largest customer.

Mr. Stillman, as Frank always called him, was one of the one hundred wealthiest men in America, with a much lower public profile than others on the list. At his death, in 1918, his fortune was estimated by the New York *Times* at over $100 million. He loved art, yachts, and the "refining graces of life."

In 1900, near of President McKinley's first term, Mr. Stillman spoke to Secretary of the Treasury Gage about Frank. "When you are through with that young man I want him to sit over there." Mr. Stillman pointed to a desk in the corner of his office. Both Secretary Gage and Frank assumed he would be offered a position such as Mr. Stillman's private secretary. That would have been fine with Frank.

An invitation arrived a few months later for Frank to dine with Mr. Stillman in New York. Frank's description of the evening gives a good insight into both men.

"Mr. Stillman was living on Fortieth Street, just off Fifth Avenue, in an old-fashioned brownstone house. In spite of my position in the government I think some of my juices ran out of me at my knees as I mounted the steps to the stoop and rang the bell; there were stories about Stillman - his eccentricities, his domineering ways, his tremendous power. Well, I went to dinner and now that I am able to compare the experience with other meals eaten during seventy years, I still think it was the most trying dinner I ever lived through."

The guest list consisted of Frank, Mr. Stillman's daughter, someone Frank described as *"a lady companion,"* and the great man himself. *"Throughout the meal Mr. Stillman hardly spoke and I was obliged in spite of my distaste for small talk to carry on a conversation with the ladies, smothering as best I could my discomfort in the knowledge that Mr. Stillman was sitting there sizing me up. I did not enjoy a mouthful of the food served to me that night."*

After dinner the group went into a sitting room, where Mr. Stillman introduced another man, Mr. Sterling, who was a lawyer. They chatted inconsequentially for about ten minutes which, *"obviously being for the purpose of giving Mr. Sterling an opportunity to size me up, did not relieve my embarrassment."*

Mr. Stillman and Mr. Sterling then went into another room, leaving Frank uncomfortably alone with the ladies, *"to fuss with my tie, smooth my big brush of a black mustache, and to perspire deep in my mind."* When the men returned, Mr. Sterling said goodnight and left.

"Now, up to that time my host had said just nothing at all, but then he started in philosophizing about New York banks, banking and bankers. I was to find out that he was much given to making personal estimates of men, which he could do with very great acumen; having just been put through his mill I should not have been surprised at that. He spoke hesitatingly; that is, over a particular word he would hang fire until under the pressure of embarrassment a listener would be tempted to supply a word, and that would be received by Mr. Stillman as if he were a graven image and, always, he would use another word when he resumed. So he talked with me for an hour or more, always

about New York banking, and with the assistance of only one or two words from Vanderlip. Then, without preliminaries, he said to me, 'When you are through with the Treasury, and I understand Mr. Gage wants you to stay there for another year, we want you to come into the City Bank as vice-president.'

"If he had suddenly struck at me with the fire-tongs, or if he had produced a telegram from McKinley offering to send me to the Court of St. James as Ambassador, I would not have been more surprised. That I said to him that I would consider his offer of a vice-presidency of his bank is proof, I think, that I kept my emotions under control."

"The American Commercial Invasion Of Europe" - 1902

Moving directly from a position at Treasury to one at a major bank would not reflect well on either entity, or on Frank. Many political appointees, on leaving government service, "spend some time with their family." Frank decided to take a fact-finding trip to Europe instead. On his return, he wrote a series of articles for *Scribners Magazine*. Fifty thousand copies were republished in 1902 as a booklet, and distributed, "With Compliments of The National City Bank of New York," in seven languages.

What is amazing today, over one hundred years later, is how true and prophetic Frank's observations were. His desire to gather masses of data, and his ability to discern patterns of business from them are encyclopedic. He was aware of the global reach of industry and American's influence on all parts of daily life.

American cash register, South Africa

American-equipped electric cars, Cairo

He illustrated his points with photographs and illustrations of American products in use throughout the world in what seemed, to his readers, unlikely settings.

The practical Ph.D. he earned while at Treasury served him well. The ways business, finance, and government interact seemed perfectly clear to him. "*Those rivulets of commerce I had been obliged to study in Scudder's investigating organization, and the business flow that I had observed as a financial reporter and editor now were revealed to me in the immensity of their currents. As a great river system at its mouth, blending itself with the tidal waters of the sea, reveals distinct colors in the convoluting mixture of fresh and sea water, so there would be disclosed to any one who sat at my post another significant mixture.*

"*I could see the great swirling currents of two forces of the people; one of the power of their will to be a nation, their political power; the other of their will to work, of their economic power, their wealth. How should these forces that grow out of the people be blended so as to accomplish the greatest good for the greatest number? I did not know then; I do not know now.*" But Frank did believe that, if the forces did not stay in balance and went too far toward government interference with business, it would be a mistake, "*causing the people to thirst, to hunger and to die.*"

Wherever he traveled, he saw American machinery in use. American exports totaled much more than the amount coming into the country, and he worried about the long term effects of such an imbalance. Now he saw, first hand, what this meant. In the railroad industry alone, "*American locomotives, running on American rails, now whistle past the Pyramids and across the long Siberian steppes. They carry the Hindoo pilgrims from all parts of their empire to the sacred waters of the Ganges. Three years ago there was but one American locomotive in the United Kingdom; today there is not a road of importance there on which trains are not being pulled by American engines.*"

American typewriter in Uganda 1901

The new century, Frank believed, was bringing instant communication to the world, along with more industrialized society. No longer did a family grow and make everything it used. People were now dependent on specialized business and manufacturing. The countries that succeeded would be those that could produce products.

Even wars no longer had the elements of bravery that they did at a time when men with drawn swords charged into battle on horseback, or faced off in lines with rifles pointed squarely at each other. Substituted instead were executive ability and technical skill with more powerful weapons. Winners would be those able to produce both.

The Germans, he stated, "*could give us valuable lessons. They are strong in two particulars - strong in the line of technical education . . . and strong in commercial training specially adapted to the needs of their representatives in foreign countries.*"

He foresaw a time when America could lose its industrial leadership for several reasons. "*It is a comparatively difficult thing to find trained business men, born in America, who speak fluently two or more Continental languages, and it follows from that difficulty that we send commercial representatives to Europe who are under the almost hopeless handicap of not speaking the language of a country in which they wish to do business.*"

Scientific discoveries were, he believed, being made more frequently in Europe than in America, and he cited a number of examples - the X-ray, the wireless telegraph, a new method of refining gold, and advances in chemistry. All of these led to paying royalties to European companies.

With his farmer's eye, he saw that one of America's strengths in manufacturing was also a weakness. Standard Russian plow harnesses did not fit onto American plows. The American manufacturer would not vary its design, forcing the Russian importer to have a special adapter made in Germany.

An American binder on Russian steppes 1901

In England, he worried about the effects of what he considered to be "*the most dangerous rock in the path of English industry - the growth of a spirit in trades-unions which attempts to regulate the business of employers in other matters than those relating to wages and hours of labor. I believe the decline of English industry can be attributed to the success of labor organizations in restricting the amount of work a man may be permitted to do, more than to any other single cause. We have encountered that spirit too frequently in our own labor field, and it is one which, if successfully persisted in, will cut the ground of advantage from under our manufacturers quicker than anything else I know of.*"

For a man who loved what he did for a living, and spent almost every waking hour trying to improve himself, the idea that a man would only want to work eight hours a day was unimaginable.

His vision of the future has, to a large extent, proved true. "*Civilization gives no patent on technical supremacy. Americans may lead the world now in her ingenious application of labor-saving machinery, but there can be no assurance of the permanent continuance of that advantage . . . We have already seen trades-unions attempting to force employers to make work rather than to produce wealth. We have seen strikes that have had for their basis only a desire for an increased power of interference and from that it is not a long step to a position where union labor may be found struggling to restrict individual production.*

"*It is the age of machinery . . . The relative importance of labor in the cost of production is lessening; the sway of machinery is increasing. The twentieth century will be the century of machinery . . . Before it is half completed we may expect to see that sort of human labor that is the painful and laborious exercise of muscle almost supplanted by automatic machinery directed by trained intelligence . . . Such development steadily increases the importance of raw material . . . those producers who can draw upon practically inexhaustible and rich supplies near at hand . . . are at tremendous advantage.*"

Frank was right about the 20th century being the age of machinery and mechanization. The only thing he could not foresee was the dawning of the age of the automobile, and how quickly the world would switch from a hunger for American coal to a continual thirst for a constant supply of Middle Eastern oil.

A Clean Desk

National City Bank's building was an old-fashioned place even when Frank entered it in 1902. A steep flight of stone steps led up to the *"twilight of the main floor,"* where tellers stood behind long counters, separated from the customers by ornate iron bars that, to Frank, made them seem as if they were in cages.

National City Bank at 52 Wall Street, on right 1903
Old Customs House on left would be remodeled in 1908 to become National City Bank

Officers of the bank sat on a slightly raised platform, giving visual impact to their importance, and allowing them to watch everything that happened on the main floor. Only Mr. Stillman had a private office. All ten officers seemed to be constantly busy. *"They were technical experts of finance, but where I was concerned their noses were in the air,"* Frank reports.

Frank had $2,000 to his name on his first day at the bank. He was given one of the desks, with a big, shining, empty surface. He had not inherited responsibilities from a retiring or promoted officer, and no one gave him any direction as to what to do.

Frank A. Vanderlip 1902
Youngest vice president of National City Bank

He listened quietly to each morning's meeting about the day's forthcoming banking business. He went to another meeting each afternoon at 3:30, in Mr. Stillman's office, to review the day's events. None of the other officers were the slightest bit of help. *"I became aware that the experts around me had a feeling that the newest face in their midst was that of an upstart.*

"They were men who had grown up through the years in daily contact with the details of banking. As they discussed loans or talked of any of the things that were of general interest to them, none ever paused to interpret his speech to me nor can I think now of any reason why they should have done so,

unless it might be that then they would have been kinder. As it was, I knew that even though they were technical experts and possessed the experience of many active years, I knew more of the philosophy of banking than the whole bunch of them."

He sat uncomfortably one day through Mr. Stillman's *"long tirade of vigorous Anglo-Saxon,"* against the oldest of the bank officers, who had made some mistake. He decided that, if Mr. Stillman turned that sort of tongue lashing against him, *"we would have just one session of that sort."*

But Mr. Stillman never did unleash any wrath in Frank's direction. He was grooming Frank for important work, without giving him any direct clues. *"At the start I think I was expected to know, instinctively, just as the selected larva of a beehive becomes aware from its diet of royal jelly that it is being transformed."*

Soon, Mr. Stillman asked Frank to attend a meeting of the Board of Directors, something not done by the other officers sitting at desks on the platform. Mr. Stillman pointed to the chair beside him, and directed Frank to sit down. After that, Frank attended the weekly Board meeting each Tuesday.

In between all these meetings, Frank needed something to actually do. He never lacked imagination. *" A conservative,"* he said, *"is a man who does not think that anything should be done for the first time."*

At the Treasury Department, he had directed the storage of bonds in the vault to be flat, instead of the traditional rolling up of each one, to save $50,000 in construction of more space. Now he brought his out-of-the-box thinking to the bank.

Traditional thinking held that banking was done in a traditional way. Men met at their clubs, or over dinner, or on their boats. They would size each other up and talk of many things, but never, for the sake of dignity, would anyone solicit an account. *"Wasn't that silly,"* Frank thought.

When he was at Treasury, Frank met thousands of bankers and businessmen from all over the country. Now he wrote them letters, brazenly but politely asking for their accounts. Even the booklet of his articles, "The American Commercial Invasion of Europe," had, inside the back cover, a discreet request for new business.

The National City Bank of New York extends to its customers every accommodation consistent with a broad and liberal policy of management. Its facilities are particularly arranged to meet the requirements of merchants and manufacturers.

New accounts are desired and correspondence is invited to that end.

Front and inside back covers
of booklet published by
National City Bank 1902

Even though other vice presidents predicted disaster, Frank brought in 365 new accounts in his first year, some of them quite large. Before he left National City Bank, deposits grew from $200 million to one billion dollars.

Mr. Stillman's Protege

That first uncomfortable dinner at Mr. Stillman's home gave way to enjoyable, weekly repetitions. *"The awkwardness I had known the first time I had dined there was not experienced a second time because thereafter Mr. Stillman talked with me incessantly. He loved to talk about banks and men; especially men. He was instructing me, not in the principals of banking, but in the characters of the men with whom I should have to deal."*

On Sundays, they would ride out in *"one of the early automobiles, a German mechanism that would gasp and jump and then, with surprising swiftness vibrate us through the horsedrawn traffic . . . We regarded it then as a daring expedition to start up the Hudson for the residence of William Rockefeller; sometimes we arrived."* On the way, Mr. Stillman would impart wisdom along with the fresh air.

First Mercedes car, with 35-hp, four cylinder engine and four-speed gearbox
One of only 900 made in Germany in 1901

As he became more comfortable, Frank did more than just listen. He talked about his own ideas and the need for banking reform. Frank *"believed that the whole system of National bank-notes was unsound, wrong."* What he told Mr. Stillman of his thoughts as they lurched and dodged around horse-drawn phaetons and surreys would eventually coalesce in his mind to help form the Federal Reserve Banking Act.

Something else happened during those conversations. The two men developed a close, father-son relationship, in spite of the fact that Mr. Stillman had three sons and two daughters of his own. It was something Frank had been looking for, ever since the death of his own father. In Aurora and Chicago, he looked up to his first mentor, Joseph French Johnson. In Washington, of course, Secretary of the Treasury Lyman J. Gage took Frank under his wing.

It took a while to crack through Mr. Stillman's stern exterior, but, *"there developed in me an affection for him so strong that anything I might say about him now would be sponsored only by the wish to reveal him in his greatness."*

One aspect of Mr. Stillman that Frank had learned, uncomfortably, at their first dinner, was his belief that he could *"recognize truth from pretense merely by keeping his eyes upon the one who talked with him."*

If a promoter of a questionable nature or financial product

somehow managed to gain a meeting, "*It was his method to keep silent while such a man talked. The man would finish his talk and Mr. Stillman would remain completely silent. It was not lack of interest; simply there was no human response to the words. Disconcerted, the promoter would plunge again into his story and then more unwinking silence would start another round. I do not know that this was a trick consciously played by Mr. Stillman but repeatedly I have observed how effectively the weak points of a scheme were revealed under the test of embarrassed repetition.*"

With Mr. Stillman behind him, Frank felt comfortable with implementing new ideas. He felt he knew quite a bit about buying and selling bonds. Usually, this business of the bank's clients was handled through a bond house. Frank saw no reason the bank itself could not make those commissions. After a problematic start, this grew into a "*general bond business of vast proportions,*" known as National City Company, which "*earned as much as the bank itself.*"

If Frank's life were a musical, he would be at the end of Act I. He was thirty-eight years old, had a position to which he was devoted, a father figure that he looked up to, and a salary that was more than comfortable. His sister was well and happy, and his mother lived comfortably in Aurora. There was only one thing missing.

Everything in his life revolved around the Bank. Success had not given him any more ability to make small talk at dinner parties or to broaden his feminine contacts. Frank needed a romantic interest. He needed to find the perfect girl.

○ ○ ○

Narcissa

Narcissa Cox Vanderlip circa 1930

o o o

Narcissa

Ruth Isabel Vanderlip was a smart enough young woman to go to college, and a lucky enough woman to have a brother who could afford to send her there. She was not the type of female whose friends would be flighty or uninteresting.

She was twenty-five years old in 1902 when she went to New York to stay with her brother Frank and his former boss, Lyman J. Gage, in the apartment they shared at 661 Madison Avenue.

That winter, two of Ruth's friends from the University of Chicago came for a short visit on their way to Florida. They were Miss Mabel Narcissa Cox, known to everyone by her middle name, and her sister, Clover.

With delicate features and dark blonde, wavy hair, Narcissa was a pretty person with a warm smile. At first, Frank thought she was *"an inexperienced school-girl."*

But something about her must have appealed to him. Perhaps he sensed the intelligence and spunk she would later display. Perhaps, as Frank says, *"I was ripe for it."* Whatever created the spark in a normally tongue tied man, when Narcissa left for Florida, *"she was followed by the youngest vice president of the National City Bank."*

Love was a new experience for him. *"I had never done anything like that before; I have never had any occasion to do it since."*

They knew each other only seven days when they became engaged, and those days were not even seven in a row. No one was more surprised and delighted than Frank.

FRANK A. VANDERLIP AND MISS NARCISSA COX, WHO ARE TO BE MARRIED TUESDAY EVENING.

FRANK VANDERLIP.   NARCISSA COX.

Wedding Announcement of Frank and Narcissa Vanderlip May 16, 1903

Their wedding date was set for May 19, 1903. Narcissa was due to graduate from the University of Chicago several months after that, and gave up her graduation to be married. Given their later emphasis on education for their children, it is surprising they did not wait those few months. Love is not always rational.

Frank's best man was his old friend and fellow reporter from Chicago, Edward Walker Harden, veteran of the Manila Bay cable adventure, who was known to his friends as Ed. At some point during their bachelor days, the two men had made a wager. Whichever of them was first to get married would have his honeymoon paid for by the other one.

Friends of both the bride and the groom helpfully drew up a budget for a grand honeymoon abroad, and made sure to publish it in the Aurora *Beacon-News*, perhaps as insurance against Ed Harden backing out of the bargain.

ITEMS IN A BRIDAL TRIP TO EUROPE	
Railroad tickets Chicago to New York . . . . . $	45
on Limited	
Stateroom on train	18
Meals on train	10
Two days' hotel bill in New York	50
Passage on steamer, bridal suite	500
Ten days at Hotel Carlton, London	250
Passage to Paris	30
Ten days at Hotel Ritz, Paris	300
Fare to Berlin, first class	50
Five days at hotel in Berlin	125
Fare to Vienna	15
Five days at hotel in Vienna	100
Fare to Rome	40
Five days at hotel in Rome	100
Fare to Venice	20
Five days at hotel in Venice	100
Railroad fare to Geneva	40
Trip through the Alps	150
Fare to Madrid	75
Five days at hotel in Madrid	100
Return voyage to America, first class	300
Tips	200
Carriage from dock to new home	5
Total Cost of Bridal Trip $	2,623

Christ Reformed Episcopal Church on Michigan Avenue in Chicago was the setting for the evening ceremony, and it was, "packed to the doors with friends of the bride and groom."

Distinguished guests could be divided into three classifications: financial - former Secretary of the Treasury Lyman J. Gage and two of his former Assistant Secretaries with their wives; journalistic - humorist George Ade and Chicago cartoonist John McCutcheon; and university - the president of University of Chicago. No mention is made in any of the papers of Frank's mother and grandmother, who must surely have been there.

Narcissa, gowned in white lace with full length sleeves, a high neck and a long train, made the unusual choice to enter the church alone, and was then escorted to the altar by her father, where a proud

Frank waited for her. Narcissa's singular entrance may have been a public statement of her views a few years later on women's rights, when she was the president of the New York League of Women Voters.

Frank's sister Ruth was one of the five bridesmaids. Perhaps it was the sight of her rose colored dress and short matching veil, or the elegant evening, that gave Ed Harden the idea, but he and Ruth were married on September 9 of the same year.

Several hundred people attended the reception at Narcissa's parents' home at 3308 Calumet Avenue. The reception hall, library and stairway were banked with pink roses. The bride and groom received their guests in the drawing room, which was decorated with white lilies. One of Frank's friends, in a description to the *Chicago Tribune*, called the evening a "really an important event."

Gifts were set out for display in two upstairs rooms. Secretary Gage gave a "beautiful crescent of diamonds"; John D. Rockefeller gave a large silver dish; and Marshall Field, who had issues with Frank's reporting style at the *Tribune*, gave a "set of diamonds and emeralds."

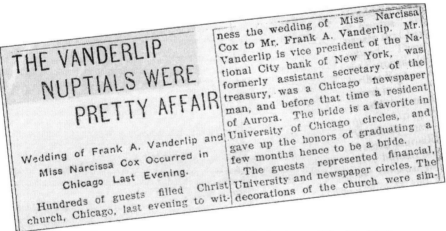

THE VANDERLIP NUPTIALS WERE PRETTY AFFAIR

Wedding of Frank A. Vanderlip and Miss Narcissa Cox Occurred in Chicago Last Evening.

Hundreds of guests filled Christ church, Chicago, last evening to wit-ness the wedding of Miss Narcissa Cox to Mr. Frank A. Vanderlip. Mr. Vanderlip is vice president of the National City bank of New York, was formerly assistant secretary of the treasury, was a Chicago newspaper man, and before that time a resident of Aurora. The bride is a favorite in University of Chicago circles, and gave up the honors of graduating a few months hence to be a bride.

The guests represented financial, University and newspaper circles. The decorations of the church were sim-

Wedding Announcement, Aurora Daily News May 20, 1903

Leaving the reception to start their honeymoon in Europe, Narcissa wore a blue "going-away" gown, and a hat of green leaves. They would return in September and move into 6637 Madison Avenue. No newspaper mentions whether Ed Harden paid for the honeymoon.

o   o   o

Beechwood

Teahouse, Beechwood, New York circa 1915

o o o

Beechwood

Marriage changes a man, even a workaholic like Frank Vanderlip. He and Narcissa did not stay at 6637 Madison very long. They moved to a rented house with an option to purchase it, on Fifty-first Street, just west of Park Avenue.

The following summer, they had their first taste of grand country life. Mr. Stillman generously lent them his gentleman's estate, at Cornwall, on the west shore of the Hudson. Narcissa and their new baby, also named Narcissa, moved there to escape the summer heat in the city. Frank worked and stayed in the town house on Mondays and Tuesdays, then again on Thursdays and Fridays. In case anyone should think he was going to *"develop permanently into a slacker,"* he carefully explained that he *"always had a thick bundle of papers with me when I came home on Tuesday and Friday evenings."*

Mr. Stillman's place was *"the loveliest, I think, that I had ever been in."* It had fine, comfortable, English style furniture, cheery chintz curtains, boats and a dock on the Hudson River, a stable full of riding horses that thrilled Frank, a carriage to take out for drives, and a garden where Frank and Narcissa spent peaceful hours.

It was more than just a house. It was several hundred acres, including Mr. Stillman's parent's home and a large farm, where he showed his Texas roots, raising Black Angus and Jersey cattle.

Mr. Stillman's Hudson River home
Now a Jesuit retreat house 2013

Staying there, Frank enjoyed *"the feeling of being a country squire. I seemed to be arriving somewhere."*

The "somewhere" was just ahead, around a few bends in the Hudson. Frank was about to be a squire in his own home.

A Grand Purchase - 1905

By 1905, Frank and Narcissa had a second daughter, Charlotte, named after Frank's beloved mother, and they were *"eager to have a country place."*

They found a home on the Hudson. It was, Frank says, *"a pretentious estate, a very old place, that sheltered a relative of the Vanderbilt family,"* who felt it was too large now that her children were grown.

Frank's first impression was that, *"If it was too big for a Vanderbilt I was quite certain it was too big for a Vanderlip."*

"Buy it," Mr. Stillman told him.

"Suddenly, I realized I wanted it passionately; my hesitation had been largely because it seemed such a startling step for the boy I had been to own an estate on the Hudson."

Beechwood before Vanderlip remodel 1907

Once again, Frank gives the reader a colorfully written tale, in which he may be forgiven for condensing some of the actual facts, as shown in the researched back-story of the property. As with much else in any historical account, the truth is never simple.

Back-Story of Beechwood

Large estates have names. This one was Beechwood. Built in 1790, it was purchased in 1833 by Benjamin Folger, at a time when the area was called Sing Sing, now Ossining, known today mainly for its famous prison. Folger and his wife Ann became followers of a man who named the property Mount Zion. He was known as Matthias the Prophet, or Matthias the Imposter, depending on who was giving the description.

By whatever name, Matthias, a colorful personality to say the least, lived there in 1834 and 1835, driving around in an unusual chariot drawn by a pair of grey horses. He claimed to be the Angel of Revelation, and sermonized from his own version of the Gospel to a circle of devoted followers. His story was worth a soap opera plot, involving several wife swappings, a trial, a poisoning, two exhumations

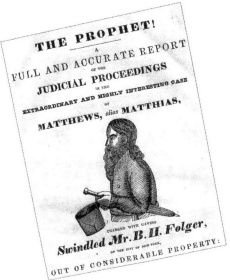

Pamphlet with trial report 1834
With portrait drawing of Matthias

of the same poor corpse, a vengeful mob, and a property swindle.

Matthias apparently murdered one of his disciples, Mr. Pierson, in 1835. He was acquitted for lack of evidence at a sensational trial. After a long, colorful affair with Ann Folger that began in 1834, and after a possible attempt to murder Ann and her long suffering husband, Matthias left the area ahead of a mob bent on shaving his beard. Benjamin Folger, more concerned about his wife than his business, went bankrupt and lost the house in 1835.

Over one hundred years after Matthias, when Frank's grandchildren heard floorboards on the upper levels creaking, they were certain it was the ghost of Matthias, returning with a knife to kill the ghost of Ann Folger. Frank, Jr. assured his nieces and nephews it was only changing temperatures that made the wooden floors creak.

One of the individuals who lived in the house and was unwittingly involved in the Matthias incident was a former slave claiming mystical powers named Isabella Baumfree, later known as Sojourner Truth. She had escaped to freedom in 1826 with her infant daughter, and was the first black woman to win in court against a white man when, later, she successfully sued for the return of her son. She was an early fighter for abolition and women's rights, giving a famous speech to the Ohio Women's Rights Convention in 1851. Narcissa, who was heavily involved in the women's rights movement seventy-five years

Sojourner Truth circa 1864

later, may not have known that Sojourner Truth, an early heroine of her favorite cause, had lived in her house.

Parts of an unusual type of carriage were found in the attic at Beechwood in 1982, and are believed to have been remnants left behind by Matthias.

An 1835 writer who told Matthias' story thoughtfully included a map of the ground floor of the home, intended, in the article, to give the reader an image of who was sleeping where during the whole episode.

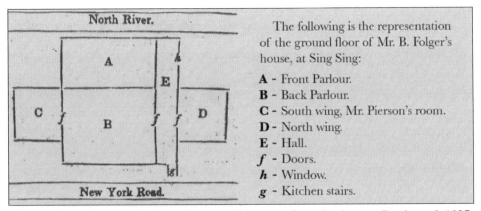

The following is the representation of the ground floor of Mr. B. Folger's house, at Sing Sing:

A - Front Parlour.
B - Back Parlour.
C - South wing, Mr. Pierson's room.
D - North wing.
E - Hall.
f - Doors.
h - Window.
g - Kitchen stairs.

Ground floor drawing of original house which was enlarged to become Beechwood 1835
North River is Hudson River, New York Road is Albany Road, Rte. 9
Scale not accurate, does not show extensive grounds on river and road sides of house

The property sold in 1893 to H. Walter Webb and his wife, whose maiden name was Leila Howard Griswold. Walter Webb was a vice president of New York Central Railroad, owned by the Vanderbilt family. Leila's name is important, as she is part of a confusion in Frank's story of his Beechwood purchase.

Architect Robert H. Robertson was hired to enlarge the original building, and the Webbs named the estate Beechwood. Walter died unexpectedly after a walk in his parkland in 1900. His widow, Leila, married famous interior decorator Ogdan Codman in 1904, which is why she sold the property to Frank. As far as can be determined from original documents, Leila was not related to any of the Vanderbilts.

Walter had a brother, Seward Webb. Seward's wife was, just for the sake of confusion, named Lila. She was the daughter of Walter's boss at the New York Central Railroad, Cornelius Vanderbilt II. Just to add to the muddle, Lila's sister Margaret Louisa (also a Vanderbilt), and her husband Elliott Shepard, owned Woodlea, the property across the road.

All of this is only of consequence to this tale because of Frank's charming sentence, speaking of his first impression of Beechwood, "*If it was too big for a Vanderbilt I was quite certain it was too big for a Vanderlip.*" Beechwood was never owned by a Vanderbilt.

Frank may have confused Leila and Lila from the start. Or, more likely he, or Narcissa, actually made this remark when Frank, along with William Rockefeller, purchased Woodlea, and developed the Sleepy Hollow Country Club. After buying Beechwood, when Woodlea became available, Frank considered buying the larger place for his home instead. Narcissa proclaimed that Woodlea was too large, and that she would never move in there. Whatever the truth may be, the story illustrates Frank's dry wit and story telling ability more than it gives a newspaper man's set of facts.

Woodlea circa 1905
Became Sleepy Hollow Country Club

Making A Home

Along with the house, Frank acquired twenty-three acres, then added 102 more. He and Narcissa soon hired architect William Welles Bosworth for a grand expansion. The original landscaping credit went to William Welles Bosworth and Narcissa. In 1913, Frederick Law Olmsted, designer of Central Park and of the 1893 Columbian Exposition in Chicago, added his genius.

Beechwood as expanded by Bosworth, from roadway on the property circa 1910
Before addition of library

A great expanse of lawn sloped down to the Hudson. A "well manicured wilderness" of elm and giant beech trees had a brook and pathways of slate meandering through giant rhododendron bushes. There were gardens "transplanted whole from European castles."

Swimming pool at Beechwood 1918

There was a swimming pool edged in white Italian marble that sparkled in the sunlight, "shining like loaves of fine grained sugar." Scattered about the grounds were reflecting pools, formal gardens, a small building styled after a Greek temple known as a *tempietto*, a pergola, wisteria covered trellises, and a tea house. Eventually there would also be a home for grown daughter Charlotte and another for Frank's personal doctor.

By the time they were finished, the property had two porticoed entries, over 100 rooms, a hunting lodge, a carriage house, a gate house, a squash court, and an artist's studio called Beech Twig, later rented by author John Cheever. A music room held glass cases of antique instruments. The rooms were decorated with dark wood, early English furniture, old silver, fine carpets, silk curtains, and a collection of oil paintings, in a style that was the standard of an elegant country home.

The French Room, Beechwood 1923

Beechwood Library 1919
With Andromeda painting

One of the paintings, a huge canvas of Andromeda, from Greek mythology, chained to a rock because her mother bragged of her beauty, was thought at the time to be by Anthony Van Dyck. Frank's boss and mentor, Mr. Stillman, also collected paintings and had a Van Dyck of his own. Mr. Stillman declared that he enjoyed Frank's much more than his own, because whenever he looked at his, he saw, as if on the canvas, the dollar figure of the interest his money could have been earning somewhere instead of hanging on his wall. The painting, since judged to be by an imitator, is now owned by the Los Angeles County Museum.

Pergola at Beechwood circa 1912

Narcissa Vanderlip 1917
Cultivating potatoes at Beechwood
For World War I food effort

Garden temple 1915

Although they lived a life of elegance, Frank and Narcissa always kept their Midwestern roots. Narcissa took an active role in the gardens and in growing plants from seeds and cuttings. During World War I, she turned part of Beechwood into a large vegetable garden, and did more than simply order her staff to plant crops. She enlisted her friends from the suffragette movement as helpers. The ladies did part of the field work themselves, wielding hoes and cultivators, as well as picking the crops.

For the entrance gate, Frank decided to bring in two columns that had been a part of what was called the Old Custom House in New York City. When it became the National City Bank in 1899, upper floors and a second level of columns were added in 1907. The two columns moved to Beechwood in 1908 from the lower level were apparently extraneous.

The *New York Times* reports that the columns, weighing thirteen tons each, were delivered by railway from New York. Five "powerful teams of horses" were not even enough to haul them to Beechwood, and a system of block and tackle was used to get the columns up the hill. They still stand today, at a rather unused entrance, on each side of an ornate iron gate. They are powerful guardians, even with half of their height now buried below ground level.

Old Custom House columns in original location 1899

Old Customs House columns at Beechwood gate circa 2012

Library ante-room circa 1926
Palos Verdes model on tabletop

The Neoclassical-styled library had a skylit, octagonal ante-room. When Frank was developing the area of Palos Verdes, California, he used the ante-room as a display space for the detailed plaster model he commissioned in Paris. Reflecting his lifelong love of reading, Frank wanted the library to be large enough for 100 men to read in peace or, possibly, large enough that he could find a place to read that was as peaceful as on his boyhood farm, when he carried a book in the bib of his overalls out into the fields while herding cows.

A Party House

Beechwood was much more than just a family home. As a man who continually marveled at his inability to "play", Frank had no trouble enjoying himself and entertaining guests when he was there. He often brought guests home for dinner from the city, to talk business and to show off his estate with pride. He and Narcissa freely opened the grounds for large parties, yearly for the bank employees, and often to benefit some worthy cause.

Six months after Frank took over as bank president, in January 1909, all 400 of the bank's employees and their companions or spouses rode a special train of ten brand new cars out to Beechwood on a Saturday, after the bank closed at noon. They were delivered to the gate in automobiles, where they were greeted by Frank and Narcissa. After walking through the greenhouses and the vegetable garden, and across the lawn and tennis courts, they spent the afternoon in athletic contests - a 100 yard dash, a one mile race, high and broad jumps, and a shot put. Prizes were gold seal rings. To relax, there was a musical concert, followed by dinner on the lawn and a vaudeville performance.

It is hard to imagine Mr. Stillman, Frank's predecessor as president, inviting such a crowd to his own estate on the river.

On the 100th anniversary of the bank, the party theme was a circus. The crowd arriving by train numbered over 1,000. A tent was set up for the performance of acrobats, equestrians, wirewalkers, jugglers and clowns. Frank, Narcissa and their children enjoyed front row seats.

After the performance, Frank hoisted Virginia, his youngest daughter, onto his shoulders and led the throng back to the lawn, where dinner was served under umbrellas, due to a light rain.

The *Times* reports, "The flower and Italian gardens of Mr. Vanderlip, as well as his spacious house, were thrown open to the visitors during the day, and despite the menacing looks of the gardeners, the young ladies and their escorts, and the older women with their children ran hither and thither plucking nosegays."

National City Bank party on Beechwood lawn June 1914

In June 1914, the group was serenaded on the lawn by the 71st Regiment band, and an orchestra played for dancing in a specially built pavilion. Professional athletes gave exhibitions on various parts of the grounds. Dinner on the lawn was catered by the bank's own restaurant. After dark, movies were shown on a screen in front of the house, the concerts continued, and the new Roman pool glowed with illumination.

Evening was special, with the grounds lit by a 15,000 candle power lamp, the largest incandescent electric light ever made. Frank must have personally selected this detail himself. As a man who had originally wanted to study electricity in college and counted Thomas Edison as a friend, how could he resist such a marvel?

Other events were charity oriented. Two hundred soldiers and sailors were entertained in 1918.

The following year, one thousand children, mostly wards of Westchester County, had a party at Beechwood in 1919. The children watched marionettes in the open air theater and saw a performance by Chow Chow, the health clown of the National Child Health Organization. A thirty piece orchestra from an orphanage performed. Some of the children were local Girl and Boy Scouts, a few others were sons and daughters of the Vanderlip's friends, along with Frank and Narcissa's own children. Adults brave enough to mingle with 1,000 children included Mr. and Mrs. John D. Rockefeller.

Frank and Narcissa in Japanese clothing 1920
Greeting guests at Beechwood party

Two parties had a Japanese theme. The first, in 1920, was a 'thank you' to members of the Japan Society, after a trip the Vanderlips took with a group of their distinguished friends. Frank and Narcissa greeted guests dressed in the custom-made kimonos they purchased while in Japan.

The second, in 1924, was a tea given to raise funds for Tsuda College, a women's school destroyed in the Great Kanto Earthquake that Narcissa visited on the trip to Japan.

Celebrities Come Calling

Other gatherings were smaller and more personal, attracting a wide range of well known personalities, all interesting people in their own fields. Annie Oakley, Sarah Bernhardt, Eleanor Roosevelt and Henry Ford were guests, as well as a number of Rockefellers. The Wright brothers even landed a plane on the lawn after circling the house.

Isadora Duncan dancing on lawn circa 1915
Photo probably taken at Beechwood

Dancer Isadora Duncan, famous for her modern, interpretive dance, sheer costumes, and bohemian lifestyle, not only danced on the Beechwood lawn, but taught the children to dance. It was summer, and to stay cool at night, the children slept in a room at the top of the house, on the fifth floor, where they could get a breeze off of the river. Isadora Duncan visited them there one night. They had a wonderful time, laughing and shrieking, leaping from bed to bed, as she taught them how to "flee from the flames and lava of the eruption of Pompeii."

Isadora Duncan's dancers circa 1915
At Beechwood

Isadora Duncan's sister Elizabeth
and young Virginia Vanderlip circa 1915

Frank and Narcissa helped fund Isadora Duncan's dance troupe while the group lived nearby during and just after World War I.

Several presidents were at the home. Before he became president, Woodrow Wilson visited Beechwood. Likewise, Herbert Hoover was there as a frequent guest.

One of Frank's favorite guests was not a famous man, but was his old friend from his days in Washington, Chief Messenger at the Treasury Department, Richard Green. Although they may have appeared, at a casual glance from afar, to have been master of the house and servant, when Frank sat in a chair on his lawn and Richard stood nearby, they were actually two gentleman happily discussing the affairs of the time. Frank says, "*It was always very fine when Richard Green was under my roof.*" Frank traveled to Washington for Richard several times, once to Richard's granddaughter's wedding, and again for Richard's funeral in 1924.

A School for the Children

With all the space at Beechwood, Frank and Narcissa had plenty of room for children. There were eventually a total of six - Narcissa in 1904, Charlotte Delight in 1905, Frank Arthur, Jr. in 1907, Virginia Jocelyn in 1909, Kelvin Cox in 1912, and John Mann in 1915. They could not have asked for a more wonderful place to grow up.

Narcissa Vanderlip with children Charlotte, Narcissa, and Frank, Jr. 1907

Most children of their time and social class went to one of the prestigious boarding schools along the east coast. Frank and Narcissa would have none of that. "*Education was what I had yearned for always and they should have it right at their front door,*" he decided.

While in Paris, they met Maria Montessori, developer of the teaching method that still bears her name. She had just begun to develop her ideas in 1897, and opened her first school in Rome in 1907.

The Montessori Method was quite radical, especially by American education standards of the time, based largely on rote memorization. Maria Montessori believed that children should be respected as being different than adults, and as individuals who were different from each other. They should be taught in a carefully prepared environment that emphasized freedom within limits. Students should be given a choice of activities within a preplanned range of options, and should learn by working with materials rather than by instruction. There should be a mixture of ages in the classroom, particularly the youngest, between the ages of three and six.

Frank and Narcissa not only brought back the idea, but also hired a teacher, first for a kindergarten originally set in Ed and Ruth Harden's home in nearby Sleepy Hollow. The school moved to Beechwood in 1913. They soon decided against using the Montessori Method, but hired architect William Welles Bosworth to build them a proper school on the grounds. It eventually had about 300 pupils, and cost Frank about a half a million dollars.

"That, I confess, was luxury. Wherever I was, in Europe, on the ocean, on trains at night, I could feel comfortable in the knowledge that my children would all be there waiting for me when I should return to play with them."

Scarborough School 1919

95

A theater was added in 1918, properly equipped with a high ceiling scene loft and the latest in a three-color lighting system. Poetry readings were given there by Robert Frost, Vachel Lindsay, and English poet laureate John Masefield. Isadora Duncan, Sarah Bernhardt, and Eleanor Roosevelt all appeared on the stage.

Where most schools have a playground, students at Scarborough could wander through Beechwood's woodlands and gardens. They could play on the broad lawns, use the tennis courts, and swim in the Olympic sized pool. A 1919 promotional booklet describes the facilities.

> "In formulating the plans, advice was sought from experienced school authorities, with the result that the structure is modern in every respect. The problem of procuring the best lighting, heating, and ventilation was given particular attention. Moreover a distinct effort was made to create an artistic whole, to surround the child with beautiful architecture, equipment and landscape."

It was a wonderful environment for Frank's children, and he could be proud of what he provided for them. But, in spite of having them at home, Frank was so involved with the bank that he did not spend as much time with them as he would have liked. *"But the truth is that by the time I really could play with them, most of them had gone right ahead and grown up,"* he says regretfully.

Eventually, after Frank passed away, the school separated as an entity from the Vanderlip family. It finally closed and, since 1981, has been used by the non-profit Clear View School, a day treatment program for emotionally troubled children.

View from Beechwood lawn to Hudson River 1918

The Pleasure of Coming Home

Beechwood from Hudson River side circa 1917

Just like thousands of other commuters, Frank would take the train into his office in New York. Unlike thousands of others, he did so in the comfort of his own train car, which was hooked to the back of the 8:26 a.m. run each morning. Being a good neighbor, he invited others in the area to ride in comfort with him. While many of them played poker or talked to each other, Frank read newspapers or worked on documents.

After Frank's return train trip home at the end of a day, he walked up the steep hill from the Scarborough station, *"not a short climb,"* he says, to his property. Another steep walk brought him to the base of a giant tree, where he would be met by his butler, a former London omnibus driver with the appropriately wonderful name Saunders. "Saundie," as the children called him, worked for Frank for ten years, beginning in 1910.

"When he met me on those days he would have for me in a tall and frosty glass, a fluid white and crinkly as lamb's wool. He called it a 'Ramos Fizz' and he would assure me that for taking the curse off a stuffy day it was the finest drink that could be concocted . . . If there was concealed in it a jigger of gin, that was entirely the fault of Saunders; I swear I never said gin to him in all the years of our association."

Recipe for Saunders' Ramos Fizz

Juice of half a lime	*Mix lime juice, powdered sugar, cream in glass*
2 teaspoons powdered sugar	*Fill glass with ice*
2 ounces of cream	*Add gin*
Ice	*Squirt full of Vichy water*
Vichy water	
1 jigger of gin	

Frank A. Vanderlip circa 1912

In spite of the luxuries surrounding his style of living, Frank was a rather conservative man, attuned to his family, his friends from the world of commerce, and the banking that consumed most of his attention until his retirement. He took his pleasure from seeing his family happy and healthy and educated at Beechwood. He never spent money on yachts, race horses, mistresses, or the idle pursuits of other rich men. The only other pasttime on which he would spend huge sums would come in 1913, when he made a purchase in far-away California.

After Frank's death, the family continued to enjoy life at Beechwood for several generations. Author Richard Yates lived there as a child when his mother taught art at Scarborough School. John Cheever rented the house on the grounds formerly lived in by Frank and Narcissa's daughter Charlotte. It was Narcissa's home for the rest of her life.

Large parts of Beechwood were sold to real estate developers in 1979. They took great care to restore the main house and divide it into three units roughly corresponding to the original 1800s structure and the two wing additions. A cluster of forty condominiums in the style of the main house was built on some of the former lawns and the orchard. Most of the old trees and the ornate landscape features, including the pool and pergola, have been preserved.

❍ ❍ ❍

Crisis

Depositors attempting to withdraw their savings from a bank, New York circa 1907

○   ○   ○

Crisis

A banker's nightmare can too easily turn into a reality. A "run" on a bank is one of the worst dreams a banker can have.

"Just fancy yourself as a banker - and discovering outside your plate glass facade an ever-lengthening column of men and women, all having bankbooks and checks clutched in their hands. Fancy those who would be best known to you, the ones with the biggest balances, pushing to the head of the line - there to bargain excitedly with the depositors holding the places nearest the wickets of the paying tellers. Even that won't give you a hint of what a banker's dread is like unless you heighten the effect with a swarm of hoarse-throated newsboys, each with his cry pitched to an hysterical scream; and then give the hideous concert an over-tone of sound from the scuffling feet of a mob."

National City Bank was the largest and most financially secure one in the country. Frank Vanderlip should have been able to sleep well. But, as he wryly notes, *"Bigness does not save an elephant staked on an ant-hill."* In 1907, someone stirred up the ants.

The Bank Panic of 1907

A forest fire begins with a single match, before grass and trees catch fire. Wind fans the flames. Smoke billows upward and animals flee. Homes burn. That is when people panic.

There was more than one match that lit the bank runs of 1907.

One was the great San Francisco earthquake of 1906, which took an unexpected amount of cash out of bank circulation, as funds went out of banks to finance the recovery, and as the Bank of England raised interest rates because of the large amounts British insurance companies paid out to U.S. policyholders.

A second, more widespread cause was a downturn in the general economy. For years, U.S. factories had been busy producing goods for a country eager to buy products. Production had finally outstripped demand and workers were let go in large numbers. At the same time, over one million mostly poor immigrants arrived in the first ten months of 1907, all looking for a place in a dwindling job market.

Immigrants arriving by ship 1907

Railroads, the backbone of the economy, were in trouble. Their infrastructure needed $12.5 billion in upgrading, according to one expert. Manufacturers had difficulty moving the goods they did produce to where they might be purchased.

Each of these problems, individually, might have worked itself out, if not for several major underlying flaws in the banking system.

How Banking Worked

It is difficult for a business person in the 21st century to imagine a world without computers, fax machines, ATMs, and all the devices bankers now take for granted. In 1907, at the end of each day, each bank stacked up all the deposits to their accounts that were drawn from other banks, and separately recorded all the withdrawals that were going out to other banks.

A person from each bank then actually hand carried all this information to a bank clearing house, where the amounts coming and going to each bank were recorded and sorted out. Even though this method sounds cumbersome, it was much less so than having each bank send different messengers out to every other bank individually.

Of course there was a lot of trust built into the system. Each bank had to know that the other bank members of the Clearing House Association had enough money to actually cover all their transactions.

Some banks carried, as part of their name, the word Trust. This was actually a deceptive title, because these were a type of bank not required to keep in their vaults as high a ratio of cash to deposits as traditional banks. They were free to lend a higher percentage out, and to make riskier loans at higher interest rates. So, they made more profit for their shareholders.

The Clearing House Association did not consider Trusts to be solvent, and did not trust them enough to let them participate in the daily morning exchanges.

Bank Clearing House, New York circa 1904

To do business easily, Trusts often made arrangements with regular banks. The Trust would have an account at a regular bank. Each day, the Trust would make a deposit in the regular bank, which would then take these funds to the clearing house.

A Speculator Starts A Run

Two of the men who used a Trust bank were F. Augustus Heinze, who had made a fortune with his United Copper Company in Montana, and his brother Otto. As the price of copper dropped, along with the rest of the stock market, the Heinze brothers decided to corner the copper market.

They went to their friend in New York, banker Charles W. Morse, who went to his friend Charles T. Barney, president of Knickerbocker Trust, the third largest Trust in the city. Even though Charles Morse cautioned the Heinze brothers against the entire maneuver, they got their loan.

When they tried to corner the market, beginning October 14, 1907, their bid failed. They miscalculated the number of outstanding shares. Holders of the short sales found places other than the Heinze brothers to buy what they needed.

Police guard failed bank, New York circa 1907

Otto and Augustus went broke, taking the Montana bank Augustus owned down with them. The Montana bank was associated with Mercantile National Bank in New York. On October 17, depositors, fearing that it, too, would collapse, started taking out their cash, and panic began to spread. As each bank reached a crisis point in the amount of cash left in their vaults, new lines of nervous depositors formed in front of other Trusts, all demanding cash.

"Extra editions of the newspapers, falling prices registered in the stock-market, wild rumors, these things contributed force to the wave of emotion that engulfed the banking system," Frank explains.

A Safe Deposit

For those nervous enough, and then lucky enough, to actually manage to withdraw their cash from a Trust bank, the question then was what to do with a large sum. Keeping it secretly stored at home was, most people knew, an unsafe option.

Sketch of Julian Street 1914

One nervous gentleman was representative of many in the same predicament. He was an acquaintance of Frank's, *"a man with black eyebrows so mobile from excitement they seemed likely, any moment, to scamper up his forehead and vanish into his hair. He was Julian Street, the young author, and he was clutching in a trousers' pocket something unprecedented in the pockets of all other authors I had ever known."* Julian Street was carrying $50,000 in $1,000 bills.

He was fresh from an adventure reclaiming part of his wife's inheritance from a Trust bank, after much heated discussion with that bank's staff. He wanted a safe place to put it. Frank was in the wonderful position of being able to assure Julian Street that his money was perfectly safe in the National City Bank. At the time, neither man had *"a clairvoyant hint of a future in which his son and my daughter would marry and make us grandfather-partners in . . . two adorable little girls."*

A Difficult Position

Every bank and banker was affected by the panic, but Frank carried an extra burden.

One night in December, 1906, Mr. Stillman had invited Frank to dinner, which was not an unusual occurrence in itself. On this particular evening, Mr. Stillman confided his intention to retire, planning to turn the bank presidency over to Frank. Mr. Stillman would then move to his Paris home, so that everyone would not still turn to him for guidance.

When the decision was announced to the other officers, there was *"considerable opposition,"* with the oldest vice president behaving *"almost as if he were going to suffer a stroke of apoplexy."*

It was decided that the turnover would not come until sometime in 1907. Mr. Stillman set sail for Paris, returning before the panic of October, 1907, as if he could foresee what was about to happen.

All during the panic, Mr. Stillman was still in charge, while Frank knew that any decisions made would affect the banking situation in the future, when he would be captain of the ship. Luckily, with cautious Mr. Stillman at the helm, Frank knew National City Bank would steer a good course.

There was much work for both men. Decisions had to be made every day, reacting quickly to each bank's distress, working with other solvent banks to decide which banks to help, and how much of National City Banks' assets to lend out. *"I was learning that banking is not a field for weaklings. If I was strong, I had need of all my strength and my own physical reserves were being drawn upon in the same way that we were having to take assets out of the bank's vaults . . . I had begun to know some of the terror that always had made the master of the City Bank preach his creed of caution. I think my graying hair became white in that panic year of 1907."*

J. P. Morgan To The Rescue

Every bank that failed had the potential to take other, more solvent ones with it, as stable banks tried to prop up the whole system by sending enough cash to the troubled institution. If a bank failed, the borrowed cash would never be paid back to the stable bank. And, even if it was, the stable bank was temporarily short of cash that would be needed if it were faced with a panic run of its own.

J. P. Morgan was a large, thickly mustached man, the most famous banker in the country. In the world of finance, his word was usually law. "*Mr. Morgan could be savage when he was out of patience, and, when he was crossed, unrelenting,*" according to Frank. If anyone could stop a run, it would be J. P. Morgan.

J. P. Morgan date unknown

When the crisis hit, he was out of town, in Virginia for a church convention. He returned, to the relief of most bankers, on Saturday, October 19, two days after the bank runs began. He had a cold, which did nothing to lighten his mood. One of the first things he did on Sunday morning was to summon the presidents of all of the Trust companies into his presence in his library on 36th Street.

"*Well, Mr. Morgan, with his back to the fireplace, watched those men as they gathered in response to his call . . . His nerves were raw that morning. He was using every fiber of his intelligence to encompass the problem of a nation. Moreover, he had, I think, a sound banker's contempt for the slovenly banking operations of some of those who were then gathering at his bidding.*"
J. P. Morgan could not believe that he actually had to introduce some of them to each other. All of the bankers in the Clearing House Association knew each other well.

J. P. Morgan's library with fireplace 1912

On Monday, Charles T. Barney was forced to resign from the Knickerbocker Trust, and the bank that acted as their clearing house said they would no longer do so. That started a run that caused Knickerbocker to close. Soon, even healthy Trusts had lines outside their doors.

Tuesday, October 22, the president of the Trust Company of America came to J. P. Morgan for help. After studying the situation with Secretary of the Treasury George B. Cortelyou and National City Bank's president, James Stillman, J. P. Morgan declared on Wednesday, "This is the place to stop the trouble, then."

The Trust Company of America had enough cash on hand to survive the rest of the day. That night, J. P. Morgan again assembled the Trust bank presidents, and held them in a meeting until they agreed to loan enough money to keep the Trust Company of America open the next day, which they hoped would restore public confidence. Secretary Cortelyou deposited $25 million, spread around various banks, the next day. John D. Rockefeller put $10 million in the National City Bank, and called the manager of the Associated Press to say that he would use half of his fortune, if necessary, to back up America's banking system.

Without ready funds to borrow for short term transactions, the stock market was having trouble doing daily trading. On Thursday,

October 24, prices of stock started to fall drastically. Once again, J. P. Morgan called in the bankers, raising $23 million to cover the day's trading and avert further disaster. When he left his office at the end of the day, he told the gathered reporters, "If people will keep their money in the banks, everything will be all right."

Bank run in the 19th Ward, New York circa 1907

The following Monday, the New York Clearing House took a drastic step and issued clearing house certificates, which the banks would recognize just the same as cash, for the purpose of moving money between themselves, freeing up actual cash for paying out to depositers. With a careful combination of all of these measures, and almost another month of daily crises that needed attention, calm finally returned by the middle of November.

Stress took a toll on them all. J. P. Morgan was seventy-one, a connoisseur of fine wine, and a heavy smoker of fat cigars that, as Frank describes them, "*had the form of a Hercules club, bulging thickly at the outer end, and they were absolutely poisonous for all but the most experienced smokers.*" Just like the others, J. P. Morgan worked late into the night all during the crisis.

Frank remembers one particular night that became a J. P. Morgan legend. "*On this night to which I refer, Mr. Morgan was listening as a report was made on the contents of the portfolio of the bank we were considering. That astonishing brain of his would take into itself a welter of facts and then, after consideration, he would speak, and we who listened would know that we were hearing wisdom. Suddenly I saw that the hand holding his cigar had relaxed on the table; his head had sunk forward until his chin was cushioned on his cravat. His breathing had become audible. The weary old man had fallen asleep.*

"Some one there, with a touch on the arm, silenced the one who was talking; another reached forward and lifted from the relaxed fingers, as one might take a rattle from a baby, the big cigar that was scorching the varnish of the table. Then we sat quietly, saying nothing whatever. One who went for a drink of water walked on tiptoes. The only sound that could be heard was the breathing of Mr. Morgan." They all sat that way for about a half an hour. When the great man woke up, *"consciousness returned abruptly; in a second he was wide awake and our conference was resumed with no reference being made to Mr. Morgan's nap."*

Crowd on Wall Street, Federal Building on right 1907

As the crisis ended, former Knickerbocker Trust president Charles T. Barney, whose bank had made the disastrous loan to the Heinze brothers, committed suicide with a pistol in his New York home.

New Ideas

When the forest fire is extinguished, or the war is won, or the bank panic is calmed, it is natural to search for causes, and to seek ways to prevent the next crisis. Like other top bankers, Frank had foreseen the economic problems. He gave much thought to a solution.

"*We would have to invent a wholesale banking mechanism that would relieve our economic system from the intolerable strains to which periodically it was being subjected.*"

Frank reached the conclusion that "*the remedy for the weakness in our banking system was the creation of some sort of a central institution to hold the reserves of the country.*" Then, "*the thing that brought about the financial paralysis, the mad scramble for individual reserves, would not have occurred.*"

A few bankers agreed with Frank, including Henry Davidson, Paul Warburg, and Ben Strong. Many others did not. Those men saw no reason for a change.

Frank and his friends did not give up. "*I wrote articles, delivered speeches and argued with every banker with whom I came in contact. The minds of legislators were somewhat quicker to grasp, to see, that there was a problem, but, for lack of banking experience, such minds were not likely to develop a blueprint of a workable machine. It was going to be a big job.*"

Many people give armchair analyses after a bad situation. Most of the time, their ideas are never put into practice. Frank was not such a person, content to daydream. He welcomed the new technology of electricity, and tried the novel Montessori approach to education. He was excited about new directions for banking. "*I was constantly after the younger officers, urging upon them the desirability of traveling more, of getting acquainted with people who were in a position to give business to the bank . . . even if it was not old-fashioned banking.*"

Frank himself brought a number of new ideas not only to his bank, but to banking in general. He was about to be one of a handful of men who would revolutionize the world of finance in America.

o o o

President

Entrance to bank president's office, National City Bank, New York 1909

o o o

President

When Frank Vanderlip walked up the steps into the National City Bank on January 12, 1909, it was into a new building, and into a new job.

Since its founding in 1812, almost one hundred years before this date, the bank operated out of its old building at what was first numbered 32 Wall Street and then, without moving, became 52 Wall Street. It had, according to Frank, a dark interior that was old-fashioned by the time he first entered it in 1902.

Mr. Stillman made a major investment for the bank in 1899, when he arranged the purchase of the New York Customs House at 55 Wall Street, for a price of $3,265,000. It was an impressive building, four

National City Bank, 52 Wall Street ca 1903

stories tall, with sixteen huge Ionic style columns, each made from a single piece of Quincy granite two stories high.

National City Bank hired Charles McKim, of the prestigious firm McKim, Mead and White, to do a complete remodel, which included removing four of the granite columns. Two of these were hauled, with difficulty, to Frank's Beechwood home. Charles McKim designed a second level, with four more floors and an upper row of Corinthian columns. The main floor glowed with light from its sixty-foot high central dome, perched above a bright, coffered ceiling. The floors and walls were of elegant grey marble.

It was, Frank said, *"breath-takingly lovely, a palatial colonnaded structure of commerce such as Mr. Stillman had wished it to be."*

Custom House
55 Wall Street
1885

National City Bank 55 Wall Street

Just after remodel with second layer added to Custom House 1909

This particular Tuesday, about three weeks after the bank moved into its new home, was monumental for Frank. It was the day he was elected president of National City Bank, the largest financial institution in the country. His mentor, Mr. Stillman, became chairman of the board. *"My new salary was $50,000. I was forty-five years old. And in six moves from overalls I had become the head of the country's biggest bank."*

National City Bank interior, new building 1910

With his new position, Frank looked for new ways to improve the bank. Having become acquainted with a number of bankers when he was in London, Frank decided to bring some British touches to his own facility. *"In a London bank the luncheon will be on a sideboard so that you may pick out what you wish to eat. There will be fine old silver with a proper polish on it; appreciative eyes will detect in that silver a delicate blue that comes with age. The hall-marks, for those who can read them, will reveal that this silver may have been used by hungry men who interrupted their eating to complain against the rebel, Washington."* Frank ordered luncheon to be served at the bank, for the officers and directors, a practice picked up by many others in the following years. He hoped it would encourage the directors to stop in more often, and pay more attention to the bank's operations.

Some European traditions just did not translate to American business. Frank's second British innovation did not fare well. "*I arranged to have tea served in the afternoon. But I did not like tea myself; nobody else seemed to, and the reporters thought it was funny - so that idea did not flourish.*"

Frank A. Vanderlip as Bank President 1909

Two Deaths in the Family

Before Frank had much time to celebrate his appointment, tragedy struck his family. It came through a phone call from Chicago at the end of March, 1909. "*In that time a voice relayed over such long stretches of wire would be faint, then loud, then faint again. By the tiniest thread of sound I learned that my mother was dying.*" Charlotte Woodworth Vanderlip had suddenly developed pneumonia, at the age of sixty-three.

Charlotte Woodworth Vanderlip circa 1907

Being president of National City Bank had advantages. Before airplanes could make a non-stop trip from New York to Chicago, the fastest way to travel was by train. Frank telephoned the president of New York Central Railroad and, "*Within an hour an engine, a couple of empty coaches and a private Pullman car came roaring up the Hudson Valley, pausing at the Scarborough station just long enough for me to step aboard, alone.*" Narcissa stayed at Beechwood, waiting for the birth of their daughter Virginia, who arrived one week later.

Frank's train made the trip in sixteen hours and seven minutes but, "*As I stepped down on the platform at Englewood and saw the concern in the blue eyes of my old friend and brother-in-law, Ed Harden, I knew I was too late. My mother had been dead for half an hour.*"

More bad news quickly followed. The *Chicago Record-Herald* told the story in their March 30 edition.

BANKER AGAIN MOURNS AFTER HIS DEATH RACE

———

Grandmother of Frank A. Vanderlip Expires Within 24 Hours of the Mother to Whose Side He Fruitlessly Hastened.

———

There will be a double funeral this morning at the home of Mrs. Charlotte Vanderlip, the mother of Frank A. Vanderlip, president of the National City Bank of New York. The gloom into which the New York financier was plunged by the death of his mother has been rendered more profound by the death of Mrs. Vanderlip's mother, Mrs. Sarah Woodworth.

. . . .

. . . .

She had been an invalid for more than two years, with long periods of unconsciousness. She had known that her daughter was gravely ill, and when consciousness returned she had asked eagerly about her condition. Something of the truth was conveyed to her by the faces of those who had assembled at the Vanderlip home. She persisted in her questioning and would not be denied. At last it was deemed wiser to tell her the truth, and the shock brought on her death.

The single funeral service will be read over both this morning. A special train then will convey mother and daughter to Aurora, where interment will take place.

No one records Frank's thoughts while hurtling across the country, alone on his private train except, for the company of a porter to cater to his needs and serve him meals. It was a far different trip than his first excursion on a train at the age of sixteen to another funeral, the elaborate one for President Garfield, when his bag refused to give up the sandwiches his mother and grandmother had so lovingly packed.

Riding The Rails

Every leader has his or her own style. Mr. Stillman's was to build bonds of friendship with other New York bankers. While Frank still maintained these connections, as he felt secure in his new position, he added more of his own touches than merely serving lunch at the bank.

He took great pleasure in seeing the country on inspection trips to other banks with which he did business. He rode in private cars belonging to various railroad companies where he was on the boards of directors. *"I wanted to talk with men, not merely to exchange written communications. So, as I rode on those trips of inspection, I was something other than a railroad director. I was a banker, yes; and I was an American, but most of all I was a human being, seeing myself in the person of every small boy who might be observed standing ankle-deep in barnyard muck watching our incredible passage.*

"No single individual ever sees all of the United States. At best the most traveled person sees only sample areas of its vastness and the aviator who spans the continent in a day sees less of it than a man who attends a push-cart in some slum street-market. Mine, however, were journeys to be enjoyed as a rule, because of that peculiar comfort that one has in a private Pullman car . . . what a home! As though the change had been accomplished by a wizard, each morning would bring to me and my companions a freshly exciting scene, with important personages arriving as visitors for breakfast; but at luncheon-time the world outside would be completely altered, and there would be other guests of consequence, and then dinner would be a quite separate adventure, even, perhaps, in another climate."

Overland passenger train circa 1910-1920

Even though Frank traveled in luxury, with equally important men who treated him with courtesy and respect, he *"had not forgotten what overalls were like."* One night, as he and his friends ate their dinner in their private car, stopped somewhere in West Virginia, he noticed a group of men and women on a hillside, watching them through the train's uncurtained windows. The men were in overalls, some of the women wore farming sun bonnets. *"We could hear them talking as the waiter placed the thick steak on the table. It was in a perfectly pleasant way that one of those spectators commented to some new-comer: 'See how those sons of witches eat!' Of course, I may have misunderstood him."*

Investment Advice

Ever since his European trip in 1902, Frank believed that investment was not only for the already rich, but it was the right and responsibility of everyone in the country, for their own wealth and for the strength of the United States. He was not afraid to talk to reporters about his views.

He had great respect for the intellect of the average man, and wanted to see more people make use of their mental abilities. He enjoyed interviews with reporters, and shared his thoughts on investing with a reporter for the *Aurora Daily News* in 1906, when Frank was still vice president, in his busy office at the bank.

"Every man should put away something. He ought to begin today, not tomorrow or next week. In the mean time, don't listen to those who promise $10 for $1. If such chances were possible they never would be advertised. When any wage earner, a carpenter, book-keeper, clerk or clergyman, has saved $200 or less, there is no reason why he cannot become the partner of Mr. Morgan in the United States Steel Corp., or of the Vanderbilts in the New York Central railroad. The shares of all those companies are for sale.

"But the wage earner ought to know the value of stocks himself. He knows the prices of flour, meat and shoes. Frequently he can tell you about the batting records of ball players. If he can master the mathematical details of pitchers, catchers and race horses he can comprehend the complexities of the stock market. Moreover, it would engage and centre his mind on something worth while. I wouldn't have him speculate, but I would like to see him invest his savings in sound stocks and become interested in the great business enterprises of the country.

"The workingman of France, even the peasants on the farms and in the vineyards, understands about stocks and bonds. If a vinedresser in wooden shoes can inform himself concerning the stocks sold in Paris, almost any American can learn the names of the stocks sold in New York."

While talking to the reporter, he "did considerable talking into the twenty-one telephones. He gave many directions and much advice. In the street below men and boys were running about like mad ants. The bellowing of curb brokers swept around the corner and joined the noise of trucks and several steam riveters at work on a high building (most likely the new 55 Wall Street location for the bank). Strangers also were waiting their turn in the reception room. Through all the din and distraction Mr. Vanderlip kept the light of good humor and patience in his face and the mellowness of a June morning in his voice."

The reporter goes on to describe Frank. "He is six feet and more, has deep, strong shoulders, long, stout legs, gray eyes and hair that is white many years ahead of schedule. The mustache, grizzled when it ought to be brown, is trimmed to the stubbiness of a shoebrush."

Public Secrets

Frank was a rich, successful man. He communicated daily with men with powerful last names such as Morgan, Rockefeller, and Harriman. He sat on boards of directors for the strongest companies, and he formed opinions not always in agreement with his peers. A lifetime that included manual labor, journalism, an inquisitive mind, and a love of learning coalesced in his thinking about banking and business in general.

Woodrow Wilson, not yet president, felt there should be a law that would force corporations to file reports of director's meetings for public inspection. "*Well, there are some of us who have been on many boards who would say such reports might not reveal much,*" Frank commented, aware that boards often simply rubberstamped whatever a strong leader proposed. But, he agreed that the public, especially stockholders, had a right to know what companies were doing with their money.

"*None of the big men of Wall Street could tolerate the thought of publicity when I arrived there. If they were suspicious of reporters, they were equally suspicious of men who would talk with reporters . . . it was an honorable but mistaken part of their creed. If I might be permitted to give a single piece of advice to my countrymen it would be to insist, as a national policy, on being given a better understanding of the affairs of business; after awhile, I think, 'insiders' would include approximately all thrifty persons.*"

To be better informed, Frank believed, the general public should have ready access to information.

"A great corporation carrying on a public service is not a private thing; it affects too many lives. From my earliest days as a reporter, when I had to cozen my way into stockholders' meetings by buying a single share of stock, I have felt that corporate secrecy generally was wrong. I thought then, and I think now, that corporation wealth would be better administered from the viewpoints of small stockholders, labor, and the public, if the affairs of corporations had a great deal more publicity . . .

"It has been my experience that honest business men greatly outnumber dishonest business men. I have found that, usually, business is fairly conducted. It is because I am so sure of this that I think that publicity rather than a ceaseless flood of new laws is what we need. Publicity would sharply curb the grasping fellows."

Frank's belief that the public should be informed, and that business should be conducted openly was about to be put to a test, in a still-controversial matter that greatly affects the country to this day.

Jekyll Island

Jekyll Island 2013

o o o

Jekyll Island

There could not be a better-named location for a secretive conclave of powerful men that, over one hundred years later, is still both praised and reviled in various circles.

After the Bank Crisis of 1907, everyone in the financial community knew changes had to be made to safeguard the monetary system of the country. No one knew quite what those changes should be.

Senator Nelson Aldrich circa 1910

Searching for answers, Congress appointed a joint commission of members of both houses to study the issue, led by Senator Nelson Aldrich, considered to be the most knowledgeable Congressman when it came to finances. "*This group had gone to Europe, had interviewed bankers and the heads of the central banks, and then, after a pleasant summer, they had returned to the United States without any definite idea of what they ought to do . . . although Senator Aldrich really had been working hard for two years.*"

Mr. Stillman wrote to Frank from Paris after seeing Senator Aldrich, emphasizing the importance of working on the problem. He felt that if Frank, Senator Aldrich, and Harry Davidson of J. P. Morgan and Company could get together free of interruptions, they might crystallize a banking plan. "*Mr. Stillman also reported to me that in his talk with Senator Aldrich he himself had not expressed any views, except as he had impressed on the senator his belief in the necessity of not being too much influenced by 'our Wall Street point of view'. But would the electorate have believed that? I question their ability to do so*

"This was how it happened that a group of us went with Senator Aldrich to the Jekyll Island Club on the coast of Georgia."

A Private Place - 1910

Jekyll Island is not as frightening as its name implies. It consists of only 4,400 acres of useable land, of which 200 acres now make up the Jekyll Island Club Historic District. The Club was founded in 1886 by a group that included J. P. Morgan, Marshall Field, of the Chicago department store, Joseph Pulitzer, after whom the journalism prize is named, and members of the Rockefeller and Vanderbilt families.

The main purpose of the Club was to be a hunting resort. A game warden kept the island plentifully stocked with pheasant, turkey, quail and deer, which were often served on the restaurant menu. Horseback riding, camping, and hunting were encouraged, even for the members who were women.

Looking like a Victorian wedding confection with its turret and gracious porches, the main Club building was an elegant, comfortable place, staffed by discreet help who knew how to care for the discerning members. In the winter season, it was almost empty, a perfect retreat.

Jekyll Island clubhouse soon after construction 1888

The Journey

A private island was the perfect place to work. In spite of Frank's belief that the public should be aware of the business of finance, he felt it was necessary to be *"as secretive, indeed, as furtive as any conspirator. None of us who participated felt that we were conspirators; on the contrary we felt we were engaged in a patriotic work. We were trying to plan a mechanism that would correct the weaknesses of our banking system as revealed under the strains and pressures of the panic of 1907."*

The men had to leave New York on the night of November 22, 1910 as a group without being spotted by reporters. "*Since it would be fatal to Senator Aldrich's plan to have it known that he was calling on anybody from Wall Street to help him in preparing his report and bill, precautions were taken that would have delighted the heart of James Stillman.*"

As though they were part of a mystery, "*We were told to leave our last names behind us. We were told, further, that we should avoid dining together on the night of our departure. We were instructed to come one at a time and as unobtrusively as possible to the railroad terminal on the New Jersey littoral of the Hudson, where Senator Aldrich's private car would be in readiness, attached to the rear end of a train for the South.*"

The number of men boarding Senator Aldrich's train car varies, depending on the source for the list. Frank says that included were the Senator; Assistant Secretary of the Treasury A. Piatt Andrew; J. P. Morgan and Company partner Henry P. Davison; Kuhn, Loeb and Company partner Paul M. Warburg; Bankers Trust of New York vice president Benjamin Strong, Jr.; and Frank himself.

Private railroad car similar to Senator Nelson Adrich's 1912
This car owned by Clara Baldwin Stocker, daughter of Lucky Baldwin

Some sources say that Benjamin Strong was not on the island, but was included in so many follow up discussions that he became a first-name-basis member of the group. Still other sources add Charles D. Norton, president of J. P. Morgan's First National Bank of New York and other sources add the Senator's personal secretary, Arthur Shelton.

However many travelers there were, they probably all enjoyed the little bit of 'cloak and dagger' work. "*When I came to that car the blinds were down and only slender threads of amber light showed the shape of the windows. Once aboard the private car we began to observe the taboo that had been fixed on last names. We addressed each other as 'Ben,' 'Paul,' 'Nelson,' 'Abe' (it is Abram Piatt Andrew). Davison and I adopted even deeper disguises, abandoning our own first names. On the theory that we were always right, he became Wilbur and I became Orville, after those two aviation pioneers, the Wright brothers.*"

They were determined to work in secret. "*Discovery, we knew, simply must not happen, or else all our time and effort would be wasted. If it were to be exposed publicly that our particular group had gotten together and written a banking bill, that bill would have no chance whatever of passage by Congress. Yet, who was there in Congress who might have drafted a sound piece of legislation dealing with the purely banking problem with which we were concerned? Indeed, there were surprisingly few bankers, besides those of us who had been called together, who had given the special matters under consideration any thorough study whatever.*"

As soon as the train was rolling, the men went to work. At first each man spoke up about his own concerns, with vague, "*scraps of ideas about as formless as the contents of a rag-bag.*"

Frank made a suggestion. " '*What we ought to do first,*' I said, '*is to set down those things about which we are agreed, then, one by one, we can take up those things about which we seem to disagree.*' " There are still many business meetings and disagreements that could benefit from this method.

His shorthand skills came in handy. Frank

Train station, Brunswick, Georgia circa 1910

became the recording secretary as the group, representing about one quarter of the world's wealth, rode the rails down the coast in the dark.

At the Brunswick, Georgia train station, Senator Aldrich's biographer tells how they were almost discovered by the press. The station master mentioned that people there recognized the group, and that reporters were waiting outside of the building. Henry Davidson took charge of the matter, and suggested to the station master that they go for a walk. Henry Davidson returned with a smile, and assured the group that they would not be revealed. No one asked Henry Davidson how the reporters were diverted. Still anonymous, the men left the station and took a boat to Jekyll Island.

On The Island

Parlor, Jekyll Island Club 1893

On Jekyll Island, they were well cared for by a staff accustomed to *"people with a taste for luxury,"* on a deserted island where they were *"completely secluded, without any contact by telephone or telegraph with the outside."*

The meals must have been outstanding, as this is almost the only time in all of Frank's writings that he bothers to mention details of what he ate. *"Without our ever stopping to hunt, deer, turkey and quail appeared on the table; there were pans of oysters not an hour old when they were scalloped; there were country hams with that incomparable flavor that is given to them in the South . . .*

Diningroom, Jekyll Island Club circa 1918

Thanksgiving occurred during that week and we ate wild turkey with oyster stuffing and went right back to work."

The Plan

Everyone agreed at the beginning that, *"what we simply had to have was a more elastic currency through a bank that would hold the reserves of all banks,"* in order to avoid a repeat of the Bank Crisis of 1907, but there were many serious questions to debate.

Questions for Debate

• *If it was to be a central bank, how was it to be owned, by the banks, by the government, or jointly?*

• *When we had fixed upon bank ownership and joint control, we took up the political problem of whether it should be a number of institutions, or only one.*

• *Should the rate of interest be the same for the whole nation or should it be higher in a community that was expanding too fast and lower in another that was lagging?*

• *Should it restrict its services to banks?*

• *What open-market operations should be engaged in?*

Frank, remembering the time twenty-five years later, says they worked, *"for a week or ten days."* Paul Warburg recounts that, after they had a basic outline, and before settling on a final recommendation, the men took a day off to go shooting, which has given the entire planning session the nickname, 'The Jekyll Island Duck Hunt.'

Writing in defense of criticism of the meeting that continues to this day, Frank asserts, *"If what we had done then had been made known publicly, the effort would have been denounced as a piece of Wall Street chicanery, which it certainly was not. Aldrich never was a man to be a mere servant of the so-called money interests. He was a conscientious, public-spirited man. He had called on the four of us who had Wall Street addresses because he knew that we had for years been studying aspects of the problem with which it was his public duty to deal."*

The Results

After they returned North, Senator Aldrich planned to present the bill the group had drafted to Congress. He fell ill, so Frank and Benjamin Strong went to Washington to write the report that would accompany the bill, known as the Aldrich Plan, introduced on January 11, 1912.

It called for a central bank, to be called the National Reserve Association, controlled by private bankers and financial experts. It would print money that would be an obligation of the private banks, and it would be the "principal fiscal agent of the United States." There would be 15 district associations, and a total of 46 directors on the board. Three-fifths of the directors would be elected by the member banks without regard to their size, an idea the Aldrich Plan said was "more democratic in form, with more liberal representation to minorities than any method in general use."

The chairman of the board of directors would be the governor of the National Reserve Association. He was to be appointed by the President and serve a ten-year term, unless he was removed by a vote of the board. The government would be represented on the board by the Secretary of the Treasury, the Secretary of Agriculture, the Secretary of Commerce and Labor, and the Comptroller of the Currency.

As explained in the originally proposed Aldrich Plan:

> "This distribution of power and control furnishes the assurance that the general interests of the country and of all communities will be conserved as well as the interests of the shareholders, as the National Reserve Association, through this form of organization, is brought into close relations of responsibility to the Government and the people. The provision that one-half of the directors elected by the branches shall fairly represent the agricultural, commercial, and other interests, and shall not be connected with banks or other financial institutions, insures the infusion of representative men into the governing board, who will have every motive to act in the public interest."

The Aldrich Plan did not pass in Congress. Senator Aldrich retired, and Democrat Woodrow Wilson, who was opposed to the idea of a central bank, became president in 1912. His party platform opposed the Aldrich Plan but supported the general idea of banking reform.

The Glass-Owen Plan

President Wilson set his own party to work on a plan that, originally, would not have a central bank at all. The chairmen of the House and Senate Banking and Currency Committees, Representative Carter Glass and Senator Robert Latham Owen, worked for months, introducing what would be known as the Glass-Owen bill on June 26, 1913.

Senator Robert Latham Owen 1910   *Congressman Carter Glass circa 1916*

Instead of a central bank, this plan called for 12 or more privately owned regional banks which would perform the same functions as one central unit. They would be under the control of one central, government controlled entity known as the Federal Reserve Board. It would co-ordinate monetary policy through the regional banks. Currency printed though the Federal Reserve Board would become an obligation of the U. S. government.

Conservative Republicans were vehemently opposed, because bankers would have no control over their own industry. Progressive

Democrats in the House, backed by William Jennings Bryan, wanted strong government oversight, and approved of the Glass-Owen bill. The bill passed the Democratic House, 285 to 85, on September 18, 1913.

The Senate was not so easily swayed. It debated and wrangled for months, with the Senate Banking Committee holding hearings from September through October. That is when Frank stepped into the fray.

Frank testified on October 6, 1913. He opposed three points in the Glass-Owen plan - the independence of regional reserve banks, the plan to have the new form of issued currency be backed by assets other than gold, and the section compelling all national banks to become members of the new association. He said there were many good qualities to the Glass-Owen bill and "took issue with many bankers who have criticized adversely different parts of the bill," according to the *New York Tribune*. Although he

New York Tribune *October 9, 1913*

believed Glass-Owen was a step in the right direction, he agreed with the banking community that it gave too much political control over the banking system.

He then threw a new plan into the ring. The names actually sponsoring his proposed bill were Senators Hitchcock, Nelson, Bristow, Crawford, McLean and Weeks, but it became known as the Vanderlip Plan. It called for a federally controlled central bank and twelve regional banks around the country. There would be nine members of the Federal Reserve board of directors, five of them representing the government and four representing banking interests, giving the government a measure of control. But, the public would be able to purchase stock in the regional banks, theoretically putting them in control as stockholders, while bankers would still have some power.

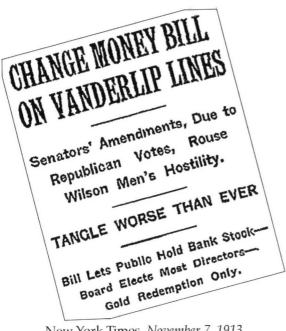

CHANGE MONEY BILL ON VANDERLIP LINES

_____

Senators' Amendments, Due to
Republican Votes, Rouse
Wilson Men's Hostility.

_____

TANGLE WORSE THAN EVER

_____

Bill Lets Public Hold Bank Stock—
Board Elects Most Directors—
Gold Redemption Only.

New York Times *November 7, 1913*

The Senate Banking Committee adopted three of the Vanderlip Plan ideas on November 6, 1913, with several of the Democrats and all of the Republicans voting for them. The public was given the right to own stock in the regional banks. The Federal Reserve Board would have the right to appoint five of the nine Directors of the regional banks. The proposed new currency was, according to the *New York Times*, "made redeemable solely in gold, instead of in gold and lawful money, a change earnestly advocated by Mr. Vanderlip and by practically every banker that testified before the committee."

It seemed for a while as if Glass-Owen would be derailed for the rest of the year while discussion went on. President Wilson was furious. Some of the Democrats called for a binding party caucus, but their leadership felt that would simply accentuate differences within the party, although the "extreme Wilson wing of the party" wanted the President to "run a freight train over the recalcitrant Democrats."

In a show of partisan politics recognizable today, Senator Simmons said, "There is no reason to suppose that the Democrats on the floor of the Senate will support a bill that did not have the support of a majority of the Democrats in committee." Another Democrat, Senator Vardaman, put it even more bluntly. "I do not propose to vote for a currency bill that is five-sixths Republican," he stated.

The following week, on November 10, 1913, Frank, Congressman Glass, and Senator Owen held a friendly debate on their two plans in front of a discerning audience. The Economic Club of New York held a dinner at the Hotel Astor attended by 1,200 bankers and businessmen.

Hotel Astor Grand Ballroom, New York circa 1910

The first speaker was Frank's original mentor, Joseph French Johnson, now Dean of the School of Commerce at New York University. He explained how the Democratic Party, of which he was a member, meant to write into their party platform the phrase "We oppose the so-called Aldrich plan for the establishment of a central bank." Instead, the word "for" was accidentally replaced with the word "or", fundamentally turning the entire party against the idea of any central bank at all, due to a "trifling typographical error, the omission of a single letter of the alphabet," according to the *New York Times*.

Frank spoke next, beginning with a spirited defense of Wall Street and bankers. *"What does this cry of government by the people really mean? Who are the people? Are not my associates and am not I one of them?"*

He explained how he and many of his associates came from simple beginnings, and went on to justify why such men should be entrusted with their positions, hinting that they knew more about the subject than the average person. *"In such a technical and intricate matter as banking and currency legislation do you want the advice of men who have started in most humble surroundings and remained there, or of men who, in spite of every handicap, have surmounted the barriers and have made a success of life?*

"I am charged with representing an institution that in the minds of some people seems to be the very fangs and claws of the 'Money Trust.' Yet in its dealings with the public the limit of interest which it has ever charged is six per cent, no matter how high the rate in the Street has gone above that. That institution has always stood ready to assist the Government in its financing at any and all times, even at the possibility of loss to itself. In its dealings with its employees, it has provided liberally for pensions and insurance without cost to them; it has created a fund larger than the endowment of some colleges for their education, and it looks after their physical welfare with the most scrupulous care.

"I decline quietly to be tagged a discredited citizen, or to come before you with an apology for the business in which I am engaged."

Believing that bankers would have to strongly support the new law in order for it to function, Frank gave the President some advice. *"It is of no moment at all to the business world whether that action is in October or January, but it is of tremendous moment that we have legislation that will work successfully, and toward the carrying out of which bankers will heartily co-operate, not through compulsion, but because their business judgment recognizes it as sound."*

Frank complimented President Wilson on his *"courage, his persistency, for the strength of his political purposes,"* before chiding him for rushing the process. *"The measure history will make of your acts will be largely influenced by the success or the failure of the legislative program which you are now with your splendid will imposing upon the country. We need legislation, but that legislation must conform to higher laws than any man or set of men can make - to the laws of economics. Those laws are greater than party platforms, they are greater than any administrative program; they will work undeviatingly whatever legislation you write upon the statute books . . . There is nothing in the financial situation that need give you cause to hurry, if by taking time for deeper consideration and for better understanding your proposed enactments can be improved."*

His next words to President Wilson are still timely advice to every political body, from the halls of Congress to local city politicians.

> *If you will now throw the tremendous weight of your influence on the side of free intellectual judgment and against the brute force of party majorities, if you will throw the great weight of your influence in a direction that will lead to an exercise of freedom of thought without political restriction, if you will see to it that decisions may be made upon the economic merit of the proposals and not be tied and hampered by party domination, you will then have earned lasting praise. Do not again permit the intellects of the men who must decide this great question to be bound and hampered by caucus rule. Do not permit partisan pride to stand in the way of achieving that which is right. See to it that there is free play for the sound and unhampered judgment of Congress and then you will indeed have brought to this country a new freedom."*

Frank added to this statement the next day, when he spoke to members of the Catholic Club, saying:

> *"It seems to me that the time has come for us to use all the force we have to make Senate and Congress see that what we want is their intelligent judgment."*

Senator Glass spoke next, and defended his bill, saying his committee had listened intently to bankers before ever crafting the legislation. "It seemed fair to me that they should be represented. When the President of the United States in conference gave it as his opinion that they should not be represented, I didn't sleep a wink that night." He added, "There are many things I can learn, but what I have been unable to learn is what the American bankers really want."

The Final Vote

The Vanderlip/Hitchcock Plan was officially entered as a proposal into the Congressional Record on November 22, 1913. The House passed the Glass-Owen Bill with the Hitchcock amendments

November 24. A slightly different version passed the Senate on December 18. After reconciliation of the two, the House voted yes on December 22, and the Senate did the same the following day. President Wilson signed the Federal Reserve Act into law on December 23, 1913.

President and Mrs. Woodrow Wilson 1920

There would be a seven member Federal Reserve Board of men appointed by the President and approved by the Senate. The Board would oversee the district banks, generally regulate the banking system, and set national monetary policy.

Each of twelve branches would have its own board of directors. There would be a single national currency, originally called Federal Reserve Bank Notes. The Notes were to be backed by one of the twelve branch banks, and would be redeemable in gold or "lawful money."

According to Frank, the Federal Reserve Act was basically the same plan proposed by the Jekyll Island group. "*It provided an organization to hold the reserves of all member banks and arranged that they would always be ready to relieve a member-bank under pressure by rediscounting loans that it held. The law as enacted provided for twelve banks instead of the one which the Aldrich plan would have created; but the intent of the law was to coordinate the twelve through the Federal Reserve Board in Washington, so that in effect they would operate as a Central Bank. There can be no question about it; Aldrich undoubtedly laid the essential, fundamental lines which finally took the form of the Federal Reserve Law.*"

The Board

First members of the Federal Reserve Board 1914
Left to right: William G. McAdoo, Secretary of the Treasury;
John S. Williams, Comptroller of the Treasury; Adolph C. Miller, economist;
Frederic A. Delano, former president of Wabash Railroad System;
Unknown man; Charles S. Hamlin, Governor of the Reserve Board;
W.P.G. Harding, Alabama banker; Paul Warburg, international banker

Moody's Magazine introduced the Board to the financial world in 1914 with a one-page article, cautiously expounding the virtues of the new system.

Not since the Civil War have the American people imposed upon seven men so arduous and so vitally important a public duty as that with which they have entrusted the members of the Federal Reserve Board, who must bear the responsibility for the success or failure of the new banking system of the United States. For fifty years the United States has prospered, except on a few notable occasions, under the National Banking System. Now that system, because of its inadequacy in financial crises, is to be revised and to a large extent superseded by a system based on European practice in which the volume of currency in the country is measured by the demands of business, and the reserves of all the banks are mobilized in central reservoirs. On paper the Federal Reserve Act promises to remedy the greatest evils of American finance. Whether that promise is to be fulfilled or not depends very largely upon the ability and the patriotism of the seven men . . . They are men of wide experience in business and finance.

The Federal Reserve System was planned especially to enable our banks to stand the shock of financial and commercial crises. Its foundations are being laid at the most critical moment in the history of the modern world. If they are finished successfully, as we believe they will be, no future crisis can shake the structure which will be erected on them.

The Legacy

There have been over 100 amendments to the original Federal Reserve Act, giving proof to Frank's statement, *"There can be no time limit beyond which you cannot change a legislative plan if by such change you will more nearly conform that plan to higher laws."*

In 1933, the gold obligation was removed, and redemption would be with current notes of equal face value. Since 1971, what are now known simply as Federal Reserve Notes are backed by all twelve of the Federal Reserve Banks. They are not convertible to gold or any other specific commodity, but only by the legal requirement that they are issued against the Bank's collateral.

The Jekyll Island experience and the following legislative battle was something Frank trained for his entire life. It let him marshal all he had studied and pondered about banking principles - how to write about them coherently, and how to make the system more fluid. He believed he was doing a service to his occupation and to the country.

"We gave, each of us, every bit of our mental energy to the job and I enjoyed that period as I never have enjoyed anything else. I lived during those days on Jekyll Island at the highest pitch of intellectual awareness that I have ever experienced. It was entirely thrilling."

o o o

Titanic

Crowd gathers outside White Star Line office to hear news, New York April 15, 1912

o o o

Titanic

Narcissa and Frank Vanderlip traveled to Europe regularly, making the five day Atlantic crossing in the best cabins on the best

Titanic leaves Southampton April 10, 1912

ships. Had they been returning from Europe on the night of April 14, 1912, it would most likely have been on White Star's newest ship, the Titanic. But, on that fateful Sunday, they were safely settled in their warm home at Beechwood on a cold night, awaiting the birth of their fifth child.

It was not until the next morning that they heard the news of the Titanic disaster. As the world knows, the grandest and newest passenger ship afloat hit an iceberg and sank in frigid waters. Somewhere between 324 and 329 of the passengers were in luxurious first class. One hundred and thirty of them died. Many of them were friends of Frank and Narcissa, and also friends of their neighbors.

Madeleine Astor   *John Jacob Astor IV*   *Margaret "Molly" Brown*
In mourning for her husband   *His body was recovered*   *Photo taken aboard rescue ship*
Titanic passengers known to Frank and Narcissa Vanderlip and their neighbors

Eleanor Widener   *George Dunton Widener*   *Benjamin Guggenheim*
Survived   *Body not recovered*   *Body not recovered*

Titanic passengers known to Frank and Narcissa Vanderlip and their neighbors

Friends On Board

Frank's friends were mainly people from the worlds of business and banking, and his circle of these men was large. He traveled frequently, mainly by private rail car, to visit bankers throughout the country. He belonged to a variety of private clubs and sat on the boards of directors of many companies, particularly in the rail industry. There were probably few Americans in first class on the Titanic with whom he would not have been familiar.

George Dunton Widener was heir to the largest fortune in Pennsylvania, and owner of a successful streetcar company. His father was on the board of directors of Fidelity Trust Company of Pennsylvania, the bank controlling International Mercantile Marine Company, a large American shipping conglomerate that owned Titanic's White Star Line. He was on board with his wife Eleanor and twenty-seven year old son Harry. He would most certainly have known Frank through banking business.

Harry was returning with his parents after a trip to purchase old and rare books in Europe to add to his distinguished collection, including one from 1598, which went down with the ship. Frank was also a collector of books, perusing auction catalogs and marking down his choices, along with his maximum offer, before sending a trusted assistant to auctions to place his bids. Once, when someone jokingly asked him if he had read all of the thousands of books in his library he answered, *"Yes, some of them twice."* He and Harry Widener had much in common.

Both George and Harry's bodies were never found. After the disaster, Eleanor donated a library to her son's alma mater, Harvard, with the stipulation that not even one stone of the building would be altered as long as it stood. The Widener Library still stands, unaltered, in the Harvard Yard.

George and Dorothy Harder and Clara Hays
Aboard the rescue ship Carpathia
Body of Clara Hays husband George recovered
Titanic passengers known to the Vanderlips

Charles Melville Hays was born in Illinois, as was Frank, and rose to be the general manager of Canada's Grand Trunk Pacific Railway. When he and his wife Clara were returning from Europe on Titanic, he was working on financing and building Canada's second transcontinental railway and related hotels. Clara got in a lifeboat and was safely rescued. Charles' body was later recovered.

George Achilles Harder and his wife Dorothy were from New York City. He was a top executive with Essex Foundry. Both of them survived, and George Harder later became chairman of the board of his company. They saved three items from the Titanic that were passed down in the family - her fur coat, the button hook for her shoes, and a bottle of brandy.

Telephone communications in 1912 were still over lines run through manual switchboards, with connections often dependent on the skill of the operator and the number of calls already on the line. The first transcontinental call would not go through for another three years. There were no telephone lines to talk directly overseas. All messages with passenger survival lists had to first be telegraphed to New York, transcribed, and then posted for viewing.

The residents of Scarsborough, N. Y. had to rely on someone in New York City constantly checking the survivor lists and relaying the information through overworked lines and overworked operators. Because of Frank's necessity to be able to do business even from his home, the connections at Beechwood were better than most.

All day on Monday, Beechwood was a gathering spot for Scarborough residents looking for answers by telephone about who survived and who perished. It was a traumatic and anxious time, and the house was filled with chaotic activity and grieving people. It would have been good to have a calm hostess in charge, dispensing food, drinks, and sympathy.

Narcissa was not able not take on that role. Instead, she was busy in the bedroom, delivering a healthy baby boy. Kelvin Cox Vanderlip was born on Monday, April 15, 1912.

Kelvin Cox Vanderlip
Age 3 1915

o o o

Palos Verdes
Part I

Lunada Bay, Palos Verdes, California 2013

○ ○ ○

Palos Verdes - Part I

Carl Schader was a desperate man. He had land to sell in California - a lot of it. And, he had no one to buy it. With only twenty days left on his exclusive option, before he lost his $36,000, he went where there was money. Carl Schader took a train from Los Angeles to New York in 1913.

Frank Vanderlip was not a gullible man, or an impulsive one. Some of his actions may have looked unplanned, but they were always well thought out means to a goal.

The story that Carl Schader sold Palos Verdes, California to Frank after a ten minute meeting may or may not be accurate but, even if true, there was much thinking on Frank's part before Carl Schader ever walked into Frank's office.

According to Frank's oldest son, Frank A. Vanderlip, Jr., the Bank Crisis of 1907 had great impact on Frank's attitude toward his investments. "He decided that he wanted to take money out of Wall Street and put it into real estate, particularly in cities or growing towns where two railroads might cross . . . he wanted to get into large pieces of real estate, at low prices, in towns that would grow because of a double railroad system."

As Frank showed with his war bond drive, his property and school at Beechwood, the development of the Sleepy Hollow Country Club, and with his work at the Bank, he never made small plans.

Freeport, Texas - 1912

Traveling in a private train car has advantages. When Frank decided to inspect a sulphur mine in Texas that one of his vice-presidents told him about, he merely ordered his rail car diverted from its route home from Palm Beach, Florida after a trip there with Narcissa, in March 1911. Impressed with what he saw, Frank became part of a pool of $700,000, including his mentor Mr. Stillman, that purchased 15,000 acres of land along the mouth of the Brazos River in Texas. Under the leadership of Eric P. Swenson, a vice president of Frank's National City Bank, a new city was founded there. It was named Freeport, and planned as a city to rival Galveston and Corpus Christi, based on the mining and shipping of large sulphur deposits.

Naming ceremony 1912
Freeport, Texas
Frank and Narcissa Vanderlip on porch
On either side of Governor Colquitt

Using the holding company name Freeport Texas Company, the Vanderlip-Stillman-Tilghman syndicate had businesses in sulphur, asphalt, transportation, a river terminal, stevedores, and oil, as well as the townsite. The headquarters were in New York, with Eric Swenson serving as president. (The Tilghman name in the original syndicate was from brothers Frederick B. and Sidell Tilghman, investors who were related by marriage to Eric Swenson.)

Early photographs show a barren, frontier town environment, with huge sulphur mounds, heavy mining equipment, and smokestacks used in the refining process. It must have been a dusty place, with the inescapable scent of rotten eggs that sulphur always carries. It was not the type of place that Frank and his friends would want to live, although he did attend the naming ceremony.

Panorama of downtown Freeport, Texas from roof of bank building 1912

Sulphur was an important component of fertilizer, and also used in the chemical, paper-making, pigment, pharma-ceutical, mining, oil refining and fiber manufacturing industries, so the syndicate was justified in expecting a good return on its investment. The company managed to double its output between 1912 and 1915. There were 300 residents when Freeport began in 1912.

Brazos River at Freeport, Texas circa 1920

Freeport never did rival Galveston, but the sulphur business was successful. Eric Swenson lost control in a proxy fight in 1930. By 1962, Freeport Sulphur was the country's largest producer. The Freeport Texas Company is now Freeport-McMoRan Copper and Gold, Inc., with sales of $1.9 billion and 10,000 employees worldwide in 2002. The 2010 Freeport census showed 12,049 inhabitants.

Texola, Texas - 1912

Another investment, in Texola, Texas, did not fare as well. The town was new when it got a post office in 1901, and a railroad line in 1902. In 1910 there were two cotton gins, corn and grist mills, four churches, three hotels, two restaurants, and 361 citizens. Frank must have believed it would become a major rail center if he purchased property. By 1930, there were two more cotton gins, a ten acre park, and a 300 seat auditorium, which would have held most of the population. Sadly, Highway 40 bypassed Texola, and the census in 2000 showed only 47 residents in what is now considered to be a ghost town.

Texola, Texas 2012

Spokane, Washington - 1911

NEW ADDITION TO BE PUT ON MARKET

Kiernan-Lawyer Company Plats Lincoln Heights Second Addition.

A new 40-acre tract of land in the southeast portion of the city has been platted into lots and will be put on the market at once by the Kiernan-Lawyer Land company, sales agents for Lincoln Land property.

The tract of land will be known as Spokane. Lincoln Heights Second addition to enth avenue. It lies between Thirty-seventh avenue and Forty-first avenue, and between Myrtle and Havana streets.

Spokane Daily Chronicle 1911

Frank met W. H. Kiernan, a Spokane friend of Mr. Stillman's, in New York. W. H. Kiernan and his partner, Jay Lawyer, must have also been known to Frank's old friend and mentor, Joseph French Johnson, who helped start the Spokane *Spokesman*, and would have vouchsafed for the two real estate developers. Frank invested in their Western Trust Investment Company of Spokane, also known as the Reynolds Development Company.

With Frank as a partner, they purchased and subdivided forty acres into one-acre lots in the southeast portion of Spokane known as Lincoln Heights and, according to Frank, Jr., bought a ranch that was the "southwest corner of Spokane," which they held until 1930.

Coos Bay, Oregon - 1912

Originally known as Marshfield, the scenic town on Coos Bay is known for a large coal field, as a center for dairy farming and, of course, for lumber. Reynolds Development Company, which included Frank, decided to buy land there in 1912, as well as one of the large docks and a dredging company. As with Frank's holdings in Freeport, Texas, he was doing more than simply selling home plots. He was building communities.

Reynolds Development ads in the local newspaper called their land "The lowest priced high class property in the city," near the high school and close to the railroad depot. The "sightly and sheltered location is the cream of the real estate market." Many of the lots were "beautifully wooded while others command a magnificent view of the city and harbor."

The ads give no clue as to how big the lots might have been, but, judging from photos of the town, they were not large. The selling price was the same for each, $300, with $25 cash down and monthly payments of $10. These were developed lots, with streets, water and, presumably, electricity, so it is difficult to compare their value to the $150 per acre Frank would pay for raw land in his biggest investment, still a year into his future.

Coos Bay, Oregon with ship M. F. Plant *in harbor circa 1911*

One piece of Coos Bay that Reynolds Development did not buy was a ship, known as the *M. F. Plant*, that made a regular circuit between Portland, Coos Bay and San Francisco. It had a circuitous connection to Frank, being the first vessel to be captured as a prize during the Spanish-American War, when it was a Spanish trading vessel. The U. S. profit from it's capture went into the same funding for the war as the $200 million Frank raised on his Treasury bond drive. The *M. F. Plant* was sold to an Alaskan company, and was wrecked there as the *Yukon* a year later.

Los Molinos, California

Frank obviously thought a lot of W. H. Kiernan and Jay Lawyer, for he put up $178,000 to join their $700,000 purchase of a ranch in Los Molinos, California. Apparently, the next land buy held much greater appeal to all of the men, as they never did develop this holding, which today is a 2 square mile area with about 2,000 people.

Palos Verdes, California - A Grander Vision - 1913

Carl Schader's offering was different. It was more than just land, or mining, or dredging. It was an opportunity to create an elegant new community on land that was almost virgin territory.

He offered 16,000 acres of gently rolling hills, spread across a peninsula jutting out into the ocean just south of Los Angeles. It was cattle ranch land, with a few natural springs, fewer trees, even less people. Part of an old Spanish land grant known as Rancho de los Palos Verdes, it was being sold by owner George Bixby and his family.

McCarrell Ranch on Bixby land, Palos Verdes, California circa 1910-1915
View across Santa Monica Bay toward Santa Monica Mountains
Eucalyptus trees planted by Phillips family

The Bixbys had already sold the land, several times. But none of the buyers were able to exercise the options for which they put down deposits. George Bixby was already $251,000 richer from the forfeited option money, which included $36,000 of Carl Schader's own money.

Even though parts of Palos Verdes overlooked the bustling Los Angeles port of San Pedro, Carl Schader saw something else. He had always "dreamed of seeing the great bluffs of the fourteen miles and more of coast line comprising the outer boundary of the ranch converted into a second Newport, a beautiful seaside city where the wealthy and well-to-do might live in enjoyment of life 365 days in the year, and where all the tawdry amusement concessions and crowds that go to make up the average shore resort might be forever barred."

The Sale

Before committing himself to a purchase, Frank sent two of his trusted younger men, Ned Courier and a man with the last name Higgins, on an inspection trip to California. When their report was favorable, Frank put together a syndicate of just over fifty investors. They were a number of his long time associates and friends, including Harry P. Davidson, of J. P. Morgan Company, and Benjamin Strong, president of Bankers' Trust Company of New York, both of whom were in the famous Jekyll Island group. Other members were James Stillman; E. C. Converse, of Bankers' Trust; J. P. Morgan; Frank Trumbull, chairman of the board of Chesapeake and Ohio Railroad; Edwyn Levinson; and Frank's sister and brother-in-law, Ruth and Ed Harden. Frank would be the controlling member and guiding light.

The final purchase price was, "about $2,400,000," for 16,004 acres, equaling $150 an acre, according to Harry Benedict, who worked for Frank for many years. Converting 1913 dollars to 2013 value, using the Economic Power conversion of a share of the Gross Domestic Product, the price would be $926,400,000, or $57,885 per acre.

Los Angeles Times *Nov. 1, 1913*

One of the originally planned purchasers, Walter L. Fundenburg, got part of the money back that he had paid the Bixbys, in the form of a $150,000 second mortgage. Carl Schader got a large enough commission that the *Los Angeles Times* reported he had "a smile that simply refuses to budge from his lips."

Arrival

Getting to Palos Verdes was not easy. Frank's first trip was in 1914, and mirrored the route taken by his family when they first brought the children in 1916. According to Frank, Jr., "The syndicate had an enormous Packard touring car, which met us at the railroad station in Los Angeles. We came out Western Avenue as far as it went at the time, and then had to switch over to Narbonne Avenue. We came by the Phillips' ranch house, he being the top superintendent of the time

. . . we ended up at the top of the hill which is now Crenshaw and Crest, and started down Paint Brush Canyon. Well, the view from that spot down on the plateaus below, and Catalina beyond, was the most incredibly dramatic thing that anybody had ever seen. And our trip, our introductory trip, was very carefully planned so that we got the dramatic impressions."

1915 Packard touring car photo 2012

That view from the top of the hill was the same one that took Frank's breath away when he first saw it. He uses the most romantic of his journalistic skills in his description. *"When I did see it I came to a mental halt: although I had become used to handling large projects I was overwhelmed by this possession. It was almost the size of Manhattan Island; but it was the complete antithesis of that swarming city where in mingled squalor and magnificence all the ancient problems of mankind can be seen to have survived with the virility of weeds."*

Palos Verdes in early stage of development of homes 1929

"I had grown up on a farm that was a mile square and in my boyhood eyes that was a broad range of land. When I encountered this new possession, which was equal to twenty-five of my boyhood farms, and found the opportunity of exploring it over ranch trails, it seemed like an empire. An exquisitely beautiful empire it is, too, with more than ten miles of seacoast, the whole surface in picturesque rolling hills and occasionally more picturesque canyons. Even the ocean view is more beautiful than ordinary, for the mauve and purple hills of Catalina Island make a central point of interest that adds as

much to the pictures as do the Palisades to the view across the Hudson; but it is an infinitely grander picture."

Palos Verdes looking south from Portuguese Bend with Catalina Island photo 2012

Frank immediately realized what he purchased, and the responsibility that came with it. *"At first I was nonplussed. I had grown used to tackling pretty large financial measures, but the problems of sixteen thousand acres of land in the edge of a great city cannot be condensed on a sheet of paper as neatly as can a very great financial undertaking . . .*

"It made every creative fiber in me cry out for expression, for those hills were not much altered from the day that Dana stood on them when he was accumulating those experiences that were preserved in Two Years Before the Mast *. . . For the space of my toiling journey to the ranch house I was a colonizer in my soul, a Raleigh."*

The Land

Rancho de los Palos Verdes was actually a working cattle ranch, under the control of Bixby manager Harry F. Phillips, Sr. and his family, who grazed two thousand head of cattle on the hillsides.

Some of the coastal land was rented out to Japanese farming families, who grew mainly tomatoes, sweet peas and flowers, using a method known as dry farming, where water from springs was carefully utilized during the dry summer months.

Frank's first step was to learn about his new land. He hired the engineering firm of Koebig and Koebig for a study that lasted several years. They did an extensive survey on five-foot contour lines, and platted "every foot of the ranch." The finished map was twenty-one by seventeen feet, and was the most detailed ever made in the country.

They found that the soil varied from sedimentary deposits of clay, shale, and even diatomaceous earth to other areas that were volcanic rock. Some canyons had underground springs that flowed all year, some hillsides were perfectly dry. Weather testing stations showed that parts of the coastline and hilltops were often cloaked in fog, other parts were almost eternally sunny.

Along the western cliffs, the view was all the way up the coastal curve toward Santa Monica. Closer along the curve was the developing area of small beach homes and a popular pier, known as Redondo Beach, that was the type of community Carl Schader was trying to prevent in Palos Verdes. The eastern side faced the port area of San Pedro. The northern view was toward downtown Los Angeles, with the San Bernardino Mountains on the far horizon.

Entire 16,000 acres of Palos Verdes, looking north toward Los Angeles circa 1930
Development since 1914 includes road around coastline and a few homes
All land shown is Palos Verdes up to road running from upper left side to center top side

The finest spot, after all considerations, was deemed to be the area at the southern edge known as Portuguese Bend. It was here that Frank decided to put up his first structure, a house for his own family.

The engineers did not recognize that Portuguese Bend was perched on top of tilted layers that were much like the layers of a cake with soft icing. About forty years later, the icing would start to give way, and Portuguese Bend would begin an inexorable slide toward the ocean, taking some of the homes built in the 1950s along for the ride.

The Cottage - 1916

When the house known as the Old Ranch Cottage was built, Frank apparently had not yet settled on his vision of developing the entire peninsula in the style of Italian architecture that makes Palos Verdes so unique to this day. It is generally accepted that the Cottage, as it is now known, was built to resemble Frank and Narcissa's New York home, Beechwood. While the exterior has the same white, Hudson River design, with the same shutters and casemate windows, all of the original area of the Cottage would probably fit into Beechwood's library.

The Cottage, Frank Vanderlip's original Palos Verdes house photo 2011
First section built is to the left of what is now the front door

Frank, Jr., had a different theory about the Cottage's design origin. The family had a small retreat beside a brook, about twenty miles from Beechwood, at Shrub Oak, New York. "It was a simple house that happened to be twenty-six feet square, with a living room in the front that faced the brook, a kitchen, and a dressing room - bathroom behind. There was a staircase that went upstairs, and the whole top floor was one sleeping porch. There was no telephone, there was no electric light, there was a spring that sent water into a tank at about forty degrees . . . where we kept our milk and eggs and the like, cold. And Pa did enjoy swimming in the brook, and letting his six children do the same."

It was simple living for the family, away from business and servants. It was, as Frank, Jr., says, their "contact."

Narcissa wanted the California experience to be the same. "My mother wanted to repeat this house. It wasn't entirely practical, so it was done with a staircase going up to the two bedrooms that faced the ocean and two quite large bathrooms that had huge tubs." On the lower floor originally were the living room with a fireplace, a tiny kitchen, and a bedroom and bath for one maid. All six children, who had their own domains in the 100 room Beechwood home, must have slept together in the same bedroom at The Cottage.

Narcissa planned the setting carefully, wanting to have a view of the cliffs and the breakers. In 1916, "She put the four stakes in the ground," Frank, Jr., relates, and then Frank and Narcissa went to Europe.

The house was partially pre-assembled and brought overland from San Pedro in wagons. "When they got back here the builder had decided that everybody wanted to look straight out to sea at Catalina. So, the house wasn't oriented the way she wanted it, and she burst into tears. So Pa, presently, built the second wing, which was the living room, and the two bedrooms above that." The old living room became the present dining room, and the original upstairs became a large master bedroom with a spectacular ocean view. Frank was never afraid of construction.

The Cottage with modern additions photo 2011
Original two-story section is in center with original porch

Harry Benedict, known in later years as Frank's, "right hand man," gives a description of conditions at the Cottage in his unpublished autobiography.

The first visit of my wife Frances to the Palos Verdes Ranch pleased and interested her and, in later years, elicited comments of disbelief, in light of the modern facilities that came to be a part of the scene. On that occasion we left the electric train in San Pedro. I rented a Model T Ford and drove Frances out to the Vanderlip Cottage over the farmers' dirt roads, winding around high on the hills above the Coast on a one-track road, mumbling a prayer that we wouldn't meet a Japanese farm truck loaded and on the way to the harbor.

At the Cottage (this was long before the present living room and bedrooms were added), we made do with water brought up on a horse by a Mexican hostler, kerosene lamps and some sort of kerosene grates for cooking. Frances reveled in it. There was not a house or a paved road in sight in any direction.

On one of my trips out on business about this time, Mr. Vanderlip was at the Cottage with a couple old friends. I spent a day or two on business; then, in order to get to the terminal of the electric line at South Redondo Beach on my way to the railway station in Los Angeles, our Mexican produced three horses. I rode one, he rode one, and led one over whose back were slung my two suitcases. We followed a trail north along the top of the hills down into what is now the Riviera."

The First Plan

One of Frank's first priorities was improving access to his holdings. "*As a boy I had been in a situation where in common with all my neighbors, because of lack of roads and transportation, we were in effect serfs on the soil. At that time, it was a great event to go as much as twenty miles from home. Fifteen miles was the range of the average individual's wanderings from the site of his bed. That was about as far as a horse could take him and bring him back in a day . . . With the early background I had, road building was naturally the first enterprise we undertook on the ranch . . . The automobile, the airplane and other gadgets of our times had not been developed in 1912 as we know them, but they were at least on the horizon of our minds; they were a part of my vision.*"

The *Los Angeles Times* reported, "More than 100 miles of contour roads will be laid out in the tract, and these are to be lined with trees. A wide, paved highway, extending from the northern line of the property, to the southern edge of the ranch, just above San Pedro, will be thrown open to public use by the syndicate. This magnificent highway, which will follow the brink of the rugged Palos Verdes ocean bluffs for more than fourteen miles, will be the most scenically beautiful automobile route in Southern California, overlooking at every turn a new panorama of sea and rugged coast and inland hills."

Palos Verdes Drive South
Portuguese Bend 1926
Road recently graded,
Not paved for decades

Palos Verdes Drive South
Portuguese Bend 2013
Road lowered by 1956 landslide
And constant land movement since

Grading flat roadbeds over miles of hillsides does not happen overnight, even now, with 21st century equipment. It would take about ten years to lay out all of the streets in Palos Verdes, with the work done by wagons pulled by teams of mules. Even into the 1930s, when Harry Benedict's sons grew up along Palos Verdes Drive South, they would sit beside the dirt road in front of their parents' villa and watch for the occasional car to drive past, kicking up clouds of dust.

*Palos Verdes Boulevard
curving into
Palos Verdes Drive West
(then Granvia La Costa)
under construction 1923*

*Palos Verdes Boulevard
curving into
Palos Verdes Drive West
2013
Malaga Cove Plaza
shown at top right of curve*

Frank's original idea for Palos Verdes was an enclave of large homes set on lots ranging from several acres up to 100, with a country club up on the bluff that would be one of the finest in the world. It would have private dining rooms, a large pool, polo grounds, a concrete pier down at the shoreline, 150 guest rooms, and everything that "wealthy lovers of outdoor sports could desire."

Preliminary sketch for planned Los Palos Verdes Country Club 1914

He hired landscape architects Frederick Law Olmsted, Jr., and his stepbrother John C. Olmsted, to develop a master plan for the entire hill, pleased with their work at Beechwood. Their famous father, Frederick Law Olmsted, Sr., had designed both Central Park in New York and the Chicago Columbian Exposition that Frank attended in

1893. There was no design firm more suited to undertake such a large project.

The brothers laid out three model villages, one especially for artisans. Frank commissioned a large plaster model, detailing the style concepts. Streets would follow the contour of the land, rather than running in a grid pattern. Each lot would be situated to take advantage of carefully landscaped views. There would be restrictions on building styles, and the natural landscape would be conserved and enhanced. Heavy traffic would be routed away from homes, and only a few roads would direct anyone onto the hill. Throughout the area, there would be plenty of parkland, with fountains, trees, schools and libraries. Frederick Law Olmsted, Jr. loved the area so much that he built a home for himself on a cliff top with a spectacular view in 1928.

Diorama made in France of planned artisan village above Golden Cove circa 1916

Where Frank's ideas differed from those of other planned communities was that he envisioned all of the construction in a particularly harmonious blend of Spanish and Italian architecture, with stone or whitewashed walls, red tile roofs, Mediterranean trees, and colorful flowers. On-site nurseries cradled 100,000 small trees by 1914, and it was estimated that a total of 500,000 would be planted, not including those put in by future individual homeowners. It was, indeed, an *"infinitely grand picture,"* that might have been completed, if America had not gone to war.

Palos Verdes residents twenty, or fifty, or now one hundred years later will understand how easy it would be to spend a life of contentment without ever leaving the area. Frank was happy and involved in those early days of development, but had a much broader set of responsibilities.

There was a huge banking operation to run, which could only be done from New York. There was his sprawling home on the Hudson and its school for his children to oversee. And, there was a war in Europe that needed the financial resources of the United States, and of Frank's National City Bank.

Livingroom at the Cottage with Frank Vanderlip original portrait over fireplace 2012
Books, shelves, painting, Chinese decor and fireplace tools in place since Frank's lifetime

o   o   o

The War Years

Narcissa Vanderlip canning homegrown vegetables for War effort, Beechwood 1918

o o o

The War Years

Even when one spark ignites a forest fire, usually there are embers that smolder in flammable underbrush long before any flames are visible.

On June 28, 1914, the sudden spark that started a world war was the assassination of Archduke Franz Ferdinand, heir to the throne of the Austro-Hungarian Empire. It was a sudden, public attack, planned for its shock value as much as it was for the actual killing of a member of a powerful ruling family. No one was quite prepared for the inevitable events that followed.

Capture of Archduke's assassin June 28, 1914

Bankers do not like surprises, or putting out fires, especially ones that involve stock prices or battlefields.

As President of the country's largest bank, Frank Vanderlip carefully tracked the world's economy and politics. He knew there was great unrest in Europe, and that various alliance agreements had been signed by a rotating series of countries ever since about 1870 to try to maintain peace. He knew that Britain, France, and Russia had interlocking understandings to support each other, known as the Triple Entente.

He also knew there was a race between Germany and Britain for naval dominance. Between 1908 and 1913, European military spending increased by fifty percent.

In 1908, Austria-Hungary annexed Bosnia-Herzegovina, angering Serbia and Russia and starting the First Balkan War in 1912. The Treaty of London should have maintained peace but, instead, the redistribution of borders gave several small countries enough courage to attack their neighbors in an attempt to grab more territory.

In this roiling mix of posturing and land grabbing, a terrorist cell known as the Black Hand trained a group of young Serbians, armed them with pistols and bombs, and snuck them across the border with the help of some Serbian officers and officials, to kill the Austrian Archduke.

Frank's mentor, Mr. Stillman, was in Paris at the time. Like a deer in the forest that picks up the scent of smoke in the air long before flames lick at tree branches, Mr. Stillman saw hints of the coming conflagration. Before sailing for New York just after the assassination, he wrote to Frank about the warning signs. French banks were refusing to give out credit, preferring to keep their funds close at hand, and they were forcing merchants to pay up on their outstanding loans. Mr. Stillman even noted that *"pearl necklaces of any considerable value could be purchased for cash at sixty percent of what they formerly had brought,"* as Frenchmen hoarded cash to prepare for bad times ahead.

The Austrians, wanting international approval for their actions, gave the Serbians a list of demands that, if met, would settle the situation, but it was a list they knew would never be approved. When it was not, the Austrians declared war.

Russia mobilized the next day, to counteract Austrian power. Germany mobilized on July 30, planning to quickly invade France and then turn toward Russia. When Germany marched through neutral Belgium and attacked French troops there, a chain reaction set off that spread to colonies and other countries in Africa, the Middle East, and all the way to Asia.

Washington Times August 1, 1914

Over the next four years, nine million soldiers would die. Twenty-one million more would be wounded, many of them permanently incapacitated by the effects of poison gas and the horrors of trench warfare.

French soldiers in trench 1914-1918   Wounded, captured German soldier 1914-1918

Wars can never be fought without money. Frank understood that fact well. *"Banking is an essential function in the existence of a society in which masses of individuals have removed themselves, or are born away from the soil. The average man, I think, looks upon bankers as a group apart from the herd and, in the main, leeches. Yet that average man's breakfast really reaches him only because it has been constantly attended by banking processes. Somebody has to furnish credit to buy the wheat from the farmer; there has to be credit first to build and then to operate the railroad that carries the wheat to an elevator and then to a miller; and the miller has to have credit while transforming the wheat into flour and then a baker has to have credit while he changes the flour into bread. These self-liquidating processes of commerce are the unseen forces by which chains of people are induced, in their proper turns, to cooperate in society, to serve others far removed from their presence. What is true in peace is true in war. The soldier generally gets his breakfast as a result of banking processes and it is*

Soldiers unloading armored car 1914-1918

by those same processes that guns and ammunition are started on their way to a battle-field."

A Looming Financial Crisis

European governments needed funds. They wanted gold, to be able to buy whatever was necessary for the war effort from whoever could supply it. They were selling out their American securities at low value to stockpile cash. Prices were dropping. *"A fearful strain existed in every part of the financial mechanism,"* Frank observed. *"As in 1907, the foremost problem was how to create an extraordinary amount of sound currency."*

Some bankers, including Frank, believed arrangements should be made to issue Clearing House Certificates, which were, in effect, notes exchanged solely between banks to keep money flowing on paper, without any actual currency changing hands.

The Secretary of the Treasury, William McAdoo, disagreed. He believed enough money could be put out with National Bank Notes. This was a solution Congress, foreseeing a monetary crisis, had passed after the bank crisis of 1907. It was known as the Aldrich-Vreeland Act. The Act allowed National Banks, in an emergency, to temporarily borrow from the government, in the form of National Bank Notes, using as collateral amounts they expected to recover from outstanding business loans. Secretary McAdoo estimated this amount would be over $150 million.

Frank believed the Secretary was wrong. From his own research, he felt that the amount available to banks, estimated against their outstanding loans, would be considerably less.

When Secretary McAdoo came to New York, Frank proved that he was right. At a meeting with the heads of New York's major banks, *"I read off the amount of currency which was available for each bank. Every time I spoke an amount and named a bank, somewhere around the room an informed head nodded confirmation."* The Comptroller of the Currency, John Williams, who was with the Secretary, was not amused.

The information Frank gathered was from his careful appraisal of facts. His man in Washington had bypassed the Comptroller, who should have had the correct figures, and had gone straight to the custodian of the emergency currency. Frank also kept index cards with basic financial information for each National Bank, which his staff updated for him each day.

Everything Frank knew was legally public information. No one else had bothered to gather it.

Frank's actions certainly helped keep the financial world stable in the days ahead, but they did not endear him to Comptroller John Williams and his allies. This would not be the last time Frank's belief in doing what he felt was right for the country came into conflict with other important men in the worlds of money and politics.

The next morning, Clearing House Certificates were issued, and the banks were able to meet their responsibilities.

Still worried about the overseas demand for gold and falling stock prices, the New York Stock Exchange closed for months, slowing the volume of sales to a trickle. Frank became chairman of a committee that "*raised a pool of $100 million in gold to ship abroad to preserve American credit. Just as soon as it was known overseas that we had that gold and would ship it on demand, the demand eased. None of the $100 million of gold was exported. What began to come over then were orders for goods and requests for credits.*"

News vendor July 31, 1914

European governments wanted farm wagons from Studebaker's factory, and large numbers of horses to pull them. One million dollars in credit was lent out just for nitroglycerin. "*These were but the first drops splashing down ahead of a rainstorm of orders. Those people overseas quickly ceased to want us to ship them gold; they wanted something much more vital to them. They wanted to hire the productive energy of the most effectively industrialized nation that has ever existed; they wanted to buy all the food that we would sell them; they wanted everything that was required to keep them alive and to kill their enemies. And they wanted everything quickly. The one French word I never can forget is* vite". By 1916, forty percent of all Allied war supplies came from North America.

President McKinley tried to keep the U. S. out of the war by remaining neutral, and refused to give loans to combatants on either side. While Mr. Stillman also counseled neutrality, telling Frank to keep the bank *"snug"*, he was anything but impartial. *"The Germans cannot violate my beautiful France,"* he declared passionately.

National City Bank closed out their accounts with German banks. A representative of the French government *"thanked me very prettily for the action we had taken."* National City Bank then agreed to a large loan to the French government, much to the displeasure of J. P. Morgan, Jr., who considered the French government to be his bank's prerogative, even after he had already refused to give the French a loan. It took a certain amount of finesse by Frank and one of his men to calm J. P. Morgan, Jr. and maintain the friendship between the two banks.

Talent Search

As if Frank did not have enough to occupy him, with financing a war, daily running of the bank, planning Palos Verdes and his other land developments, and spending time with his family and school at Beechwood, he was always searching out promising young men to bring into executive positions at the bank.

"I was always on the lookout for men for the City Bank's service. Whether I was in other banks, in the homes of friends, or encountering people on steamships or trains I felt that I was, after a fashion, Fortune's adjutant for some people." Within the banking profession, it was a great honor to be recruited by National City Bank. A number of the men Frank hired were already successful in their own field, and soon became vice-presidents.

Describing his eight vice-presidents, when speaking to the Economic Club of New York, Frank said, *"With a single exception, they are men whose boyhood started in poverty. One of our vice-presidents' memories begins as a cotton picker in the fields of Louisiana; another was a teacher of a country school in Kansas; another was a newsboy on the streets of Chicago. I could go through the whole list and show that these men forged their way to the top from humble beginnings by making sacrifices, by improvement of opportunity and by fidelity to duty."* He could, of course, have been giving a description of himself.

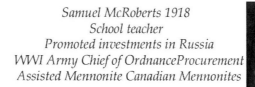

Samuel McRoberts 1918
School teacher
Promoted investments in Russia
WWI Army Chief of OrdnanceProcurement
Assisted Mennonite Canadian Mennonites

Joseph Truitt Talbert 1909
Picked cotton and worked in grocery when young
"Few if any bankers in New York possessed a wider acquaintance in
banking circles throughout the country. He was noted for his
knowledge of credits and currency" New York Times May 9, 1920

Two of National City Bank's vice-presidents in 1914

Representative of the group was John H. McEldowney, the cited man who started as a newsboy, who had been Frank's assistant all the way back when Frank was financial editor of the *Chicago Tribune*. *"When he came to the City Bank he knew nothing of practical banking, but he quickly caught the idea of banking."* He became a vice-president in five years. Indicative of how the bank looked on their men as family, when John McEldowney's heart weakened, Mr. Stillman searched across Europe for a doctor who could help. Sadly, no one could, and John McEldowney died.

Frank enjoyed discovering and promoting these men, seeing himself in the same mentoring role that others had played for him. A young man named James Perkins so impressed Frank in 1914 that Frank immediately offered him a position as vice-president, telling Mr. Stillman, *"his selection will be one of the best things I have ever been able to do for the bank."* Speaking of James Perkins' ascension to chairman of the board twenty years later, Frank commented, *"I take pride in seeing my judgment so well confirmed."*

Going into the bank, as joining the staff was called, was more than a profession. It was considered to be a family. One way to promote this idea was through the City Bank Club, described as "probably the most active and efficient organization of bank employees in the country." The bank had been founded in 1812 and, on its 100th anniversary, Mr. Stillman gave the club $100,000, matched by a similar amount from the board of directors. This was invested, and the income was used for "education, entertainment and benevolence."

Education, in Frank's eyes, was always a priority. Moody's Magazine reported, "The basement of the bank building is fitted up in class rooms and courses in English, mathematics, economics, Spanish, French, German and stenography are provided free for all employees. The faculty of the educational courses is composed mainly of professors from New York University. At the monthly meetings of the club high-grade literary and other entertainments are given and at least once a year a dramatic performance and a ball are given in the main banking rooms."

National City Bank main floor, ball given by City Bank Club March 25, 1914

Frank looked for good men not only at his own social and professional level, but anywhere he might find them. "*It was always exciting to me to realize that the green eye-shade of any one of the hundreds of young fellows in the bank might mask the face of a James Stillman of the future. Any messenger or office-boy who came into my presence was as interesting in his potentialities as a lottery-ticket.*"

As the bank grew, and expanded into foreign branches, "*I scoured the world for the right kind of men.*" He needed "*cultured professional bankers able to speak and write and think in several languages - and such men were rare.*"

So, Frank invented a way to cultivate his own bankers. It was "*a scheme I had for the creation in the City Bank of a kind of West Point for the training of selected young men.*" He started with a group of fifteen, later enlarged the scope to sixty men. They lived in a community dorm, spent time working in the various departments of the bank, and had classes in practical banking matters.

"*The way banks have been run, in feeding their executive force with uneducated office boys, and trusting here and there to a development of some exceptional mind, is about on a par with the old-fashioned way of farming, where a man used the small potatoes for seed and sold the large ones. The modern farmer gives as much attention to his seed . . . That is just what we are doing now in the Bank and instead of having to trust to some boy here and there with only a grammar school education developing exceptional capacity, we are getting young men in with trained minds, of good families, and with a vision that banking is a profession instead of merely a job.*"

Internships such as Frank instituted were a new idea. He made arrangements with various colleges to select one man from each at the end of their sophomore year who would become part of the program during each of their next two summers, and who would spend the last half of their senior year working in the bank for college credit. "*It will furnish a picked lot of men, particularly for foreign service, who are educated and will be adapted to that field and it will give the bank an unique position as being the training school for bankers.*" Such programs, now a normal part of many businesses, helped Frank's bank remain, according to Moody's Magazine in 1914, "the largest and strongest financial institution in the United States."

Harry E. Benedict was one of the young men whose life took a different path because of Frank and the bank. Born on a Wisconsin farm in 1890, young Harry worked jobs that varied from page in the state Legislature to railroad worker, before taking Frank's route and learning shorthand at a business school. That led to a one year secretarial post with the Indian agent on a rather isolated reservation where, among other duties, he settled the estate of a "dead

Harry E. Benedict circa 1918

Indian who had married nine times, with an occasional foray outside," which "offered moments of humor." Next, he was appointed to the Wisconsin Highway Commission, where he managed the office and learned much from the earliest experiments using cement for paving roads.

Convinced by some of the engineers to go to college, Harry worked part time at the Commission while getting his degree. When he was offered the National City Bank internship in New York at fifty dollars a month, it was quite a comedown from his four thousand dollar monthly salary with the Highway Commission but, like the other thirty-four men selected that year, Harry jumped at the chance.

In the years that followed, Harry would be known as Frank's right hand man. He would accompany his boss to Washington, Europe, and Japan, meet most of the leading bankers, railroad men and politicians of his time, and eventually build his own home near Frank's on the Palos Verdes land in California.

Taking Stock - 1915

Two large homes. Forty thousand acres of land. Six children. (The youngest, John Mann Vanderlip, was born in November, 1915.) One million dollars. Frank accumulated all of these by 1915.

His yearly salary as bank president was $100,000. Not much, Frank reasoned, when, "*In six months of 1915 the enterprise under my command had net earnings of $3,406,000.*"

He had a lifestyle to maintain that came with his title, which was "*one of the most conspicuous banking positions in the world.*" For a man of humble background, Frank felt the need to justify his quest to secure his own fortune. His job "*entailed an expensive life. Moreover, I had some excuse for entertaining a notion of riches different from that of most; during fourteen years I had been associating with men who possessed gigantic fortunes; Stillman, Morgan, Frick, Carnegie, Baker, Harriman, William Rockefeller and others.*"

Mr. Stillman was ill. "*For months on end he was completely an invalid, barred by the feebleness of his hold on life from receiving any news of the bank."* He was given so many morphine injections that *"he told me it became difficult to find space upon his legs where a needle could be inserted. Physically and mentally he was sore to the touch."* It was only a matter of time before he would no longer be chairman of the board, and Frank's greatest supporter. Frank wanted security.

J. P. Morgan, Jr. offered to sell Frank a large block of the Morgan stock in National City Bank, which Frank hoped to purchase, re-sell part of at a profit in time, then repay the loan, make something for himself, and own a substantial interest in the bank. Frank wrote an almost apologetic letter to Mr. Stillman, asking to borrow the four million dollars needed for J. P. Morgan, Jr.'s 10,000 shares. He also asked Mr. Stillman to give him a five year option on a large part of Mr. Stillman's own shares. The reason Frank cited for such an audacious request was not to control the bank, or to "keep up with the Joneses", but goes to the heart of what he always believed was his highest duty. *"I only cite as my excuse for writing this letter, the fact that I have been having a flash-light revelation as to the responsibilities which I have in regard to a large family and a quite reasonable desire, which is very strongly upon me just now for definitely crystallizing the means properly to safeguard that responsibility for the future."*

National City Bank stock certificate circa 1930s

One can only imagine Frank's shock, anger, and embarrassment when Mr. Stillman, his mentor and hero, turned him down.

Payment for the first quarter of the Morgan stock was to be made on a certain date. *"The day came and I did not have the million. However, Mr. Morgan earned my lasting gratitude by carrying the stock for me until I was ready to take it up. I took it all up, rather grimly."*

Loving Mr. Stillman as he would a father, and looking back on the incident twenty years later, Frank came to understand his actions. *"My affection for him has been undimmed in the years since his death. I quite understand him, I think, in the attitude he took toward my request. Of course he did not want to surrender any of it! It was a piece of himself that I was asking for."*

In spite of Frank's forgiveness, and their close relationship, it was obvious that Mr. Stillman did not consider Frank a member of his own family. On Mr. Stillman's death three years later, all of his stock went to his son, James A. Stillman. When that happened, Frank's fears would all become reality.

Casting His Own Shadow

Most bankers of Frank's time feared change, expansion, and publicity. Frank thrived on all three. *"I was, in addition to being a banker, a publicist. To be a publicist banker you have got to think, you have got to have something to say. It was because of those extramural activities of mine that the City Bank was taken out of the groove in which it previously had gone in comfort."*

The war in Europe was brutally continuing. Mr. Stillman was not alone in his solid defense of the French and, by extension, of the British. "For France, which for me stands for Humanity and Civilization, I will gladly run the risk of shedding my blood, if I could see any sensible way of doing it," Mr. Stillman declared in 1915, even though his illness prevented him, in actuality, from any type of action.

Frank, on the other hand, was less radically inclined. Having traveled in countries now on both sides of the fighting, he found traits to admire in each. *"I believe . . . the impelling factors that have led to this terrible war have more to do with greed and desire for trade expansion, a dislike of the too efficient Germans, and other motives that are none too worthy."* Even though he was younger and healthier than Mr. Stillman, *"I do not feel like enlisting under any of the colors, and the dominant feeling in my mind is one of resentment that it has been possible to lead the world into such a catastrophe."*

What Frank and Mr. Stillman did agree on was that the bank should be making itself more secure, and not overly involved in war-related financing. Frank feared that the high demand for American goods, coupled with a labor shortage, was driving prices unnaturally high and that, when the war ended, there would be a depression in American manufacturing industries if other outlets were not found to sell their products.

He wanted the bank to diversify its loans, and to open branches in neutral countries, and in those that were underdeveloped. The first foreign branch was opened in Buenos Aires, Argentina, in 1914. Others followed throughout South America and Europe. By 1920, the bank's subsidiary, International Banking Corporation, had 132 overseas offices.

The Panama Canal was just opening for business in August, 1914, a great feat of engineering and construction which was sure to bring great profits for any financiers involved. Because of the war, and Frank's expansive vision, there were similar, but smaller, "*marvelous opportunities that a banker ordinarily would have to boot out of his path for sheer lack of time.*" He wanted to be able to "*take a foreign business enterprise of great possibilities or even a good idea with management behind it and finance it into strength.*" Even if it was not with his own hands, Frank wanted to create real things, just as his father had built a farm wagon and Frank had turned out machine parts on a lathe.

The group he helped put together in November, 1915, was grandly christened the American International Corporation (AIC). He boldly described it as "*the most important business thing I have ever done.*" Frank's goals for the company included the financing of business enterprises, foreign or domestic, that would bring construction or other collateral benefit to an area, such as industrial or machine construction, ship building, and shipping. (One loan went out to a tea importer.

First ship through Panama Canal August 5, 1914

Even though Frank never did personally like tea, he did admire the British tradition of elegant afternoon tea service. Under a loose definition, a tea importer would fall under the category of a collateral benefit.) AIC planned to promote U. S. banking, business and engineering interests around the world.

Even though Frank believed long-term profits would come from businesses not related to the war, AIC quickly got involved. The federal government created the Emergency Fleet Corporation to build merchant vessels for shipping all the U. S. goods to war-torn Europe. In 1917, AIC's American International Shipping Corporation got the majority of the Emergency Fleet contract, and built the largest shipyard in the world at Hog Island, Pennsylvania, on the site of what is now the Philadelphia International Airport.

War poster circa 1917

Hog Island, Pennsylvania ship yard 1919

In the next four years, 122 cargo and troop transport ships were built there. None saw action before the war was over, but the lessons learned about ship construction on a grand scale from prefabricated parts would serve well in the wars that followed, particularly in building World War II Victory ships.

Wartime poster circa 1917

Another AIC wartime interest was in a commodity that has a controversial reputation in the 21st century, but is vital to any war effort. Symington Forge Corporation supplied shells for guns to fight the enemy, and Remington Arms supplied the hardware. Both those and others were owned or heavily financed by AIC. Frank may have thought the U. S. should not get into the war but, once it did, he wanted to be sure the Americans were on the winning side.

Wall Street obviously was excited about this enterprise. Directors and major investors included most of the corporate and banking giants of the time, including members of the Du Pont, Rockefeller, and

Armour families. The corporation started with $50 million in capitalization. Huge amounts of this went into companies dealing in steel, rubber, shipbuilding, and heavy machinery, in the U. S. and in Latin America, China and Russia. United States Rubber, United Fruit, American Balsa, and Allied Sugar Machinery were all backed by AIC.

*U. S. Rubber Company
Tire advertisement 1919*

By the end of 1918, the corporation was doing large amounts of business in seventeen countries. Frank sincerely hoped this would be the foundation of his own true fortune.

It was work Frank loved. *"What days those were!"* he exclaimed, adding, *"The very idea of the thing was exciting in Wall Street."*

One person not overly thrilled was Mr. Stillman, even though he backed Frank's efforts. He worried that once the war was over, both German and British banks would regain their influence, and America would lose long term prospects for world-wide financing. Mr. Stillman urged caution with the bank's resources.

For someone with a vision, who had been cautious with finances for his entire career, it was time for bolder action.

Health Matters

Coordinating the business of a large bank, two related corporations and a similarly related company, as well as writing articles and giving talks about finance, was more than a full time job. It was no wonder that Frank had no time or need for the stress-relieving hobbies of his friends, such as golf and cards.

Hard work had never bothered Frank. He told a reporter, *"Work is my definition of success. Two days work in one."* But, he added, *"A man must be strong if he is to put two days' work into one."* Believing strength came from health, Frank told a reporter that he only ate two simple meals each day. *"The stomach is the boiler room of human energy,"* he said. It took a lot of energy to carry out his busy schedule.

Another reporter described Frank at this busy time in his career. *"He looked the part of the big man. He was tall and strong and handsome . . . his hair was snow white, but his face was young. His eyes were clear and his color high. A mustached closely clipped was masculine and becoming."*

Frank A. Vanderlip 1917

Frank not only enjoyed his work, he enjoyed his good health. He needed a lot of stamina to be able to keep up with his own schedule. Along with his position as bank president, he was a director in about forty corporations. *"Every morning at the office I would find on my desk a card about a foot in depth, and it was numbered with the minutes of the day. There were never fewer than four engagements to the hour during the periods I was at my desk."* He prepared with a morning routine before leaving his house. *"My days began early and lasted long. After 1914 I really did get a bit of exercise; as late into the season as Thanksgiving I would start the day by plunging into the lovely blue of the outdoor swimming-pool that Wells Bosworth had designed for us at Beechwood. Consequently, I would be wide-awake and steaming with energy as I arrived at the station and* entered a private club-car hooked to the rear of the 8:26 train."

Swimming pool at Beechwood 1918

No one, however, is immune to overwork, stress, and aging. *"Between meetings I had to move swiftly to keep pace with a schedule that in time began to be a kind of slavery. It was no simple knapsack burden that I carried. I could not put it down. Indeed, that onrolling, overpowering mass of work was far too much for me. It was a frightful load. My job followed me wherever I went."*

Frank was tiring out. *"It is no wonder to me now that I was quite exhausted at the end of each day. I was paying an impossible price for the bank-account I was building up in the black; physically, I was going swiftly into the red."* He did not realize it at the time, but Frank was developing diabetes. He would not be diagnosed until 1920, after suffering its effects for three years. When insulin treatment was discovered in 1922, Frank would become one of the first diabetics to use the treatment.

What Frank enjoyed was the excitement of planning and creating financial innovations. Now, in the midst of constant and overwhelming activity, he was tired and bored. *"When the novelty had worn off, there was considerably less zest to the exercise of power, I found; and I grew weary of the repetitions involved in work that could not be delegated. Each problem that was laid before me I had to understand right down to its roots before I could make a sound decision. If I had not possessed a physique of extraordinary vigor I could not have stood it. Remember, I had been going at top speed in the City Bank since the summer of 1901 and there had been no let-up, except as I was occasionally permitted to enjoy an illness."*

Changing Focus - 1916

January of 1916 was something of a breaking point for Frank. Discouraged by Mr. Stillman's refusal to help him acquire a large amount of National City Bank stock, and exhausted from work and the beginning of an illness, Frank decided to take a trip to his Palos Verdes property in California. *"I was about as thoroughly tired as a man could be."*

When he informed the bank's attorney, John Sterling, that he would be gone for six weeks, the lawyer was horrified. " *'Suppose something should occur? A panic! Suppose we lost $100 million in deposits. What then?'*

" *'Is that your notion of the worst that might happen?' I asked him.*

" *'Yes,' he said, and drummed his fingers on his waistcoat.*

" *'Well, Mr. Sterling,' I said gaily, ' be quite easy in your mind. The City Bank could pay $100 million back to its depositors without a quiver.' Then I recited figures to prove my case until he was chuckling with relief."*

Frank had reason to be proud of his role at the bank. Now, he wanted something different. He wanted to turn over the presidency to someone qualified, and spend his time coordinating the activities of the associated company and two corporations he had been instrumental in forming, while becoming some sort of vice-chairman of the bank's board of directors. The problem was that he was not willing to turn full control of the bank over to someone who would not still give Frank a measure of control.

Before Frank left, *"Again and again in my letters to Mr. Stillman I brought up the question of a successor."* No one was deemed worthy.

It was a bloody year in Europe. According to one British writer, "1916 is seen as the year when the armies of Britain, France, and Germany were bled to death." During the Battle of Verdun, the fortress changed hands sixteen times, with huge loss of life on both sides. The Battle of the Somme pitted 386 Allied aircraft against 126 German planes.

Europe became more and more dependent on the U. S. for supplies. Food rationing was common in both Britain and Germany. Armies were fed first, with food lines forming for limited supplies on both sides of the combat. The Russian government wanted, *"saddles, harness, shoes, ammunition, cloth and food."* All of the transactions required financial assistance. *"The excitements, the pressures, the chaos of the war days added much to the load of a Wall Street banker. All of us down there had to readjust our mental attitudes toward money. We had to calculate utterly unpredictable forces and weigh terrifying hazards."*

British women in bread line 1916

German supply lines 1916

Relief came for both Europe and for Frank when President Woodrow Wilson finally decided the U. S. could not remain neutral. He asked Congress for a "war to end all wars," in order to "make the world safe for democracy." On April 6, 1917, Congress voted to go to war against the empires of Germany, Austria-Hungary and the Ottomans, as well as against Bulgaria.

A Banker At War - 1917

Wars run on money, as Frank had noted many times. Only a month after Congress' declaration, the Liberty Loan campaign kicked off. It was a bond drive to raise $5 billion, at an interest rate of 3 ½ percent, maturing in thirty years, redeemable after fifteen years. At first, there was not much excitement among the public for the bonds.

Frank became a member of the Liberty Loan Committee, and was appointed chairman of the sub-committee to publicize the effort. *"I found, somehow, new sources of energy. I suppose I could find enthusiasm for that work that I could not produce just then for the heavy routine of the City*

Bank . . . Week after week I had a schedule crowded with speaking engagements." He was a good man for the job, with all of his practice at giving speeches about finance. He was not the only financier working on the drive. Rallies and parades were held across the country, featuring bankers, actors, even teams of pilots offering airplane rides to anyone who purchased a bond.

Liberty Loan parade 1917
Frank A.Vanderlip on left, J. P. Morgan, Jr. on right

As the publicist-banker, Frank's first wartime assignment was to travel the East Coast and West as far as Chicago, meeting with bankers, directing their thinking about bond drives, and about what would need financing, the tightening of money, and what would be generally expected of them. He was given a private rail car, two bank officers, and his secretary, Harry Benedict, as his assistants.

As always, more funds were needed. Taking a lesson from the Spanish-American War in 1898, Congress decided to find a way to have smaller investors feel that they were involved in the war effort, and passed the War Savings Act. There was no specific plan on what to do, but "*it was intended that a way should be found to capture the small change from the pockets of the nation.*"

This was something that was familiar to Frank from his time at Treasury during the Spanish-American War, yet it was new and exciting. He took a leave of absence from the bank and, taking his private secretary, Harry Benedict with him, *"soon afterward, having relinquished my salary of $100,000 a year, I set out for Washington, to become a dollar-a-year man. There were a lot of us."*

The President Goes To Washington - 1917

The first time Frank worked in the nation's capital, he was a young, single man without much money, on his way up, proud of the carriage and two horses that came with his position. This time, he was a respected and well-known fifty-three year old with a wife, six children, and a string of fine automobiles on both coasts.

Instead of the grand office at Treasury that Frank shared in 1898 with Secretary of the Treasury Lyman Gage, or the smaller but quiet office he called his own as Assistant Secretary of the Treasury, this time Frank shared a small one with Harry Benedict. It opened directly onto the public hallway, with no anteroom, a decided comedown. Frank did not mind.

His living quarters were more spacious. He leased the former French Embassy house at 1640 Rhode Island Avenue NW, making it comfortable with furniture from Beechwood. Frank, Harry Benedict, and five servants moved in. Narcissa visited occasionally, but was usually occupied in New York with the care of the children and her work for the suffrage movement.

French Embassy, 1640 Rhode Island Ave. 1901 Washington, D.C. Frank Vanderlip's leased home 1917-1918

Two men living a busy working life as bachelors, with Narcissa often absent, would not seem to need the services of five servants. However, Frank was a meticulous dresser, and certainly expected Harry Benedict to be the same. Someone had to tend to their clothes, keep the large house clean, polish the old silver serving ware Frank was so fond of, and prepare and serve meals to the constant stream of important men who were invited to dinner. Except for the amount of time Frank spent in resting at his Palos Verdes home in early 1918, the Rhode Island Avenue house was a center of social activity.

Frank's title was Chairman of the Educational Committee for the sale of War Savings Certificates. Just as in the Spanish-American War fund drive, the certificates were designed to involve people who could not afford to buy larger bonds. The smaller certificates would not only generate funds, but would boost public support for the war.

Savings stamp poster 1918

There were a number of distinguished names on the committee, including Henry Ford, but Frank could not later recall them all meeting together even once. In reality, Frank had virtually free reign to plan as he wished, mainly with the help of former Wabash Railroad president Frederick A. Delano, whose nephew was future president Franklin Delano Roosevelt.

Metropolitan Bank 1907
Washington, D. C.

To have space for the operation, Frank leased a floor of the Metropolitan Bank building, near their office at Treasury, and filled it with a crew of capable young men, who were area directors, to distribute the securities, and with a staff of over one thousand women. Frank and Harry Benedict would often get their morning exercise by walking to the bank building from the house on K Street, through Lafayette Square. They were accompanied some days by former president and future Supreme Court Justice William Howard Taft, who Harry Benedict reported, was, "as big and cheerful as he had been painted."

The first issue of certificates would be worth five dollars at maturity, in five years, on January 1, 1923. If they were purchased on December 3, 1917, the first day of the one-year drive, each one would cost $4.12. Every month thereafter, the price would go up one penny until sales ended in December, 1918. A profit maximum of eight-eight cents may not seem like much almost one hundred years later, but at the time, coffee was thirty cents a pound, and a loaf of bread cost about one dime.

For the many Americans who would find it impossible to put up the required $4.12, Frank and Frederick Delano came up with the idea for twenty-five cent Thrift Stamps. They could be purchased at post offices, with no interest, saved up, then traded in for a War Savings Certificate. Each stamp could be pasted into a tri-fold cardboard holder that was sized to fit into a man's shirt pocket, or conveniently into a woman's purse. *"It was an admirable arrangement for the promotion of savings among persons who ordinarily let their money trickle through their fingers."*

To promote sales, Frank adapted a strategy used by politicians up to the present time. He invited a man from each of the twelve Federal Reserve districts onto a committee that appointed state chairmen. These, in turn, appointed county chairmen and on down, until someone in each election precinct was involved.

Circular explaining stamp program 1918

Calling on his writing skills, Frank produced a circular explaining the process, *"simple enough for a child to understand."* To distribute them to twenty million citizens, he employed a method that became the bane and business of the post office at least until the spread of the internet. He sent bundles of circulars to each post office, to have them delivered to every address along with the regular mail.

Savings stamp poster 1918

Through contests, artists submitted poster designs. Plays were presented at schools. *"Eventually we succeeded so well that in all the schools a large proportion of the children were saving their pennies, nickels and dimes by lending them to the Government."*

The first drive brought in $1 billion in sales of Thrift Stamps alone, with a total of $4 billion sold in all three issues. *"I kept pondering on that astounding revelation: There had been accumulated in the space of a single year, from the loose change in the pockets of the American public, money enough to create an institution as great as the nation's biggest bank."*

End Of The War - 1918

Armistice Day, November 11, 1918, brought celebrations in Washington, New York and across the country, as the horrors of World War I came to an end. The Savings Stamp program would continue for another two years, but Frank's work in Washington was finished.

He was exhausted, even after a one month trip to California in February, and tried to find the energy to face the battles waiting for him back at National City Bank in New York.

End of World War I celebration December 5, 1918
Wall Street, New York
National City Bank just out of photo on lower left

The world around him was changing, not only because of the political and economic upheaval war leaves behind, but for a more personal reason. His mentor and protector, Mr. Stillman, was dead.

o o o

The Shield

Rendering for James J. Stillman mausoleum, Woodlawn Cemetery, New York 1918

○　○　○

The Shield

When an army goes to war, it does so with its best defensive shields firmly in place.

James Jewett Stillman, who, "*in good health was all the shield that I ever would have needed,*" died on March 15, 1918. He was worth somewhere around $100 million. That made him one of the wealthiest men in the country.

Converting that figure to 2013 dollars, using the Economic Power conversion of a share of the Gross Domestic Product, his fortune would be $38 billion. Few people outside of the banking business even knew his name, let alone the fact that his wealth was in the range of others, like J. P. Morgan, who were both envied and reviled.

Mr. Stillman, as Frank Vanderlip always referred to him, was so averse to personal publicity that, in his later years, he actually took the subway from his home at 9 East 72nd Street in Manhattan to get to the bank, going in through the back, alley-like door. "*I myself had to know him a good many years before I fully understood that he imposed silence upon himself solely because of his feeling of responsibility for the bank.*" It was not until most of the bank responsibilities fell on Frank's shoulders that "*it was amazing to me to find him on occasions warmly, humanly garrulous.*"

It was Mr. Stillman who saw Frank's potential and brought him into the bank as a vice-president, promoted him to president, steered Frank into the purchase of Beechwood, included Frank in investments

JAMES STILLMAN, HEAD OF CITY BANK, DIES SUDDENLY

In Ill-Health for a Month, but His Condition Was Not Regarded as Alarming.

ACTIVE UP TO LAST WEEK

His Efforts Resulted in the National City Becoming the Most Powerful Bank in America.

BACKED BY ROCKEFELLERS

Banker's Wealth Estimated at $100,000,000—Gave Great Aid to French War Sufferers.

New York Times obituary March 16, 1918

like Freeport, Texas, and stood behind Frank's sometimes controversial and new banking ideas, explaining once, with evident pride, "I cannot control that young man."

What Mr. Stillman could control was much of the banking world, with the ties he created using his personal fortune. He breathed, ate and slept thinking about the world of finance, and what would be best for his beloved bank. "*If any man possessed power to look into the future, that man was Mr. Stillman,*" Frank said. "*His mind was ceaselessly trying to fit together the things that he knew, so as to give him a better understanding of what was coming. It was not precisely like having a crystal ball to have access to Mr. Stillman's intelligence, but it was, I think, the next thing to it. Often the proposal that Mr. Stillman uttered quietly was the thing that Mr. Morgan executed; but Mr. Stillman was above the struggle, rather than in it.*"

Mr. Stillman gave Frank the backing, confidence, and space to excel as a banker. But, inside, the man was quite sensitive. "*I shudder now to think how many times I may have hurt him, and I realize that his harshness with some of those he loved was because the unintentional hurts he received from them were sometimes intolerable. He was, really, as sensitive as a child during all those years that he was one of the most influential of Americans.*" As Frank also became a visionary and Mr. Stillman took ill in the last three years of his life, their philosophies began to diverge, and the hurts were magnified. Neither man ever got over Mr. Stillman's refusal to help Frank purchase a large block of National City Bank stock.

Above all, it was Mr. Stillman who acted as a shield against the enmity of William Rockefeller, a major stockholder in the bank, and controller of the Standard Oil funds that were deposited there.

There could not have been a better shield. Not only was Mr. Stillman's sister married to William Rockefeller, but his two daughters were married to two sons of John D. Rockefeller.

William Rockefeller circa 1915

196

By the time Mr. Stillman died, he and William Rockefeller were old men. *"Physically and mentally,"* Frank says, *"he was sore to the touch. Many of his letters from abroad contained pathetic appeals to me, his friend, to be careful not to wound him. Any unconsidered word was apt to fester in his mind long after the one who carelessly had uttered it had forgotten entirely that it had been said."* The morphine Mr. Stillman took for pain probably did not help his personality.

William Rockefeller was not known as the most patient of men. Mr. Stillman was having trouble with his eyes, and William Rockefeller's hearing was failing. *"In spite of their respective crotchets, Mr. Stillman and Mr. Rockefeller seemed to enjoy each other's society. Apart they were unfailingly and harshly critical of one another, but when together they seemed to enjoy life. Sometimes they were really jovial."*

Frank's relationship with William Rockefeller was another matter. They were neighbors, with the Rockefeller estate just across the road from Beechwood. The two men had disagreements over everything from Frank's purchase of the estate that became the Sleepy Hollow Country Club, to a misunderstanding about some connected land, to the ownership of a large block of National City Bank shares, to the propriety of a particular railroad bond sale where Rockefeller, as a director of both the bank and the railroad, was both buyer and seller.

When Mr. Stillman died in his New York City town house, no one was able to broker peace between William Rockefeller and Frank. There was bound to be a battle over who would control the bank.

James Stillman's town house, 9 East 72nd Street, New York 1905

○ ○ ○

Russia

Postcard, St. Petersburg, Russia 1904

○ ○ ○

Russia

In darkness just before midnight, an Orthodox bishop in a long golden robe held up one single candle. Around him, a chorus of bearded men sang *"one of the most moving songs I have ever heard, though I understood not one of the words; only the feeling of sorrow and hope expressed in moody bass voices."* The only other sound was the jostling, breathing, and occasional whispering of thousands of worshippers packed into the cathedral.

Orthodox Patriarch at Easter service Moscow, Russia 2012

As if by magic, or by the hand of the divine, his candle wick suddenly burst into an orange flame. The priest touched his candle to those held out by people crowding in close to him. *"Each person there lighted the candle of his neighbor and all the faces, the women's that were like rosy masks tightly framed in shawls, the men's dark with beard and shadowy eye-sockets, these faces ceased to have any trace of human coarseness and became, each one, as refined as an icon picture; and the gilded effulgence seemed to be that of myriads of haloes.*

"These people had been fasting but on this night they held, every one, a small loaf of bread.

"Then a robed figure touched a candle-flame to a fuse-end dangling just off the floor beneath the place where echoes of the rich voices of the choir told the shape of an enormous dome. I saw the fuse-end as a sputtering galaxy of golden stars rise higher and higher into the darkness and then it began to travel horizontally. Once it seemed to go out and there was a gasp of concern from thousands of throats. That would have meant bad luck. I do not know if it was stage management, but the hidden light suddenly reappeared and the moan changed almost to a shout."

"One by one a great ring of candles took fire from the fuse and that moment it became Easter Morning in St. Isaac's. Then all those people began to eat their bread, and I, who almost never went to church, began to feel the kinship of my work with that of the spiritual leaders of humanity."

St. Isaac's Cathedral 1901
St. Petersburg, Russia

Frank Vanderlip stood inside the Cathedral of St. Isaac's in St. Petersburg on the first hour of Easter, 1901. *"We were taken up into the chancel so that we were close enough to touch the bishop in his golden robe."* On a portion of his European travels before taking his new position as vice-president of National City Bank, Frank was in Russia to interview financial and business leaders, but he also visited farms, factories and shops, trying to fully understand the economic flow of each country he visited.

Frank was not a particularly church-going man. When he was growing up, even if he had been, there probably was not a single Orthodox church, with all of its ritual and symbolism, in his home town of Aurora, Illinois.

What he witnessed on that Easter morning had such a lasting impact on him that he described the incident and his reaction in great and moving detail twenty-five years later.

Bread and Prayers

The lesson that Frank carried away from St. Isaac's was not one of resurrection, but of the mechanics of human survival. *"Abundance in the fields will not place bread on our tables. The least understanding man is beginning to appreciate this fact nowadays, but there in St. Isaac's I was fully aware that prayers for bread in a world where there are so many crowded cities, would have to embrace not only agriculture but the functions of banking as well. It is by a series of steps in credit that grain in the shape of bread reaches the tables of most of humanity's two billions."*

While this realization certainly gave Frank an affirmation of the importance of his profession, it may have also contributed to his reaction, during and after World War I, to the starvation in Europe and in Russia. He witnessed first hand the starvation after the war's end, and strongly believed that the war-torn countries would endure much more suffering without wise and generous American and international financial help to restart their transportation lines and industries.

The Bank Goes To Russia - 1914

At the start of World War I, National City Bank opened a $5 million line of credit for Russia to buy supplies. While this was definitely in the bank's interest, as it became Russia's purchasing agent in the U. S., Frank believed this was the right and necessary thing to do. The bank followed later with two more loans totaling $75 million.

Before the U. S. entered the combat, and while Tsar Nicholas II was still in power, the bank took the radical step of opening a branch office in St. Petersburg in January, 1917. Two months later, the tsar's regime collapsed. The Red and White Russian factions battled for power, both sides heavily armed.

Turkish Embassy, St. Petersburg 1903
Became National City Bank, St. Petersburg

First, Prince Georgy Lvov tried to form a stable government, and then Alexander Kerensky tried to do the same. Between them, they ran Russia from March through November, 1917.

Although Frank took his leave of absence from the bank to work in Washington, D. C. in September, 1917, he and his men at the bank apparently felt Russia was secure enough to go ahead with a planned branch opening in Moscow in November, just as Vladimir Lenin and Leon Trotsky seized power and the Red Army forces overcame the less radical White Army.

Vladimir Lenin speaks to a crowd 1920
Leon Trotsky on lower platform

It was a colossal mistake. The new government declared that the huge loans given by the bank to Russia under the tsar were no longer Russia's problem. On December 17, 1917, they decreed that all banks, along with other businesses, were nationalized, and they claimed $26 million that depositors had entrusted to National City Bank in Russia. The bank's vice president Samuel McRoberts, one of the promising men Frank had brought on board, who had negotiated the various Russian loans and branch offices, resigned.

National City Bank stood to lose millions, possibly 40 per cent of its capital, or $33 million. It was everything Mr. Stillman had feared might happen. He summoned Frank from Washington to New York in February, 1918, where, "the two men apparently had a major confrontation, probably over the question of who was ultimately to blame for the National City's still undetermined Russian losses."

Fresh from the quarrel, worn out, suffering from undiagnosed diabetes, probably sick at heart over the loss of the bank's money and his mentor's good will, Frank left for Palos Verdes in late February, 1918. He was there when Mr. Stillman died not even one month later.

Mr. Stillman's son, James A. Stillman, who had no love for the man his father had practically adopted for the last sixteen years, became chairman of the board. He, like major stockholder William Rockefeller, did not approve of Frank's, "lengthy absence and his preoccupation with public affairs."

Still believing that Russian investment of some sort was a good idea, Frank went so far as to attend a conference in April, 1918, titled "League to Aid and Cooperate with Russia," organized by American businessmen. When World War I ended in November, 1918, the bank must have agreed with Frank's assessment. In February, 1919, the bank opened a branch in Vladivostok, a gathering spot for retreating White Army soldiers and refugees fleeing Bolshevik power.

Russian children on refugee train 1919 Vladivostok, Russia

Future Strategy

Later writers, looking at the actions of Frank, his bank and other financiers, with the advantage of hindsight, have labeled them all communist sympathizers, or worse. At the time, the world was still a bloody battlefield where millions were dying, not only from wounds, but from starvation. Even when hostilities ended, Frank saw first hand the bombed cities and factories, the devastated farmland, and the emaciated people. To a large extent, he and many others did not particularly care who was in charge. They just wanted to set the world on a strategic road to recovery.

Frank did, however, worry greatly about the spread of what he termed Bolshevism. *"It cannot too often be repeated, or too clearly kept in mind, that paralyzed industry, idle workmen, stoppage in the flow of manufactured things, and the want and hunger which must follow as a consequence, all of which is emphasized by the breakdown of domestic transportation, spell Bolshevism . . . There cannot be security in an atmosphere where Bolshevism is contagious, and where an outbreak in one center is almost certain to be communicated to adjacent regions."*

 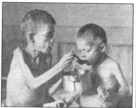 

Women search trash bin   Starving boys in orphanage   Women wait for food
Scenes of the effects of food supply disruption, Russia 1917-1920

He believed that the world was, properly, headed in the direction of giving workers a greater share in profits and a greater say in running and organizing businesses. *"I found the situation the same in every labor community where I had the opportunity to observe conditions. There is a determination on the part of labor to have more to say about conditions of its job . . . to have a larger share in the profits of industry . . . to see to it that society no longer regards labor as a mere commodity . . . that society shall grant to labor, not as a concession but as a right, a voice in determining immediate industrial surroundings, rules and regulations under which labor will work."*

But, he looked to the English, rather than the Russian, method of achieving this goal. In England, in spite of labor strikes after the war, *"The great fundamental common sense of the English people had asserted itself. The intelligence of the working classes and the labor attitude of the government, the public and the employers, had united in at least a temporary solution."*

Frank did not visit Russia on his 1919 trip to Europe. He did talk to several men who were there, and he studied events extensively. He did not believe that a minority such as the Bolshevik regime could do what was right for the whole population. *"Perhaps 100 million people of the 175 million that once constituted Russia have passed under the sway of a Bolshevik regime, although the true adherents to that political theory probably numbered less than five per cent of the population involved. The most centralized and autocratic government in modern times has sprung up in Russia, although ninety-five percent of the people involved did not adhere to the political theories and would repudiate the authority if they could."*

Bolshevik cavalry, unknown Russian town 1917

Part of what he believed was wrong with this system was the logistics of moving and allocating scarce resources when workers are not motivated to do so. *"Every shop in Petrograd is closed and the windows shuttered . . . Literally, starvation is a matter of daily occurrence, because of the impossibility of moving food into the city over the broken-down transportation system . . . There is not a ton of coal in all Bolshevik Russia, and locomotives must be fired with wood . . . Starvation follows the breakdown of transportation, and would continue no matter what sources of food there were at the end of these broken down lines of railways."*

As opposed to the Russian model, in England, he saw *"a sort of dogged optimism in the minds of all classes and a belief in the power and intelligence of England and Englishmen, a more or less conscious impression, that they would work out eventually a relationship between labor and capital in which all apparent sacrifices that capital might have to make would be more than compensated for by the increased efficiency which would come from a body of satisfied workmen."*

By the time he returned from his 1919 European trip, he put his faith not in the worshippers in St. Isaac's Cathedral clutching their bread and waiting for a spark to light the darkness, or in the Bolshevik revolution promising to give everything to everyone, but in the education and common sense he saw in British workers.

There was no time to readjust his banking theories accordingly. At the end of his fact-finding excursion to Europe, his days at the bank were numbered.

○ ○ ○

Europe

*Frank Vanderlip, Harry Meserve, Duke of Tovar, Madrid, Spain April 1919
Entering Royal Palace to meet with King Alphonso XIII*

o   o   o

Europe

Harry Benedict had the flu. He was so desperate to get well that he submitted to shock treatment while he was in bed at New York's Yale Club.

Whether it was such a radical remedy, or his own determination to not miss out on the once-in-a-lifetime experience, he appeared, slightly pale and weak, at the dock to sail for Europe in January, 1919.

Joining him on board were his boss, Frank Vanderlip, Frank's wife Narcissa, and two National City Bank vice presidents. Harry Meserve was the man who headed the bank's Petrograd office when the tsar was overthrown during the Russian Revolution. Paul Grosjean was the son of a prominent Belgian banker, and was fluent in French and a number of other languages.

The purpose of the trip, according to Frank, was to *"take a hurried glance at financial conditions in London and on the Continent,"* following the end of World War I. He found *"the process of learning so fascinating,"* that he extended the stay by an extra month. Before they went home, the group *"visited seven countries and had received impressions from interviews with hundreds of people of importance, representing at least fifteen countries."*

Claridge's Hotel, London 1908

First stop was Liverpool, in the middle of a typically cold English winter. They went directly to the warmth of London's Claridge's Hotel, where they first saw the war's effects. Even in such a privileged setting, both the quantity and selection of food was limited.

Being president of America's largest bank guaranteed that whoever Frank wanted to meet in the financial world would go out of their way to talk with him.

England

At the beginning of February, Frank met with the British ministers of Finance, Labor, and Reconstruction, as well as the leaders of several of the labor unions and the two heads of the government employment administration. He talked to bankers and financial editors of leading newspapers. He visited mill towns for the cotton spinning industry, and studied the plight of coal miners. He witnessed railroad strikes, coal shortages, a threatened strike by electric company employees, and saw a "*rapidly growing army of unemployed which was increasing directly as the demobilization of the army proceeded.*"

Typical English mill town of Crompton with smokestacks circa 1890

The country had been at war for four years. Everyone had sacrificed for the war effort, and now they were tired of struggling. In the coal mines, children working all day was a common sight. Labor demanded better working conditions, a shorter work day, and higher pay. The men Frank spoke to on both sides of the issues agreed on

Child coal miners on strike, England 1919

one thing. "*England was in for such a fight with labor as she had never known and the outcome was anything but clear and had in it possibilities of revolutionary import.*"

When Frank returned to England at the end of his trip, in May, he found *"the situation as completely changed as it would be possible to imagine."* He reported with relief, *"The great fundamental common sense of the English people had asserted itself."* The government, business leaders, and union representatives had found ways to negotiate.

These were men, on both sides, who Frank understood. *"They were patriotic Englishmen with a great love for their country and with hope for its future. Some of them were men with no great amount of culture, but with wide knowledge. They had an understanding of economics that could only have been obtained by men who recognized that these laws were of transcendent importance and that the principles of action under which they led unions embracing half a million men must be formulated in accordance with sound economic principles or the leadership would go astray."* No wonder Frank admired Englishmen. He could have been describing himself.

Paris

The Versailles Peace Conference was underway when Frank and his party arrived in Paris. The Ritz Hotel was, as Harry Benedict described the scene, "pretty much the public hub of the official and private groups." Of course, that was where Frank and his party stayed. Most of the historic personalities involved in the peace talks could be seen, at some time, in the hotel lobby.

Place Vendome, Ritz Hotel on left, Paris, France circa 1890

Herbert Hoover 1917

One of them was a friend Frank greatly admired. Herbert Hoover, who would become president ten years later, was then directing the Commission for Relief in Belgium. Throughout the war, Herbert Hoover ran a delicate gauntlet between the Allied and German forces to deliver food to five million starving people in 2,500 villages, cities, and towns of Belgium and northern France. Part of his task, he believed, was "to maintain the laughter of the children, not to dry their tears." He did the job well. By 1917, three fourths of Belgium's children were getting hot meals at special locations.

The two men dined together several times in Herbert Hoover's rooms at the Ritz. They had much in common. Herbert Hoover, born in Iowa, was the orphaned son of a blacksmith and a self-made millionaire who, before entering the political arena, was interested in purchasing a newspaper. He believed America had an obligation to help Europe recover and that, in the summation of a man's lifetime, it was his accomplishments that were most important.

Always influenced by those men he admired, some of Frank's actions in the next few years for which he paid a high personal price, when he felt that he was doing what was best for the country, may have partially been the influence of Herbert Hoover's philosophies.

Another of Frank's old friends in Paris for the peace talks was Ignace Jan Paderewski, pianist, composer, and newly installed Prime Minister of Poland. They spent three days together, discussing the establishment of a "sound banking facility" in Poland. Frank must have helped with more than just advice for, at a dinner in New York for 4,000 honoring the prime minister nine years later, he thanked "Mr. Vanderlip and others who by their encouragement, by their constant work and otherwise, had helped me to establish the foundations of my entire activity in this country, the Polish Victims Relief Fund."

France filled Frank with *"admiration that there was in the world a nation of such superb valor,"* but he sighed over its problems at the war's end. *"France never stopped to count the price in courage and manhood that she must pay to defend herself."* The country also did not, he felt, pay attention to the finances involved. *"There was never any reckoning as to what the future had in store. All things were possible to that patriotism which is unsurpassed. And no more did France count the financial cost."*

The war left France with an almost impossible devaluation of its currency. Frank did not think the French even wanted to acknowledge how badly off their financial situation was. *"Indeed I think the French mind grows bewildered when the unit of a billion is reached. They call it a milliard and after you have annexed nine ciphers to a figure, the French mind no longer follows. It got to be all the same when the debt of France piled up to a hundred milliards and then two hundred, and then engagements were made that will take it far beyond that figure. It got to be like figures in astronomy that are so great that they are represented by conventional symbols."*

The Battlefields of France

Frank's group traveled along the entire line of what had been the French defensive lines against the Germans. *"France had a visible aspect of having been bled white . . . The pathos of that devastated territory is beyond words - the all but homeless people camping in wrecked buildings with windows screened with paper. Patient peasants toiling northward with scanty furnishings for the home they hoped to return to, were poignant sights, when one had come fresh from the regions toward which they were going and knew that no roof stood in all the land."*

Refugees returning home, France and Belgium 1919

It was here that Narcissa noticed how quickly the devastated, war-scarred battlefields were being covered with new growth of what the French called Argonne ivy, known on the other side of the channel as English ivy. She picked some shoots, and smuggled them back home stuffed into the lining of her mink muff. At Beechwood, her gardeners nurtured them until she had enough to offer a plant to any of the mothers of the 116,000 Americans who died in the war. Many of their bodies lay in European graves, and Narcissa felt this was a way to bring a piece of rejuvenated France into the mothers' gardens.

Newly dug soldiers' cemetery near Boullonville, France 1919

As a banker, Frank's way to make sense of a problem was to break it down into manageable numbers that could be summed up on paper. And, as a farm boy, he liked to throw in an occasional farming analogy. He noted that, before the war, France's national debt was about $160 per person. By 1919, that amount ballooned to $650 per person.

He worried that the French felt this situation would be solved by indemnity payments to them from the Germans. *"They were hazy on how that indemnity was to be paid."* They did not, however, want German factories to be up and running before France's own industries were reconstructed.

Frank did not see how Germany could pay anyone anything if their businesses were not making money to pay taxes that would pay the reparations. *"A Dutch banker in talking with me one day threw up his hands in despair over the French mind. 'They want to milk the cow and cut its throat at the same time,' he said."* That brought to Frank's mind his own farm days, with a dash of his particular brand of Midwestern humor. *"Cutting a cow's throat while you milk her interferes with that maternal quietude of mind which is conducive to a generous down-giving of milk."*

With a prescient look at the future, he continued, "*Whatever the French mind is, it is usually logical. It can be forgiven in this case, however, for utterly neglecting logic, for it must be remembered that triumphant as France stands, she is still in abject terror of the future, if that future holds a military Germany.*"

Perhaps because of what had transpired in Russia, Frank watched for signs that more of Europe would embrace the Bolshevik socialist philosophy. He was relieved to report that, because "*The great anchor of France, so far as its internal political safety is concerned, lies in the fact that there are six million landowners, and that the whole nation is made up of small investors . . . France would not seem good soil in which to propagate the ideals of Bolshevik Communism.*"

Holland

From their Paris base, Frank's party branched out into Belgium and also on to Holland, where they were honored with a dinner at The Hague. It was attended by leading Dutch bankers and businessmen.

While they were there, an intriguing call came through. It was from Kaiser Wilhelm II of Germany. After abdicating his throne in November, 1918, he had crossed the border and was now living in Holland. At the ongoing Versailles Peace Conference, a special international tribunal would be established to try him for war crimes, but Holland would refuse to surrender him and the trial never took place.

Kaiser Wilhelm II of Germany 1918

The Kaiser issued an invitation for Frank to visit him for a talk. As Harry Benedict remarked with some of his boss's flair for colorful writing, Frank's "lifelong journalism instinct made this opportunity blaze like a beacon in its possibilities of discussing a world of matters leading to, during, and after the war."

It took the combined efforts of Harry Meserve, Paul Grosjean, and Harry Benedict to dissuade Frank. They had motored past, "great fields fenced high with wire in which were tens of thousands of German war prisoners." The American public would not have appreciated the head of their largest bank interviewing a man who most of them considered to be a war criminal. Frank must have been disappointed.

The group did take some time for tourist activities. In Amsterdam, they visited the Rijksmuseum and, like thousands of others for centuries, stood in awe in front of Rembrandt's *The Night Watch*. In Leiden, they researched Frank's family name, still to be found there under the spelling Van Der Lippe. The family study Frank privately published in 1914 showed Vanderlips, listed under various spellings, in Holland, Scandinavia and Germany.

Belgium

When Frank's group drove through Belgium, he remarked, "*an observer who looked only at the surface of things would see well tilled fields, and cities presenting a normal external appearance.*" But, Frank was never one to simply look at the surface.

"*The Germans did horrible material harm to Belgium, harm that went beyond all military necessity, some of it seemingly done in madness in the early days . . . Toward the end of the war theirs was a destruction of Machiavellian cunning, a destruction designed purely to prevent what might be left of Belgian industries from coming into early competition with German production.*"

Motoring through destroyed towns between France and Belgium 1919
On road to battle site of Messines near Ypres, Belgium

Frank was fresh from his talks in Paris with Herbert Hoover, who had spent the last four years helping to fend off starvation in Belgium. *"The harm that was done in Belgium was by no means entirely material; a harm was done to the moral fiber of her people . . . Four and a half years under such occupation, with the whole normal industrial life disorganized, when the question of securing somehow one's daily bread was the paramount question . . . when that situation has been borne by a people for so long a time, an impression of it will be left that no terms that could be written into an armistice will remove."*

He believed recovery was dependent on restarting industry and putting people back to work, which was going to take time, and plenty of banking credit. *"Outside of the few cotton mills . . . the industry of Belgium has ceased . . . The destruction has been so complete that it will be impossible to restart industry in anything like its full momentum for a least three years, if there were not a single financial or political obstacle in the way. Buildings in many cases must first be torn down . . . Machinery is in every state of wreckage . . . The future relation of the franc to the dollar no one would quite venture to predict."*

Destruction in Ypres, Belgium 1919

Looking beyond the world of finance, Frank worried about the spirit of the country. *"It seems to me that the greatest injury that Belgium has suffered, and God knows the total list is an unparalleled one, is in the deterioration of the moral fiber of her common people. How quickly that can be rebuilt no one can say. The inherent desire to right wrong tendencies in humanity is unmeasurable."*

There was hope, Frank concluded, because the government of Belgium was *"in strong, capable, patriotic hands,"* and because Belgian businessmen with "*trained intelligence*," only needed capital to get the country moving. Frank hoped those funds would come from American investments.

Italy

Leaving the worst destruction behind them, Frank's group fell under the spell of northern Italy. They drove through Perugia and Bologna. In the wine country town of Orvieto, Harry Benedict says, "the white wine was said to have so delighted a Cardinal in early times that he stopped there and drank himself happily to death."

It was already past the lunch hour when the group arrived at a small Orvieto restaurant and, after some persuasion, the owner agreed to "whip up something." The two Harrys, Benedict and Meserve, were given the keys to the wine cellar and instructed to choose something. Returning with dusty bottles in hand, they were surprised to find the president of National City Bank, undoubtedly in one of his elegant three-piece suits, "sitting astride a sort of shoemaker's bench grating cheese with a curious contrivance." Lunch was apparently a success, "with perhaps too much wine but good cheese and spaghetti."

Florence was a highlight of the Italian trip, with its great Duomo and artwork by Michaelangelo and Botticelli. On the morning after their arrival, Harry Benedict was stunned and hurt when Frank told him, "I will handle meetings here for the next day or two.

Florence, Italy 1905

I don't want you around." With time on his hands, Harry wandered through the city for the day, taking the same route as centuries of tourists, studying the buildings and the art.

That evening, on his return, he found preparations for a large dinner party. Before it began, Frank took Harry aside and said, "Tell us where you have been and what you did on your first day in Florence." His relief at Frank's motives gave life to his descriptions and seemed to please his boss. "This amazing man had felt that no more national financial discussions could equal the value of turning me loose with no sense of time or duties for a day or two in Florence."

In Rome, they found the streets filled with Italian soldiers, and met with a number of high financial officials. Then it was on to Pisa and Sienna, before heading to Genoa.

Along the way, Frank and Narcissa were accumulating "a few van loads," of furniture and antiques to ship back to Beechwood, much of it planned for use in the Italian villa they were designing for Palos Verdes. Credit cards had not yet been invented, and even a bank president could not simply go into a branch and retrieve cash from a U.S. account. Frank did not carry enough cash with him for so many purchases. He sent Harry Benedict into National City Bank's Genoa office to arrange a loan for $30,000 in lira. The exchange rate between the dollar and the lira was so high in the months ahead that Frank was able to repay the loan for only $10,000.

Frank's own comments on each country paid close attention to specific financial problems. Italy, he found, was "*wonderfully rich in man power, moderately well-to-do in agricultural resources. She has partly developed her great potential resources of water power, but she has not a pound of good native coal, little mineral of any kind, and none of the great staple raw materials.*"

One of the large industries was silk production, from the raising of cocoons to the spinning of skeins of silk thread. The "*lovely skeins of yellow silk*" were then exported to France, Switzerland, and Austria to be woven.

Other items that were exported were olive oil and, of course, pasta, cheese, and wine. None of these were in large enough quantities to make up for the "*absolutely insistent need for very considerable imports.*"

In Frank's view of the world, there must be a constant and equal flow of value, within countries and across borders, to keep the economic world on a steady course. "*No matter how rich a nation may be within itself, if it is deficient in some essential that must be imported, it must have some commodity of equal value that the world wants and will pay for.*"

Before the war, the world wanted Italy's beauty and culture. Tourists brought with them much of the currency Italy needed. Frank estimated that, for the war years and for the several which would follow, Italy's loss would be not less than $200 million each year.

Another income source that had diminished was money sent home by emigrants to their families. Many of these young men had returned during the war to enlist, cutting off a large source of external funding, and now adding to the ranks of the unemployed.

There was hope, Frank believed, for the country's recovery.

"These Northern Italians seem to have a genius for industrial organization." He admired the Fiat works at Turin, and the Ansaldo Company, which had foreseen the war and converted their factories to manufacture large guns well before they even had an order from the Italian army or any cash from

Ansaldo munitions plant, Genoa 1918

the government to pay for them.

But, like the rest of Europe, Italy had no money to buy the raw materials to make her products or to get them to international markets. *"It all amounts to the inevitable logic of two plus two. There is no getting away from the few fundamental factors that are involved in international trade. To buy anything abroad Italy must sell her own products or make loans to counteract the lack of balance. If she cannot make those loans, things essential to her industrial life cannot be imported. Her industrial life must halt, production cease, workmen stand in idleness and face want."*

If this should happen, Frank foresaw *"revolutionary outbreaks, a disorganization of the social order, industrial chaos."* Just after Frank left Europe, in September, 1919, what he predicted came to pass. Workers, in the Turin and Milan factories that he admired, started a revolt lasting two years and involving four million people, known as the Biennio Rosso. Their takeover of factories brought heavy business and military retaliation that, in the coming years, led to the rise of the fascist movement in Italy.

Armed worker guarding factory gate   *Labor meeting at worker-seized Fiat factory*
Factory takeovers by workers, Northern Italy 1920

A Short Rest

From Italy, the group took a steamer to Gibraltar, where they checked in to the Maria Cristina Hotel. Even after the necessity for overseas communications during the war, getting information back and forth between New York and most of Europe was a lengthy process. Frank and Narcissa learned that their youngest child, John, was sick with pneumonia back at Beechwood. Narcissa refused to move on to another town and another hotel until she could be certain that he was all right.

Hotel Maria Cristina, Gibraltar c 1910

John, still an infant, was probably very lucky. The so-called Spanish flu was sweeping the world, carried by returning soldiers and their ships to all parts of the globe. Somewhere between 20 and 50 million people died, with some estimates as high as 100 million. Symptoms started with blue-hued skin, as a virus invaded the lungs and they filled with fluid, causing the same pneumonia afflicting John. The Vanderlips did not lose any family members in the terrible epidemic.

While waiting and hoping for John to get better, they spent "an otherwise delightful several days . . . in an acre or more of bright flowers and looked across the Straits to North Africa."

Spain

Finally taking a train to Sevilla, the group went on to Granada, where Harry Benedict commented, "Time shrinks as you stand in the room where Columbus conferred with Ferdinand and Isabella on his project to sail west."

King Alphonso XIII of Spain circa 1915

In Madrid, Frank met with King Alphonso XIII, "*a conversation hampered by no ceremonies of royal dignity.*" They spoke about conditions in Spain and Europe, "*with the same freedom that one might have talked with any intelligent statesman or, I think I would rather say, with an intelligent business man, for His Majesty showed a knowledge of business conditions . . . and an understanding of the principles of foreign trade such as a good many statesmen would be quite innocent of.*" High praise, indeed, from a serious banker.

Spain was lucky because it had been cut off from the war partly by the daunting mass of the Pyrennes mountains. "*The Great War,*" Frank noted, "*brought to Spain almost nothing but profit.*"

There was a huge market for anything Spain could sell, and not much available to buy from outside of the borders. As a result, "*there lie in the vaults of the Bank of Spain in Madrid great pyramids of bricks of gold and long rows of sacked sovereigns and eagles. There is now piled in that vault gold to a value of $440 million,*" more than Frank guessed was even in the country when Spain was at the height of New World conquest.

He was treated to a view of this incredible treasure. "*I was taken down to the bullion vaults of the Bank of Spain accompanied by four elderly guardians, each carrying a massive key. These four keys were simultaneously inserted through the ancient escutcheons and a door which would amuse some of my Sing Sing neighbors if they could note the ease with which they might,*" *unaided by any keys, pass through it, was thrown open on a view of these piled masses of gold."* As the man whose bank was the proud possessor of what *Harper's Weekly Magazine* called, "the most powerful steel-vault door in the world," it must have been an amusing experience.

Just before Frank's visit, a citywide strike began in Barcelona with maintenance workers at a hydro-electric plant known as La Canadiense. It was backed by a labor group known as the Syndicate, later known as the CNT, or National Conference of Workers. The strike was finally stopped in March,

Spanish newspaper headline about strikers 1919

after a state of war was declared and troops were called in. Another strike, spreading over most of Catalonia, ran from March until April.

Strikers demonstrate in Barcelona 1919

Frank saw the Syndicate to be *"the most menacing, the most extra-ordinary, the most terrifying organization with which I have ever come in contact . . . Syndicalism proposes no compromise with the present order of society. It is Bolshevik in its aspirations and its methods. It refuses to accept the present capitalistic organization of society and is determined to overthrow the present social order completely in order that it may build a socialistic state on the ruins of the capitalistic state."* He learned of threats, assassinations, and destruction.

Even worse, from Frank's perspective as a former newsman, was the Syndicate censorship of newspapers, using fines backed by violence against editors and their presses. When Frank was in Barcelona, not one single paper had published for the last two weeks.

In spite of his personal admiration for King Alphonso, Frank could see reasons for the unrest. "*The Government in some particulars is bad and in many ways is inefficient. There still exists a privileged class of nobles, living for pleasure and blind to the responsibilities of their position. Great land holding leave large sections of agricultural population little better than old time serfs.*"

He had hopes Spain's combination of rich natural resources and all that gold in the vaults would "*make the country blossom with an era of great internal development and prosperity.*" But, he was not certain business leaders would find any ways to compromise with the worker unrest. "*What the result of the reaction of these forces may be I would not attempt to guess.*" The Spanish Civil War and Socialist takeover would engulf the country in 1936, about a year before Frank died.

Spanish Civil War poster c 1936 Communist party

Spanish Civil War poster c 1936 Falangist party

Paris Again

Retracing their steps, Frank's group returned to Paris before crossing the channel once again to London. While still in Paris, Frank accepted an invitation from General Pershing to visit his Paris headquarters, where they talked about the General's bitterness toward his reputation in America. "He was a bitter man," Harry Benedict says. "The American public accused him of being a butcher." Many people felt the war was practically ended in October, 1918, and thought Pershing should not have thrown his 50,000 fresh troops into the slaughter that followed in the next month. Pershing believed, he told Frank, that if he had not done so, winter would have set in, giving the Germans time to recuperate and raise fresh troops, bringing "a great further loss of men and much suffering."

Intending to stay in Paris for a few more days, Frank and his party were rather summarily expelled from the Ritz, a hotel not to be intimidated by the title of an American bank president. The hotel had no grand suites to spare because of the ongoing Peace Conference. The Vanderlips had to give up their rooms for the arrival of royal guests, Queen Marie of Romania and two of her daughters. Harry Benedict stood at the entrance and watched her arrive "with her small army of attendants."

*Queen Marie of Romania in front of Ritz Hotel
Queen on left, daughter Elizabeth on right 1919*

London

One last dinner in London, given by Frank, brought together the leading bankers of the city, who "had been and still were stiff-necked in regard to the provincial bankers of New York," Harry Benedict says. "It was an noteworthy occasion, and Mr. Vanderlip felt some trepidation as to whether his guests would accept and come. It was a tribute to their respect for Mr. Vanderlip, coupled, of course, with genuine interest and curiosity. He gave them a banker's report on Europe. They showed a deep interest, and accepted him as worthy of the best financial minds they could muster. Their reaction gave Mr. Vanderlip a deep satisfaction."

When Frank finally arrived back in New York, events must have made him wish to return to the praise he received that evening.

Frank's Conclusions

Witnessing first hand the destruction and misery all over war-torn Europe made Frank feel a need to improve the world. He realized many travelers, not looking as closely as he did, would see cattle placidly grazing and the colorful tulip fields of Holland, and might conclude *"Europe was almost ready to resume its old life in the old way."*

However, "*no one with open eyes could have escaped the horrid marks of war.*" Frank's view about his mission in life and the direction in which he should lead the bank began to change. He did not want his children to ever suffer what he saw happening in Europe.

Frank and his group boarded Titanic's sister ship, S. S. Olympic, on May 10, 1919, at Southampton, headed for Halifax, Nova Scotia, and then New York. During the five day crossing, he dictated notes to Harry Benedict in the comfort of their suite, using "frequent discussions of our common memory of interviews and opinions, and references to notes," that Harry Benedict made throughout the trip.

On their return, Harry Benedict dictated the manuscript to "a staff of women stenographers," It was published under the title *What Happened to Europe.*

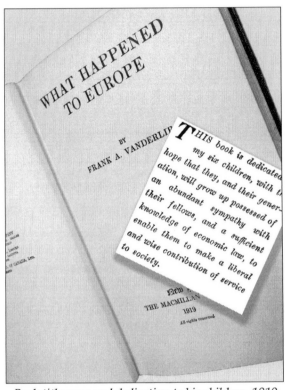

Book title page and dedication to his children 1919

Many in his bank were not happy with Frank's thoughts on putting up large loans super-ceding all others, to help Europe recover. They tried to convince Frank not to publish his book.

Much of what Frank foresaw came to pass in the following years. Some of his conclusions turned out to be wrong, as the world and circumstances changed. In general, any business person or financier using Frank's book as a guide for European investments would not have been too far off of the mark.

The most important effect of the war, Frank felt, was "*the disorganization and paralysis of industrial production,*" which would lead to further starvation, labor unrest, and its resulting "*danger of revolutionary development and of Bolshevik tendencies.*"

Even though Frank's group never lacked for food, or anything else throughout the trip, he knew *"Hundreds of thousands of people have starved to death in the last twelve months in Europe."* Part of this was not due to lack of food, but to the inability to get it where it was needed. He believed the situation would be even worse during the following year.

And, he believed, many people felt *"it will all come right in time, that eventually the factories will be restored, the flow of exports resumed . . . and that in the end we will witness the remarkable power of recovery which an industrious people can show."* There was one big problem with this *"easy optimism,"* he said.

"A normal man needs three meals a day. That need is immediate and he cannot wait for an adjustment which will come 'in the long run.' The human stomach cannot wait."

If the present governments and industries could not provide those meals, workers would take matters into their own hands. *"The element of time is now of prime importance. Unless there is speedy action in the direction of re-starting paralyzed industry, there may follow a quick march of events toward revolutionary outbreaks in any country where idleness is continued and is followed by hunger and want."* It was most important to put people back to work. *"The danger in not doing this promptly . . . is so extreme that it is no exaggeration to say that failure to do this may mean a breakdown in European civilization which will involve the whole world."*

There was a way to avert such a catastrophe. America must help, not simply out of sympathy, *"for charity alone cannot save Europe. America must understand how her own fortunes - her own future - are bound up with the fate of European civilization."*

Europe needed large infusions of capital. Frank suggested that Europe be considered as a whole, not country by country, and that the U. S. offer what he called *"receiver's certificates for the credit to get her going again."* These would be loans to nations, which would have a repayment obligation in front of all other outstanding debts. It was a bold and controversial idea, as it would infuriate the banks and other investors who already had funds at risk.

Frank saw a healthy Europe as the only way to stop what he feared would be a spread of Bolshevism. "*If the foregoing is a correct view, then Europe must be looked at as a unit and one must cease trying to find a nation here or there, or a loan of one character or another that in itself is thought to offer a fair basis of security. There cannot be security in an atmosphere where Bolshevism is contagious, and where an out break in one center is almost certain to be communicated to adjacent regions.*"

He came home with an expanded view of what his country, and his bank, should do. "*I believe the stability of the present order of society, the maintenance of a society based upon the principle of property rights, is bound up with the way this problem is worked out in Europe. We cannot stand a world apart in its solution. Indeed, we cannot stand a world apart in any sense. No matter how self-sufficient we may believe ourselves to be . . . we are inevitably part of what is coming to be a very small world, a world in which ideas travel with a freedom and rapidity that must force us to become internationalists in our views.*"

Frank's vision included his bank becoming a leader in the work of reconstruction, even though it would mean profits that would not be realized for quite some time. He believed it was the right, and patriotic, course to take. There were others in the bank, powerful men who had never been his friends, who disagreed. They believed the bank's first loyalty was to its own stockholders. With Mr. Stillman gone, and his son now chairman of the board, Frank's homecoming would not be a joyous one.

Frank A. Vanderlip 1919

○ ○ ○

Out Of The Bank

"Most powerful steel-vault door in the world," National City Bank of New York 1909

o o o

Out Of The Bank

 Ned Currier had bad news to deliver. He took a train from New York City, got off, waited for another train coming from the opposite direction, and stepped on board.

It was not difficult to find his boss, Frank Vanderlip, and Frank's group of travelers, returning home from their European trip at the end of World War I. They were in a private railroad car at the end of the train, having disembarked from S. S. Olympic at Halifax, Nova Scotia. In a way, the war was still with them on their Atlantic crossing. Even in their first class accommodations, they were aware of the thousands of Canadian soldiers aboard who were returning to their homes.

On board S. S. Olympic 1919
Returning soldiers leaving Europe for Canada

The news Ned Currier delivered, behind the closed door of the car's drawing room, was that a "plot," as he termed it, was developing at the National City Bank, to remove Frank from the presidency.

The move was almost inevitable. "*Jimmy,*" as Frank called the son of his mentor, James J. Stillman, never liked Frank. Neither did Jimmy Stillman's uncle, William Rockefeller. They particularly did not like Frank's enthusiasm for solving the troubles of Europe.

Neither did the Morgan bankers, who felt Frank was exaggerating the urgency of the European situation and what should be done about it. Benjamin Strong, one of the Jekyll Island 'duck hunters,' who was now governor of the New York Federal Reserve Bank, commented that, "Vanderlip gets very much excited with his experiences, always, and loses his perspective."

Ben Davidson, another Jekyll Island alum associated with the Morgans, had his own, less ambitious plan for European recovery, and the Morgans tried to persuade Frank not to publish his book. They did not succeed.

Frank was, in many ways, ready to move on. He was bored with day-to-day banking, still defending the bank's loss of funds in their Russian adventure, and looking at a larger world picture. But, he wanted the move to be his own choice. *"I wanted to get out. I did not want to be put out."*

Frank A. Vanderlip circa 1918 or 1919
In front of National City Bank

Whatever words were spoken when Frank met with Jimmy Stillman, it was short and to the point. *"We exchanged only a few words and thereafter I let it be known that I would get out gladly."*

Their go-between was a man Frank had known for a long time, William Kiernan. Involved together in land deals in Spokane, Washington and Coos Bay, Oregon, William Kiernan would eventually also work on the Palos Verdes project in California. Although he was a friend of the Stillmans, Frank obviously put his trust in the man. William Kiernan arranged Jimmy Stillman's purchase of Frank's bank stock, effectively turning over control.

Knowing he was leaving, Frank ignored the Morgan interests and gave several speeches, including one to the respected Economic Club. He talked about his concerns for the state of economics and politics in Europe, and his fear that the latent Bolshevism in many of its countries could reach the American shore if Europe was not helped quickly and thoughtfully. *"Those speeches were not well received in Wall Street, because I said that the country was facing a period of business depression. That sort of information, however true, never is well received in Wall Street. Consequently, many persons erroneously jumped to the conclusion that my speeches were the cause of my resignation."*

On June 4, 1919, Frank and Jimmy Stillman met with the board of directors. *"I announced that Jimmy wanted to be president and that I was entirely agreeable."* The two men stepped out of the room to allow the board to talk it over. *"There was some discussion; a few voices were raised. But it was settled. I resigned, packed up and walked out of the National City Bank for good."*

Office of Frank Vanderlip, president of National City Bank, New York 1914

o o o

Sparta

House with fence from National City Bank 1909 reconstruction, Sparta, New York 2012

o   o   o

Sparta

It is almost a cliche that, when a man retires who has worked his whole life, the first thing he does is re-arrange his wife's kitchen. Instead, Frank Vanderlip re-arranged a town.

Only about one-quarter mile north of Beechwood, along the Hudson River, sat the small town of Sparta, New York. It would have probably been better described as a hamlet.

Standing along the Albany Post Road since the late 1700s, Sparta encompassed about 70 acres, just three-fourths of the size of Frank's Beechwood home. To house teachers for his school, Frank had already built several houses at the edge of the town, on the Albany Post Road leading to Beechwood, and opened a community center and library.

Time For 'Play'

Kelvin Vanderlip, Sr. circa 1922
At the lathe at Beechwood

After walking out of the National City Bank, Frank did take a little time to relax, a new experience for him. "*It took me about a week, I think, to discover that if it suited me, I might sleep as late as I cared to. Let the old world spin! I could sit around and talk with my children or even, if I liked, go on a picnic. As a matter of fact, I did go on a picnic.*" He even set up a lathe at Beechwood, hoping to pass on this skill to his son Kelvin, who was eight years old. As it turned out, Frank used the lathe more often than his son. Frank does not mention whether or not he donned a pair of overalls to do so.

He also went to a reunion. When Frank was a boy, still living on his family farm, his school was an old stone building with twenty-nine students. His teacher was Christopher Duffy, a Civil War veteran, whose popularity was, the Aurora newspaper reported, "attested by the fact that the days are perpetuated in an organized body known as the Duffy association." The popular teacher had gone on to be the

Frank Vanderlip, Christopher Duffy, Emma Duffy 1919 School reunion, Oswego, Illinois

county superintendent of schools and was then elected an appellate court clerk. For the past twenty years, Frank had been invited to attend the reunion, but was always too busy.

Now, Frank had the time. He took a train to Illinois, and "*shook hands with Mr. Duffy, and wandered about looking into aging faces there for eyes that I could recognize.*" He found old friends. As many others have found after attending reunions, it was fun to reminisce about misadventures, such as the time Frank and a friend climbed on top of the school outhouse to attract attention, and how ashamed he was at the trouble he was in for doing so. He realized it was a distant part of a life of which he could be generally proud. "*If you want to know the truth, there is very little else in my life of which I am ashamed.*"

Looking Inward

Whatever thoughts he kept to himself, Frank did not commit to paper much second guessing of his past actions. Now, with time on his hands, he allowed himself a little. He wondered how Mr. Stillman would have handled the decisions Frank made that ultimately took Frank out of the bank. He decided that Mr. Stillman "*would have brought great wisdom and therefore sharp restraint to many expanding operations.*" Frank's solace, particularly as time went on, was that those years were "*confusing to the wisest and most experienced minds.*"

A New Project

Picnics and reunions were, of course, not enough to occupy Frank's energy. He turned to Sparta, a place that was not the type of community he wanted to have just down the road from Beechwood.

Sparta, New York, before Frank Vanderlip's reconstruction circa 1919 or earlier

Wherever Frank went, reporters were sure to follow. Newspaper articles detailed his plans, one declaring, "Vanderlip Buys Town to Reform It!" The *New York Tribune* went into more colorful detail.

For years undesirables have found refuge in Sparta. State constabulary troops have been called often to the little place off the beaten path to suppress disorder, drunken brawls, or to search for gentry wanted for breaking the laws of the commonwealth. Authorities at Sing Sing Prison, to the north, invariably make post haste for Sparta when a "boarder" has made a break for the open and just as invariably get their man there. Many escapes from the grey prison have been hatched there. Such conditions do not make for a wholesome, clean and attractive town.

Not everyone in Sparta thought the town was an undesirable place. Mrs. Andrew J. Robinson said, "I don't know when anything has happened in Sparta so exciting. It has been a quiet, peaceful, sweet little village as long as I can remember, and I lived here when I was a little girl." She also claimed that "The stories about Sparta being a sanctuary for escaped Sing Sing convicts in the old days is all false."

"When anybody got out of Sing Sing then, as now, he put as many miles as he could between himself and the prison. He never tarried here. I have known years to go by in this hamlet without as much excitement as somebody's horse running away. The people have always been nice, quiet country farmers and a few honest laborers on the railroad and in the quarry. Nobody ever did anything to get the village into the papers. We just lived quiet, happy lives."

Everyone's happy, quiet lives were about to be overturned, as Frank started buying up property. When he owned about half of the town, "The effect on the sleeping village was instantaneous. It awoke with a start. It put up the price of real estate." Frank was no fool. He announced that he did not *"care to buy any more unless somebody wants to sell at reasonable prices."*

Liberty Street looking east, Sparta, New York during Vanderlip remodel circa 1920

One man who thought he could best Frank was Nick Sellazzo, owner of a saloon which, theoretically, sold "soft drinks," as Prohibition was in full force at the time. He decided to hold out for more than Frank offered. He had, however, been charged several months earlier with violating the dry laws, so

Only divided building in Sparta before remodel Probably Nick Sellazzo's saloon on left side 1919

apparently his saloon did hold true to its name. Frank bought the other half of the building, and planned to renovate as far as the dividing wall, which would have left the saloon looking like a derelict in the shiny new town. The two men finally settled on a price of $19,000, and Nick Sellazzo moved out. "*Nick and I are good friends,*" Frank said in January, 1921. Six months later, Nick Sellazzo was back, somehow scooping Frank, and buying an old building across the street from his former saloon, hoping that he could also sell it to Frank. Nowhere is there a recorded comment by Frank about Nick's return.

Only The Best

Frank formed a corporation and got to work. "*I like to fuss with blue prints,*" he said, "*and study the details of an old structure and how it may be made useful without destroying the charm of its exterior or interior. I like to take old things and make them new.*"

As the architect in charge of the project, Frank hired one of the best. Arthur Loomis Harmon, another Illinois native, would later design the Empire State Building as part of the firm of Shreve, Lamb and Harmon. In 1920, he ran his own individual firm. The contractor, brought in from New York City, was William Crawford.

They set to work quickly. As Frank described their challenge, Sparta was "*a very tumbled-down town, a place without electricity, without gas, without baths and possessing not a single water heating plant. It had been left behind, skipped over by modern conveniences and comforts.*"

The roads were re-paved. Old fences were removed, and new ones installed. Electrical and gas lines went in. Frank and his men were not afraid to jack houses up off of their foundations and move them. Some houses were pulled back from the street, to give them a more gracious front yard. Some were turned around to face the Hudson River. Some were given extreme makeovers or new additions. Those that were deemed not worth saving were demolished.

Sparta's oldest resident, great-grandmother Mrs. Trathen, "over eighty, beloved by everybody in the hamlet," watched it all with interest. She apparently was one of the landowners who sold her home to Frank, for she moved into a tiny place "near her descendants."

Wooden houses are, of course, easier to move than ones of brick. The frame house that is now at #9 Liberty Street was picked up, moved from across the street, and turned sideways. Its new neighbor at #7 Liberty Street merely had the front door and the porch moved from the street to the side of the house, for privacy.

House now at #9 Liberty Street, Sparta, New York
Facing street before the move   Facing river after the move
Photo from left side circa 1920   Photo from right side 2006

A few of the houses dated back as early as the 1780s, others to the 1820s. Two were, according to lore, associated with the first president. Both were made of red brick, and faced each other across the road at the intersection of Liberty and Rockledge Streets.

George Washington is said to have spent the night at #12 Liberty Street. It was known, not surprisingly, as the Washington Hotel. A simple, almost square building with a steeply pitched roof, it sat on the curved corner of two main streets. A new wing on the left, designed to follow the line of the road, gave a, "graceful, curved facade."

House at #12 Liberty Street, Sparta New York
After remodel, addition on center & right 2006   Original hotel circa 1919

Across the street, #1 Rock-ledge Avenue, also made of brick, was George Washington's head-quarters while he spent the night at #12 Liberty Street, according to legend. It got a new wing on each side. As a further claim to historical fame, from 1932 to 1936, Harry Hopkins, of the Franklin Roosevelt administration, lived there as a

#1 Rockledge, Sparta, Illinois 2006

Vanderlip tenant, possibly connected to Narcissa's friendship with Eleanor Roosevelt, dating from their work together in the suffrage movement.

One house that Frank did not get, at #6 Rockledge Avenue, was owned by his own Beechwood gardener, who learned of Frank's plans for the town and held out for a high price. He did not succeed in besting the former president of the country's largest bank. Any remodeling to be done would be out of the gardener's own pocket.

Once the village restoration was complete, Frank planned to populate it with teachers, artists, and "folks who would appreciate the beauty of the surroundings much more than the present Sparta folks do." Some of the homes he would be happy to sell off, he said, for twenty percent less than he put into them, which was over $15,000 in some cases. Others, he would rent at a price that would give him three or four percent on his investment, a modest return for a real estate developer of the time.

Interviewed at his new private office in one of New York City's tall buildings overlooking Trinity Church, Frank's "attitude and the tone of his voice as he spoke of the many nice things he planned for the old homes of his neighboring town were sufficient evidence of the man's enthusiasm for the project."

The houses began to be sold off in the 1930s, but others were still held by the corporation Frank formed until the 1970s. Into the 21st century, they are lovingly tended by a new set of owners who appreciate Frank Vanderlip's salvation of their little village almost 100 years ago.

Liberty Street looking west, Sparta, New York, house at #12 on left 2013

Frank could never get the world of bankers and financiers to work on his vision for a timely restoration of the European economy. It gave him great satisfaction to be able to make positive changes, for the benefit of many, nearer to his own home.

Frank A. Vanderlip 1920

ɔ ɔ ɔ

Japan

Vanderlip party in Japan 1920
Front: Mr. Suzuki, Frank Vanderlip, Narcissa Cox Vanderlip Mrs. Suzuki, Lyman Gage
Back: Mr. Inamua, Mr. Sumitomo, Harry Benedict, Narcissa Vanderlip

○ ○ ○

Japan

Just because a man wants to retire from the world's business, the world does not necessarily retire from him.

Frank Vanderlip may have thought he would simply spend a year remodeling his village of Sparta, but there was still plenty of business for him to take care of from his New York office. Part of that still involved the National City Bank.

Because of Frank's leadership, the bank had branches and contacts throughout the world. One country that was of growing interest to U. S. business was Japan.

The Back Story

Ever since the 1860s, Japan eagerly embraced much of American culture, even though its government was based on a European parliamentary system with an emperor at the top. Immigrants started arriving on American soil, particularly on the West Coast. By 1897, there were 65,000 Japanese in Hawaii, and 40,000 in the U. S.

Like the Chinese laborers before them, it was difficult for Japanese people to be absorbed into the general population. Their appearance and culture were more foreign, and more difficult to disguise, than that of any Irishman who merely had to lose his brogue when arriving in Boston. Beatings, racial slurs, mob violence, and

Broken Japanese store windows, Vancouver 1907

various forms of segregation were not uncommon.

San Francisco passed a law in 1906 that ordered Japanese schoolchildren to be sent to separate schools alongside Chinese and

other minority students. Furious at the measure and its damage, not only to the children, but to international relations, President Teddy Roosevelt called the lawmakers the "idiots of the California legislature."

Some of the 93 segregated Japanese children San Francisco, California 1906

After much negotiation between California, Congress, and Japan, a settlement was worked out. In what was later known as the First Gentlemen's Agreement. California allowed the children back into regular classes, and Japan agreed to slow the flood of immigration by restricting exit visas.

At the same time, an organization known as the Japan Society was formed in New York in 1907. Its goal was forming better relations between the two countries, particularly along cultural and business lines.

By 1915, National City Bank had branches in Japan, China, India and the Philippines, and they were interested in participating in the Japan Society. The organization's second president, installed in 1919, was National City Bank vice-president Gerald M. Dahl. Still spiritually connected to the world of finance, Frank added another commitment to his retirement in 1920, and became the Society's third president.

Relations between the two countries should have improved after World War I, as they were on the same side of the fighting. But, there were obvious differences between the "open door" trade policy advocated by the U. S. toward China and Japan's trade expansion going on there. The Versailles Peace Conference brought out America's opposition to Japan's eye on Germany's formerly owned Pacific Islands. Japan was not happy that the charter for the new League of Nations did not address racial equality.

To top off the problems, a California group, involved in the quashed 1906 segregation effort, revived itself. The Exclusion League wanted to cancel the Gentlemen's Agreement, stop Japanese immigration, even amend the U. S. Constitution to say that a child born in America could not be a citizen unless both parents were "of a race eligible for citizenship." William Randolph Hearst's newspapers gave the League plenty of publicity. He and Frank "disagreed on many subjects," according to Frank, Jr. The Japanese question was certainly one of them.

PROTEST ON NATURALIZATION

Exclusion League Formed to Oppose Action.

[BY A P NIGHT WIRE]

SAN FRANCISCO, Sept 2 —Resolutions protesting against the reported acceptance by the State Department of a plan to naturalize the Japanese living in this country were adopted by the Japanese Exclusion League of California, an organization formed here today to work for the initiative amendment to the California anti-alien land law.

Article about Exclusion League sentiment
Los Angeles Times *1920*

The Japanese people and government did not want a problem with the United States. Former prime minister Marquis Shigenobu Okuma sent a message, through the Japan Society bulletin, saying, "I have often expressed my view of the absurdity of talking of a conflict between Japan and America, as I firmly believe there is no serious reason for such a conflict, while there is every need for the cooperation of the two nations."

An Invitation - 1920

To help find ways to improve relations, a Japanese group called the Welcome Association, led by Prince Tokugawa Iyesato, issued an invitation to Frank for him to visit Japan. He was welcome to bring along with him, according to Harry Benedict, "such representative men of importance as he might choose to ask." Frank's choices were an eclectic group. They were: Henry W. Taft, brother of former president William Howard Taft, his wife, and her maid; George Eastman, president of Eastman Kodak and his physician; former Secretary of the Treasury Lyman Gage; the presidents of Cornell University, New York Life Insurance, and the Exchange National Bank, with their respective wives, one daughter and her governess; writer Julian Street and his wife, daughter, and a maid; a prominent St. Louis attorney and his wife; a male secretary to the Exchange National Bank president, and, of course, Frank's wife Narcissa, and their fifteen-year old daughter Narcissa. Surprised to be included after he organized the trip, Harry Benedict gives a detailed account of their journey.

Accompanying the group was a special gentleman, Yamato Ichihashi, one of the first academics of Asian ancestry to reside in the United States. The son of a former samurai, he had come to America in 1894 at the age of sixteen. After public school in San Francisco, he earned a bachelors and then a masters degree in economics at Stanford, and a Ph.D. at Harvard. In 1920, he was back at Stanford as a professor. He would remain there until his death in 1963, except for the years during World War II, which he spent in the Tule Lake Relocation

Yamato Ichihashi date unknown

Camp. He met the group's train in Chicago, and would be their travel companion, teacher of Japan's history, manners and culture, and translator during meetings.

On Board Ship

The group boarded the *Kashima Maru*, sailing out of Seattle, for a Pacific crossing that was "pleasant, amusing and often interesting," with

Steamship Kashima Maru 1920

plenty of time for discussions. Harry Benedict relates, "with men like Mr. Taft and Mr. Vanderlip in the group, it was not surprising that our long and lazy evenings became seminars for discussion of subjects over a wide range. The opinions were often serious and always in an amusing tone and atmosphere. Mr. Taft was a particularly interesting man. Street was almost professionally humorous, Dr. Shurman needed no needling, and Mr. Vanderlip reveled in the seminar tone of the talks. Few remarks were offered by Mr. Eastman, Mr. Gage or Mr. Clarke, interested as they might be." It is possible that, surrounded by four loquacious men, the others just could not get a word into the conversation.

George Eastman's photograph
On board the Kashima Maru
Return journey June 8, 1920

On board the Kashima Maru
Frank Vanderlip, lower R
Narcissa Vanderlip, upper R
April 1920

Elegant Quarters

Rather than the impersonal rooms available even in the finest hotels, most of the members of Frank's group were hosted in the residences or villas of prominent men, most of whom were barons. Only three of the couples stayed at the Imperial Hotel.

The Vanderlips, Harry Benedict, and Lyman Gage all stayed at the villa of Baron Yeiji Shibusawa, who was the 'Frank Vanderlip' of Japan. He was considered the founder of the country's modern economy, and a great businessman. A few of his enterprises were Japan's First National Bank, the Imperial Hotel in Tokyo, and the Oji Paper Company, the first Western-style paper manufacturer in Japan.

Everyone was treated with the utmost hospitality and traditional Japanese formality. Baron Shibusawa specially brought European furniture into part of the residence to make his visitors comfortable, and put velvet rugs over matting floor so the Americans would not have to take their shoes off when entering the home. He even installed a European bath tub, *"which we afterwards completely discarded in favor of the real joy of the native bath located in the main part of the house which had been left in Japanese style."* After several days, the Americans began to feel clumsy, clumping about inside the home in their hard-soled shoes.

Baron Yeiji Shibusawa's villa, Tokyo, Japan April 1920
From left: Frank & Narcissa Vanderlip, Baron Shibusawa, Lyman Gage,
Narcissa Vanderlip (daughter), Harry Benedict, 3 Japanese gentlemen

"Our life in the villa came directly out of a storybook," Harry Benedict says. "As we left each morning for appointments or for social affairs, our servants were wont to assemble in the entrance veranda, a roofed and beautiful open-sided area, in two lines through which we walked in stately manner as they bowed from the waist. There were 35 of them." At the door, Frank added, there was usually *"a distinguished elderly person with a long beard whose exact position we were never able quite to define."* Harry Benedict finishes the description. "We were accustomed to dress in long coats or cutaways, wing collars and silk hats. The door lintels were of a height about right to scalp us if we forgot or failed to bow or stoop as we passed through."

Tea And Dinners

Their first formal welcome was at the Peer's Club in Tokyo, on April 25, which is where they held "daily meetings with selected groups, almost always followed by extraordinary formal and beautiful dinners," at the same location. There were tours, luncheons at special places, theater parties and performances.

At a speech after the first dinner, before a socially distinguished audience of two hundred, plus those invited to dine, the baron gave a welcoming speech, during which he *"facetiously mentioned that we would not, as Commodore Perry had, find the people of Japan wearing top-knots and wearing two swords."* Frank responded with a bit of his dry humor. It would not be the first or last time someone speaking in front of reporters should stick to the script.

"I hit on this bit of his address in making reply, and said that I regretted that some of my own countrymen were wearing a top-knot, a top-knot of national conceit, and were wearing two swords, one of prejudice and one of ignorance." When this remark appeared in the local press, some of the American residents objected, declaring, *"that we Americans should never admit that there was anything to criticize about America, or that there was ever anything wrong about her attitude or aims."* Frank did not agree that he said anything wrong.

"It proved to be the happiest chance that lead me to this attitude, for I think it changed the whole temper of future discussions. It was made much of through Japan by the press, and was always taken as sufficient reason for the Japanese in turn to admit they had made many blunders and mistakes themselves."

Meetings were held with business leaders, politicians and diplomats. Before each event, they were "properly coached and advised" on matters of etiquette. "We never lost the sense of seriousness of our visit, and never had a truly idle hour."

Harry Benedict gives particular emphasis on a dinner in Tokyo, to illustrate the "magnificence," they enjoyed. "The scene was a peerate house of our hosts, built for this purpose. Our group attending, plus the Japanese guests, made a dinner party of seventy." Before the meal, there was an orchestra performance in a reception room filled with fine Japanese art.

"The party of seventy was seated at one table, an oval, perhaps twelve or fifteen feet wide at the center. Before each guest was a red lacquer tray with gold decoration. Behind each chair was a geisha in the splendid silks and obis they wear so well. They were to direct the serving to their particular guest. The food was brought in by serving girls - one to each guest. It appears therefore, that it required 140 Japanese girls to serve our party."

Not every event was a lavish meal. At Narcissa's urging, she and Frank visited *"the reverse of the picture,"* one of Tokyo's slums where an American woman, Mrs. Horace Coleman, had established a day nursery for young children, so that their older siblings could go to school without taking the babies along with them. Frank noted the children's plight, the size and condition of the small houses and their numerous occupants. *"The houses are far from water proof, and although the day we visited them was sunny, the front was wide open to dry out the interiors. The people looked miserable and lethargic, but in no case did we see a cross or unkind face."*

Another memorable event was hosted by the Emperor at his seaside palace. They were also entertained in Kobe and Kyoto, and

visited Nikko, with its lavishly decorated shrine and mausoleum to Tokugawa Ieyasu, founder of the Tokugawa shogunate. In each city, they met with "important figures," and saw the sites. Narcissa and the other women toured Tsuda University, which played a part in a later event at Beechwood.

Shrine at Nikko, Japan 2010

After about a week, there was a rumor in the baron's villa about a bustle of preparations for a special breakfast for the guests, prepared under the direction of a famous Japanese cook. The baron and two of his grandsons would attend. *"It was served in the Japanese portion of the house in full Japanese style. It was a breakfast only in name and consisted of uncountable dishes, with turtle soup appearing at almost any stray moment. It was obviously prepared with the utmost delicacy, but as a substitute for one's coffee and soft boiled eggs, it was a harrowing experience."*

Seeing The Country

In Osaka, their dinner was hosted by Asahi Shinbun, one of the major newspapers. As a man with newspaper ink in his veins, Frank was curious to see the typesetting methods of Japanese type. He and Narcissa and their daughter were given a tour. He was interested to learn that, because of the great number of Japanese symbols, only those most used were kept near the typesetters. When they needed something a little more unusual, an assistant had to run off to get it, slowing down the entire printing process.

*Narcissa Vanderlip feeding deer
Nara, Japan May 8, 1920*

In the city of Nara, after more tea, they went into a park that was home to several hundred deer, and given rice cakes to feed them. That evening, Frank had a particularly moving experience.

"We started out in rickshaws after dinner. We did not know just where were we going, but soon recognized that we were in the great criptameria avenue leading to the temple of three thousand lanterns. Then came the greatest sensation we had had in Japan."

The three thousand lanterns were only lighted once a year, during a festival, but the governor arranged a special lighting in their honor. *"We were all affected more deeply by this whole scene than by anything that had happened in our whole Japanese experience. The grandeur of the trees, the mystery of the lanterns, the endless rows of them as we approached nearer to the temples, all affected us deeply. It seemed to me like a welcome from the ancestors, and it was on the whole the culmination of Japanese courtesy."*

A Trip Summary

At the last dinner, on the last night, Frank responded to Viscount Kaneko's speech *"in a manner which aroused the indignation of all the lady members of our party because I had spoken only of the men. Mrs. Vanderlip followed in a way that properly put me in my place."*

"What was the purpose of this hospitality and these conferences?" Harry Benedict asks. "The Japanese Leaders sensed the growing strain in international affairs. A visit by leading Americans, who would also be opinion makers, could result in important advances in understanding of their thinking, economics and political problems."

On returning home, Frank wrote and talked about his belief in the need for good relations and trade. Julian Street wrote his book *Mysterious Japan*, and others used their new knowledge and contacts in various ways. George Eastman helped introduce Japan to their love of photography and photographic equipment that exists to this day.

Last dinner in Japan, with some members in Japanese clothing May 13, 1920
Back row, L to R: Dr. Edward Mulligan, Darwin Kingsley, Seymour Cromwell,
Mrs. Kingsley, Henry W. Taft, Mrs. Cromwell, Frank A. Vanderlip, Lyman J. Gage,
Harry Benedict, Dr. J. G. Shurman, Lionberger Davis
Front row, L to R: George Eastman, Mrs. Davis, Mrs. Taft,
Narcissa Vanderlip (daughter), Narcissa Vanderlip (wife), Mrs. (Ada) Street,
Mrs. Shurman, Harry Serenbetz, Julian Street

A Thank You Gift, Vanderlip Style

The trip to Japan lasted three weeks. Such hospitality deserved more than a gift wrapped box to say, "thank you." Instead, Frank and Narcissa threw a party, as only they could do, at Beechwood.

Six hundred guests were invited, through the Japan Society, for the afternoon and evening, many of them arriving on a special train from New York City, including the Japanese ambassador. Most wore traditional Japanese clothing.

As usual at Beechwood, it was an extravaganza. There were judo and kendo exhibitions, "swimming exercises" in the pool, and a fencing exhibition. In the Beechwood school's theater, there was a concert of Japanese music with a soprano from the Imperial Opera Company of Tokyo, and a play put on by Japanese students from Columbia University. The evening ended with dancing.

Japan Society party on lawn at Beechwood June 26, 1920
Narcissa and Frank Vanderlip with two Japanese opera stars

Spreading Good Words

As Benjamin Strong said of Frank, he got "very much excited," with his experiences. Frank was impressed with what he saw in Japan. He was not afraid to say so. In a speech at the Japanese Business Men's Mission to the United States in New York in 1921, Frank tried to promote trade relations between the two countries, and to find some rationalization for the racist attitudes of some Americans, a view he did not share.

He said, according to the *New York Times*, "*much of the racial antagonism toward the Japanese in parts of the United States was caused by jealousy and the Japanese ought to be proud of it, because it was founded upon their virtues of industry and thrift.*" No Japanese laborer facing a street gang would care that the prejudice he faced was caused by his hard work, but Frank meant his words as the sincerest of compliments.

Frank was also aware of Japan's ballooning population on the small enclosure of her islands, which did not have a great land mass to farm. "*I can't suggest the solution. There probably will be several, and it seems probable that Japan will develop along industrial lines. In that we ought not to look upon Japan as a competitor we will have to fight, but should co-operate in her efforts for industrial development.*" He would not have been surprised by Japan's 20th and 21st century technological growth.

The Great Kanto Earthquake - 1923

Ellis Zacharias, a young U. S. naval officer, stood on Yokohama's pier just before noon on September 1, 1923, as a crowd waved goodbye to passengers on the luxury steamship Empress of Victoria, ready to leave for Vancouver. Suddenly, "The smiles vanished, and for an appreciable instant everyone stood transfixed." They heard "the sound of thunder." The pier collapsed. People and cars plunged into the water.

Collapsed harbor, Kanto, Japan September 1923
S.S. Empress of Australia *giving aid to survivors*

It was the Great Kanto Earthquake, the worst natural disaster in Japan up to that date. A few minutes after the jolt, a forty-foot high tsunami pulled thousands away in a series of high waves. Most of Yokohama's buildings, built of light wooden frames and sliding paper walls, collapsed. Fires broke out everywhere. With water mains severed, there was no way to stop the flames.

In Tokyo, forty thousand of those who survived the fallen buildings retreated to an open space in the downtown area. Uncontrollable fires roared toward the area from all directions, creating a giant pillar of flames. Only about 300 of the 40,000 survived. Throughout Japan, about 140,000 people died.

Destruction from Kanto earthquake, Yokohama, Japan September 1923

Umeko Tsuda And Her College

One of the thousands of casualties was a school for Japanese women started in 1900 by a remarkable woman named Umeko Tsuda. At age six, she was the youngest of five women chosen in 1870 to go to the U. S. to study. She grew up in the home of an American who worked at the Japanese legation in Washington, D. C. He and his wife had no children, and raised her as if she were their own. She excelled in math, science, music, Latin and French, and was so proficient in English that, when she went back to Japan, she had trouble speaking Japanese.

Umeko Tsuda date unknown

Umeko Tsuda faced culture shock when she returned to Japan at age 18, in 1882, and was not happy to see schooling for women aimed at making them obedient wives and good mothers. She returned to the United States., studied at Bryn Mawr College, then went on to further schooling at Oxford.

With speeches and other fund-raising efforts, Umeko Tsuda raised enough to open the Women's Institute for English Studies in Tokyo in 1900, which grew into Tsuda College. Its goal was a liberal arts education for all women, regardless of their parentage.

Although she strongly wanted social reform for Japanese women, Umeko Tsuda did not endorse the feminist movement of her time. Surprisingly, she was opposed to the suffrage movement so dear to Narcissa's heart. She suffered a stroke in 1919, just before Frank and Narcissa's visit, but her college was thriving when they were there.

Umeko Tsuda's college crashed to the ground, along with much of the rest of Tokyo, in the Kanto earthquake. Narcissa, a great promoter of education and women's rights, wanted to help put the school back together.

Narcissa threw one of her spectacular parties at Beechwood in June, 1924, for 1,000 people, to benefit Tsuda College. As their star guests, they wanted to invite Secretary of State Charles E. Hughes, and the Japanese ambassador to the United States. Since the two men were in Washington, Frank devised a novel method of sending their invitations.

Frank knew the value of publicity, and his love of birds would develop into a serious hobby at his Palos Verdes home in California. So, he hired a flock of carrier pigeons to carry invitations to Washington, and enlisted the help of a pilot from the 102nd Aviation Squadron of the National Guard at Staten Island, and his Curtiss "Jenny" airplane to do the same.

Curtiss "Jenny" biplane 1918

Birds and plane left Staten Island's Miller Field at the same time, with the birds soaring high above the "Jenny". The pilot had to touch down at both Philadelphia and Baltimore for fuel, but he still beat the birds to Washington by two hours and forty-one minutes, taking three and one half hours to make the trip. Narcissa's party was a success, as always.

The following year, Narcissa was still on the fund-raising circuit. She was the guest of honor for a tea at Vassar College, where daughter Narcissa was a senior. She lobbied for a $2,000 donation to build a new, "necessary classroom." To heighten interest, Narcissa displayed some of her mementoes from the Japanese trip - clothing, tapestries, and carved opium cases. In her talk, she "advocated not only a warm friendship between these two college but an increasing friendliness between the two nations."

Charlotte & Narcissa Vanderlip
Lawn party for Tsuda College
Beechwood June 1924

Japanese In Palos Verdes

Frank had another, more personal reason for his interest in Japanese culture besides international relations. He had his own group of Japanese tenants on his Palos Verdes land in California.

When he acquired the 16,000 acres in 1913, most of the land was covered in sparse vegetation only suitable for cattle grazing of the Bixby herds. But, along the coastal cliffs, there was a quiet community of immigrant Japanese farmers who had been there since at least 1910, when Kumekichi Ishibashi, C. Hayashi, and K. Osaki signed a lease for fifty acres at a one-year price of six dollars per acre, paid to the Bixby Ranch, "in Gold Coins of the United States."

By 1923, there were at least forty Japanese families on the peninsula. They used dry farming techniques learned in their homeland, without irrigation, and grew beans, cucumbers, peas, tomatoes and flowers. To supply electricity along the barren landscape, they resourcefully used a boat generator and automobile batteries. Drinking water came from a well in the Portuguese Bend area.

With farming instincts still in his heart, even after so many years away from his childhood and his overalls, Frank had a natural affinity and respect for these people.

He welcomed local Japanese couples to the Villa Narcissa, which was a popular place for them to pose for portrait photographs at the foot of Narcissa's cypress allee. In 1928, he hosted visiting Japanese dignitaries at the Cottage.

Frank Vanderlip with Japanese dignitaries
The Cottage, Palos Verdes, California 1928

Japanese farmers continued to work the land throughout Frank's life. The Ishibashi family sold off, in 2011, the last of the land they purchased after Japanese ownership became legal.

All of the farm families were removed from Palos Verdes during World War II, most of them to internment camps. In appreciation for the way they had been welcomed on the peninsula before the internment, a group of the Japanese families sent, from their internment, twenty-five dollars to the Palos Verdes Estates school, to be used as the teachers thought best. Many of them never came back to the area after the war.

Had Frank still been alive in the 1940s, even he probably could not have stopped the farmers' relocation. But, he would certainly have done everything possible to see to the welfare of people for whom he had the highest respect.

○ ○ ○

Palos Verdes
Part II

Poseidon statue, Malaga Cove, Palos Verdes, California dedicated 1930 photo 2013

o o o

Palos Verdes - Part II

A man with Frank Vanderlip's vision, in a position such as his, is bound to encounter others who are the same way. Not all of them are as financially reliable as Frank.

Returning from Japan, Frank decided to visit his ranch. While the rest of the travelers went on to New York, Frank and Harry Benedict rode horses from Redondo Beach, up the empty hillsides, and around the coast to the Cottage. It was Harry Benedict's first visit. "We looked down over that pretty wonderful hillside to the ocean - no houses - no roads - no traffic of any kind. Mr. Vanderlip was interested in the impression this made on me, a former farmer boy. He said, 'Isn't that a great piece of property?' I was somewhat overpowered by the scene. Mr. Vanderlip said: 'Benedict, that is going to be part of your job to see what we do with it.' " Possibly tiring of such big projects, Frank felt "that it was time to begin a liquidation of the ranch acreage."

Portuguese Bend hills, Palos Verdes, California circa 1920

It was not going to be easy. Land that is now Bel Air, Westwood, and further West was still open fields. Powerful developers in Los Angeles were driving expansion toward this westward land. Palos Verdes still had no easy access, no water, no electricity. Who would want to live all the way out there?

E. G. Lewis - A Man With Grand Ideas - 1904

That was when Edward Gardner Lewis came on the scene. Better known as simply E. G. Lewis, he was "a born promoter, with enormous enthusiasms and a flair for salesmanship." In a particular suburb of St. Louis, Missouri, there are monuments to him. In Palos Verdes lore, opinions are quite different.

Born in Connecticut, E. G. Lewis was about thirty years old when he showed up in St. Louis, selling insect extermination products and patent medicine. He soon changed professions, and bought a magazine, renamed *Woman's Magazine*. It sold for only ten cents per yearly subscription, being delivered cheaply with penny-per-pound mass circulation and Rural Free Delivery rates. With hundreds of thousands of subscribers and plenty of advertisers, he made a fortune.

When his business outgrew its downtown quarters, E. G. Lewis' ambitions expanded with it. He bought eighty-five acres near the construction for the St. Louis 1904 World's Fair, added more land in the next few years, and founded University City.

E. G. Lewis circa 1920s

The post office did not look kindly on his magazines being delivered as second class mail, calling them pure advertising, and denied him privileges. E. G. Lewis sued, and won his case, but his subscriptions dropped because of the bad publicity. Undeterred, he blamed the postal service for a vendetta against him, and came up with a new idea. He formed the American Woman's League, a sales arm for his magazine that took the commission usually given to salesmen and, as members sold subscriptions, put the funds into a foundation supposedly for local social organizations, education, and a women's retirement fund. He also established the American Woman's Republic, which charged a membership fee, taught about government and politics, and prepared women for the day when they could to vote.

Within the next few years, he put up a six-story, octagonal building topped with a dome, that is now the city hall for University City. He added another unique building, designed to resemble an Egyptian temple, housing his magazine offices and an unusual bank that he based on an idea even Frank had not come up with.

E. G. Lewis'
American Woman's League Building
University City, Missouri 1910

His idea was to bring banking to the rural areas of the country where most of his subscribers lived. Sixty percent of post offices could not sell money orders, and farming areas had few nearby banks. E. G. Lewis suggested that his readers use his mail order bank. They sent in their deposits and got a book of certified checks that they could cash through five of the leading bank's branch offices. No interest was paid, but the depositors would feel safer than with their money under a mattress. Meanwhile, E. G. Lewis earned two percent on their funds, which he kept in other banks.

All would have been fine, if E. G. Lewis had been content with his empire, or had a partner with a good financial head and the power to keep his grand ideas in check. Instead, he invested in such ideas as artificial cork, a stamping machine company working on a way to address his mailers other than by hand, and 5-cent pay phones. They were not bad ideas. All later became standard items making money for others. But, Lewis was just a little too early, and all of his investments fizzled, taking his depositors' funds

E. G. Lewis in University City office 1910

with them. His book-juggling skills and personal charm were great enough, however, that he served as University City's mayor for three terms.

E. G. Lewis - Atascadero - 1913

E. G. Lewis finally went bankrupt in Missouri. Undeterred, he looked for new land to conquer. He found it in Atascadero, California. With barely a cent to his name, in 1913, he managed to come up with enough to buy 23,000 acres of ranchland, adding another 20,000 in 1918. His plan was to develop a Utopian community through his American Woman's Republic, with fresh air, mountain views, and orchards bringing in cash for the homeowners.

As a 21st century writer commented, "A fraud could have sold land out of a tent and moved on." Instead, E. G. Lewis built a 17-mile highway to the coast, and spent time and considerable energy developing a community. Interest in lots was so high that he was able to charge potential buyers two dollars an acre just for the privilege of going onto the list. Many of his buyers, seeing the ads in his magazine, gathered their life savings to move West to the new community. They faithfully lived in tent cities erected for them, until homes could be built. A number of them counted on income from the pear orchards that were planted on their new properties. Most of them did not know it would take at least eight years for their new young trees to bear fruit.

La Plaza Building 1919   Tent camp for land buyers 1919
Atascadero, California during E. G. Lewis' founding and construction

Once again, if he had concentrated on Atascadero, he would have been a success. But, oil wells and copper mines called their siren song, and money that should have built the town went to new projects, buoyed up by a steady stream of new investors he culled from his magazine ads. And, once again, he left a half-finished town ahead of trouble. Some of the buildings he conceived, such as the elegant city hall, still stand, and Highway 41 to Morrow Bay bears his name.

E. G. Lewis - Palos Verdes - 1921

Without much actual money in his pocket, E. G. Lewis discovered Palos Verdes in 1921. As Harry Benedict describes it, "Lewis was a promoter at heart. He had no appreciable assets or sources of capital, except as he might develop them through a public following arising from his mental picture of an ideal community and city planned before any construction would begin." Other great projects have begun with even less.

Harry Benedict did not later recall that Frank ever met E. G. Lewis. If Frank had done so, it is hard to predict whether or not the outcome would have been the same. Frank's mentor, Mr. Stillman, would certainly not have been fooled.

At first, E. G. Lewis put in an offer of $5 million for the entire 16,004 acres in 1921. "Mr. Vanderlip and a small group of us in New York had only a tolerant interest in the earlier stages of Lewis' campaign. Mr. Vanderlip did not regard it as a serious possibility of a sale . . . This became a moving situation, not at all a static one," Harry Benedict wrote later. E. G. Lewis got an option for the purchase.

With little more than his verbal skill, E. G. Lewis managed to raise between two and three million dollars, by offering subscriptions into a trust, which could later be converted into lots as the property was developed. In September, 1921, he announced that plans included a hotel and country club, miles of paved boulevards, and three business centers, basically the design Frank had drawn up before World War I.

One new addition was a plan for a $3 million mono-rail to run from downtown Los Angeles to Palos Verdes, with a branch line off to San Pedro harbor. A similar system was already in use in Germany. E. G. Lewis estimated the trip would take six

Monorail built in 1901, Wuppertal, Germany 1931

to eight minutes, and cost five cents a ride. Every Palos Verdes commuter since that time wishes E. G. Lewis had stayed the course.

March of 1922 brought the first warning that E. G. Lewis was not all he seemed to be. A telegram sent to the Los Angeles *Examiner* warned, "In my opinion he is paying for his big Palos Verdes advertising campaign with money diverted from investments in his huge unsuccessful doodlebug oil promotion in Montana." Apparently, there were not as many readers of the *Examiner* as there were of the *Los Angeles Times'* friendly articles and ads, and of E. G. Lewis' own publications.

By spring of 1922, subscriptions to the new development were selling well. There were two types. Convertible subscription holders could turn them in for land, as soon as it was ready for sale, purchasing it at actual cost plus the cost of improvements. Non-convertible subscription holders were basically buying stock in the Palos Verdes Project, and would receive profits as land was sold off. Frank called it "one of the most notable works in city building in Southern California and possibly the world." He judged the financing to be on "sound lines, with competent direction of expenditures," and added that the development should "yield large dividends in satisfaction and pleasure to great numbers of people." E. G. Lewis could not have written the words better himself.

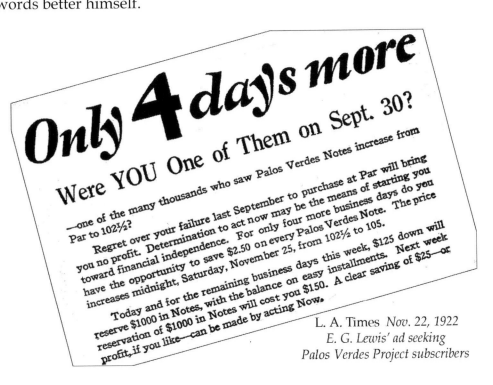

L. A. Times *Nov. 22, 1922*
E. G. Lewis' ad seeking
Palos Verdes Project subscribers

Trouble In Paradise - 1923

As funds came in, they went into an account at the Title Insurance and Trust Company (T. I. & T.) in Los Angeles. It was at this point stories began to diverge. On January 17, 1923, T. I. & T. announced that, with the installment subscriptions to be paid in the future, the total sold was about $19 million, with about ten percent actually paid in, $1,915,824.42 to be exact. That gave the project $1,500,000 to give the Vanderlip syndicate as a down payment on the $5 million, and left only $415,824.42 on hand for operating expenses.

E. G. Lewis announced, at the same time, that he was turning "the affairs of the project over to the trustee, the T. I. & T., to be worked out by engineer, contractor, and builder." He claimed to have personally put $1 million into the underwriting, and to have assigned all the fees due him to cover all the money borrowed. A vice-president of T.I. & T, John H. Coverley, became general manager.

LEWIS WITHDRAWS FROM PALOS VERDES PROJECT

Work Finished, Promoter Turns Over to Trustee Management of Great Undertaking

Los Angeles Times *headline January 7, 1923*

"My work has been largely that of one who conceives the idea, plans the construction, secures the financial resources for its carrying out, and then calls in the contractors, engineers, architects and trustee for its consummation," E. G. Lewis said. "With the completion of the general plans for the improvement of the estates and completion of the underwriting and the taking of title my own part in this undertaking is mostly finished." In other words, E. G. Lewis was an idea man, not someone to worry about all those details. "I must now be free to attend to my other interests," he added.

Whatever the real story behind this resignation was, it left no written trace. Shortly thereafter, T. I. & T. made a new announcement. They had judged that not all of the paid subscribers were "bona fide." One million dollars of the money had, in fact, been put in by E. G. Lewis as subscriptions. Another $3 million of the $19 million total was from future contractors for the project, pledging to put in twenty percent of the fees they had not yet earned. T. I. & T. was backing out of handling the account, and ready to return all cash on hand to the original subscribers. The Palos Verdes Project appeared to have come to a halt before even one building went up.

That was before anyone took E. G. Lewis' personality into account. As he had done many times before, he found the right words to make people believe in him. He managed to convince Frank's syndicate, with Frank in New York and Harry Benedict as the man on the spot, that he could salvage enough of his buyers to put a smaller deal back together. And he did.

Saving The Day

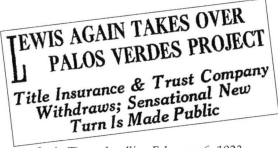

L. A. Times *headline February 6, 1923*

In St. Louis, E. G. Lewis had blamed the post office for his financial troubles. Now, he blamed everything on powerful Westside real estate developers who did not want him to succeed at the cost of their own plans. He convinced Harry Benedict these men had so much business with T. I. &. T. that the trust company could not afford to cross their plans.

At a February 5, 1923 meeting of about 3,000 subscribers, E. G. Lewis put his case to an "audience which appeared highly receptive and seized every occasion to proclaim their faith in the project and its seer." Lewis claimed T. I. & T. had been "inimical to the undertaking," and that "certain interests" had been out to ruin him financially from the start.

Frank was in Los Angeles during this important meeting, staying downtown, nearby, at the Biltmore Hotel. For once in his career, he did not take the podium to speak, probably not wanting to be associated with the undertaking if it turned into a disaster. When E. G. Lewis excited the audience into shouts of "Vanderlip!" they were told Frank had been in the building, but had already gone back to his hotel. According to Harry Benedict, the two men did not meet that day.

T. I. &. T. answered that their handling of the trust was "legitimate and careful," and said of the subscribers, "It is their money, and it is for them to say what shall be done with it." Most of the people there decided to leave their funds in E. G. Lewis' scheme.

How did a man who had faced bankruptcy multiple times, and who never had any cash of his own, manage to convince not only an eager public, but leading banker Frank Vanderlip, as well as careful businessman Harry Benedict, that he could come through on his claims? It must have been by the force of his positive personality, and probably his own true belief that he could make everything work out right. For once in his life, it was true.

"About this time," Harry Benedict says, giving weight to E. G. Lewis' claims of harassment by the trust company, "it must have become apparent to the management of the T. I. & T. Co. that this Lewis 'Caper' was becoming serious and that he might actually get enough subscriptions to purchase this large area along the ocean."

"I do not know," Harry Benedict says, "and doubt that it was publicly admitted, on what grounds the T. I & T. threw out the Lewis trust and assumed or secured the necessary legal authority for the return of the subscribed moneys. This, of course, was an almost fatal blow to the Lewis program, and to the possibility of a sale by the New York-Vanderlip syndicate."

T. I. & T. did not know E. G. Lewis very well. "Lewis, with courage and resourcefulness, advised us of his catastrophic dealing by T. I. & T." He felt that if he could find another trust company to handle his business, he could save the situation, but none of them were willing to cross more well-known interests.

One of T. I. & T.'s young lawyers was Elvon Musick, who had become a golf and social friend of Harry Benedict and his wife. The lawyer was "privately shocked at the ruthless action of his employing trust company." He came up with a plan.

He called a friend in San Francisco, who happened to be retiring bank commissioner Jonathan Dodge. Elvon Musick and Harry Benedict jumped on a train on Sunday, and rushed North to see him.

Commissioner Dodge said he had one last franchise he could give out for a new trust company before he retired the following Wednesday. If they could move that quickly, Frank's syndicate could have it.

Simple enough, but Frank, Narcissa and the children were on a much needed vacation, somewhere in Utah or Arizona, in a private railroad car, and were unreachable. Harry Benedict was on his own. He would have to come up with $300,000 to purchase the government bonds that were necessary as security to open a trust company.

Jay Lawyer 1924   Commonwealth Trust Certificate 1926   Elvon Musick 1926

Bright and early Monday morning, Harry Benedict called on a banker he knew socially, a vice-president of Farmers National Bank, whose son was also a friend of Elvon Musick. Harry Benedict had never even been in the man's bank when he sat down with Henry S. McKee and told his story. He wanted Henry McKee to understand "that this enterprise and loan was solely my responsibility to Mr. Vanderlip. Mr. McKee apparently believed me and felt that the President of the National City Bank would back the action of this young chap from his office."

Henry McKee lit a cigarette, "teetered in his swivel chair," and studied the anxious young man. "You know, Benedict, we have a rule in this bank that limits a loan to one person to $150,000." Then he paused. "But there are two of you, aren't there?" he prompted. Thinking quickly, Harry Benedict said yes, the Vanderlip interests had a ranch manager who was quite competent. It was Jay Lawyer, with whom Frank did his land purchases in Spokane, Coos Bay and Los Molinos. He would sign his name, Harry Benedict vouched, for the other half of the loan.

On Wednesday morning, they met again at the bank. Harry Benedict and Jay Lawyer each accepted a $150,000 check from Henry McKee's bank, endorsed them, handed them back to Henry McKee to deposit in his bank, and got a new check payable to the Banking Commissioner for $300,000 to form a new bank trust. Harry Benedict was "breathless as if from a long sprint, and not sure I was not out of a job." They typed up a postcard-sized name of the new organization, the Commonwealth Trust Company, inserted the card in the corner of the glass front door of a one-room office they rented, and Palos Verdes Estates was born. The first president of Commonwealth Trust Company was former Commissioner Jonathan Dodge.

As soon as Frank and his family returned from their vacation, Harry Benedict had to tell him what had transpired. The Vanderlips were staying at the new Ambassador Hotel. "I called there promptly before dinner on the day of their arrival. I was feeling pretty low. It was true that the deal was alive and progressing, but I had charged $300,000 against Mr. Vanderlip's credit in setting up the Commonwealth Trust Company. We dressed for dinner in those days, and as we walked the lower gallery of the Ambassador in dinner coats, he with his arm through mine, he said, 'Well, Benedict, I suppose you have cost me $300,000 . . . but you did just the right thing.' "

A Quick Turnover

The new Commonwealth Trust, with only one client, announced its formation on February 20, 1923. It had a competent board of directors. Besides former bank commissioner Jonathan Dodge as president, one of the two vice-presidents was Frank's brother-in-law, Ed Harden. Harry Benedict was secretary, and Jay Lawyer's son Donald Lawyer was treasurer. General manager would be John Coverley, who left T.I. & T. to join the new enterprise. Jay Lawyer would be his assistant, along with E. G. Lewis, who was described by the *Los Angeles Times* as "the original promoter of the entire development."

Within days, the situation changed again. E. G. Lewis was informed that the new directors would not accept the responsibility unless they had complete control. He sent out a letter to his faithful followers. "To this I at once agreed, since only by my doing so could I hope to protect the more than two thousand people who had made the underwriting expense advances and also assure the carrying forward of our project at all." E. G. Lewis, the man with the grand vision, would remain in the picture, for a while, simply as salesman extraordinaire.

Making The Dream Come True

On March 2, 1923, Jay Lawyer received a check from the Commonwealth Trust Company for $1 million from E. G. Lewis' efforts to form the Palos Verdes Project. Just over 3,200 acres changed hands. E. G. Lewis announced that holders of the convertible notes would be able to choose their property in Palos Verdes Estates just as soon as the maps were delivered from the printer. Harry Benedict took an early train to New York and personally, proudly, handed Frank the first returns on his syndicate's Palos Verdes investment.

In June, 1923, E. G. Lewis held a large sales rally on empty land that now houses the Malaga Cove School and some of the priciest home real estate in California. Five thousand cars showed up for a day of watching yacht races, stunt flying, and other activities, with free food included. As he had predicted the year before, "It is not men who build cities, it is the people; and we know now that the people really want Palos Verdes Estates."

NEXT Sunday, June 17th, Palos Verdes Estates will celebrate its public opening with a program of music, Spanish dancing, stunt airplane flying, athletic contests, aquaplaning and many other events. You are invited to come; all entertainment free. Bring the family and have an enjoyable picnic day on these wonderful seashore estates.

Sales rally
June 17, 1923
Near site of
future school property
Malaga Cove,
Palos Verdes

Grand Opening
Palos Verdes Estates

Ad, L. A. Times, *June 15, 1923*

Soccer match
June 16, 2013
Malaga Cove School
Palos Verdes

With new management now in control, construction quickly got underway. From the office in downtown Los Angeles, there was a mailing campaign filled with glowing promises of what was to come in Palos Verdes. Although the advertisements may seem vastly overblown in a now litigious world, they were no more misleading than any of the other developments picturing a California filled with orange trees, sunny skies, and clear blue ocean. Most of what E. G. Lewis promised actually came true.

Aug. 26, 1923

Summer Days That Are Too Short

WHAT PICTURE DO YOU SEE FROM YOUR WINDOWS?

Sept. 16, 1924

Jan. 20, 1924

L. A. Times *ads for Palos Verdes lots*

"Yes Sir, it's always fine here"

Construction Activity - 1924

A year later, 1924, there were twenty miles of paved roads, and ten miles of fourteen-inch water mains. Gas and electric power lines were in place. In October, with a blast watched by 50,000 people, a steep grade was cut from the coastline road.

Palos Verdes Country Club, newly built 1925

An eighteen-hole golf course was ready, with newly seeded grass growing and a brand new country club beside it. There were residents to enjoy the club, with about 2,500 home sites purchased, and the first homes already built.

A sales office, later known as La Venta Inn, stood proudly on top of the hill, looking across the bay all the way to Malibu. After serving its purpose for sales, it became an inn that was a favorite spot for a horseback ride to lunch, and a weekend retreat for a number of celebrities. There are now no overnight accommodations, but it is still busy welcoming hundreds of weddings each year.

La Venta Inn, newly built Palos Verdes 1924

Throughout the Estates, as the western part of the entire hill is locally known, Frank's design for a city of winding streets with Italian and Spanish buildings still holds. An art jury is responsible for keeping the theme intact on each building, in spite of numerous lawsuits to undermine its authority. E. G. Lewis would have every right to be proud of what he started.

But, he was not around to help Palos Verdes grow. In December, 1924, his pyramid of investments finally caught up with him. He was sued by a large number of his creditors from past schemes, and eventually spent six years in jail for fraud. When he got out, he retired quietly to Atascadero, where he lived until he died in 1950.

Lawyers for Palos Verdes managed to keep all of its property out of his listed assets involved in the lawsuits. At his trial in 1928, one of the Palos Verdes engineers testified that, if E. G. Lewis had simply stayed the course and continued to work on Palos Verdes, his fees and commissions would have made him a very wealthy man.

The Work Goes On

The team E. G. Lewis left behind was composed of good men. Some were people Frank had known for a long time, like Jay Lawyer and his son Donald, and the Olmsted brothers' design organization. Others, like Charles H. Cheney and Col. John C. Low, came in with E. G. Lewis and stayed to build their own homes in Palos Verdes.

The Palos Verdes Project reverted to control by Frank's syndicate in 1924, until it incorporated in 1939 as Palos Verdes Estates. With strong business management, capable engineers and designers, and an ambitious advertising campaign, Palos Verdes Estates was a success. The city now contains 5,410 homes, most of them with distinctive red tiles roofs and Italian architecture, and a similarly styled shopping plaza graced with a marble fountain, very much as Frank imagined it would be and, coincidentally, much as E. G. Lewis envisioned the Atascadero city center.

Sketch plan for Malaga Cove Plaza December 1923

Gardner Building, 1925
First shops in Malaga Cove Plaza

Malaga Cove Plaza 1926
Seen from hills with ocean below
Gardner Building in center, from back

Malaga Cove Plaza 2013 Gardner Building on right

Construction, Italian Style

There were still over 12,000 acres of Palos Verdes in the hands of Frank's syndicate in 1924. The area known as Portuguese Bend, which Frank often referred to as the Ranch, was still his isolated retreat, with the Cottage looking out to sea at the top of a gentle hillside.

At the time the Cottage was being built in 1916, a well-known Boston architect named Guy Lowell published a book that became an inspiration for many of the first Palos Verdes buildings. Guy Lowell traveled throughout Italy, photographing small buildings, farmhouses, and villas. His book was filled with examples of them all.

Frank loved the Italian ambience and look, and decided he wanted Palos Verdes to be the same. When the Palos Verdes Project bought the 3,200 acres, the designers kept Frank's Italian theme, with a plan to sell lots for comfortable family-sized homes, with some lots for larger houses. None of them would really qualify to be called 'estates', even though the city took that word as part of its name.

In the Portuguese Bend section, where Frank's own Cottage was located, and where he planned his larger house, he envisioned what would be truly grand estates, of one hundred acres or more. He used as models for his construction many of the buildings from Guy Lowell's book, and hired architect Gordon Kaufman to adapt those designs to his purposes.

The Casetta

Just next to the Cottage on the downhill side, Frank put up the first Mediterranean building, a three-bay garage with two apartments above, known as the Casetta, to house mechanics and workers. Here he stored his cars, the big, heavy touring models that were considered the best available. For some time, he sat on the board of directors of Cord and Auburn Motor Companies, and appreciated fine automobiles. His favorite Duesenbergs and Packards ran well on Palos Verdes' dirt roads.

By 1925, Frank's diabetes was causing him problems, and he often walked with a cane. When he wanted to go somewhere, he would phone the Casetta, and a driver would bring his ride uphill about one hundred feet, to the Cottage's front door, to pick him up. Almost one hundred years later, the sturdy building still stands. Frank's garages are now enclosed to be living area, and the building is a private home.

The Casetta, Portuguese Bend
With garages enclosed 2012

Frank Vanderlip and driver at the Casetta, Portuguese Bend circa 1928

Villa Narcissa

Frank and Narcissa Vanderlip with Villa Narcissa 1929

Next came a guest house, also in Italian style, named The Villetta. Although its appearance was much grander than the Cottage, Frank and Narcissa chose to stay in their familiar setting, while using Villa Narcissa, just next door, to house their guests. The famous city and suburban planners, Frederick Law Olmsted, Jr., and his brother John C. Olmsted, laid out a grand *allee* of cypress trees, which stretched over 200 steps uphill from the front door. Members of the Japanese farming community were welcome to bring their families to the *allee* to take photos.

Frank Vanderlip escorts guests ca 1935
Cypress allee, Villa Narcissa
Narcissa, back L, Frank, Jr., front R
Image from movie film

The trees were imported in a rather unusual way. "*An avenue of Italian cypress,*" Frank recalled in 1935, "*now thirty feet high, came home in Mrs. Vanderlip's pocket as seed from the Villa Palmieri, owned by my old Chicago friend, James Ellsworth.*"

These were not the only plants Narcissa brought from abroad. The first were cuttings of Argonne Ivy she imported to grow for mothers who lost sons in World War I. "My mother," Frank, Jr., confesses, "was a famous smuggler." He recalled how he and his

Cypress allee, *Villa Narcissa 2012*

sister dried the Villa Palmieri pine cones on their window sill in Florence until they could shake out the seeds. They then wrapped the seeds in clean handkerchiefs and brought them into the U. S. in their luggage. Narcissa's theory was that no one would think the children would be smugglers. She must have then put them in her pocket to carry them on the train to California, as Frank relates in his memoirs.

Villa Palmieri with cypress, Florence, Italy 1907

The Villa Palmieri, in Florence, Italy, was no ordinary home. Begun in the 15th century, it is still an elegant and beautiful landmark. Frank's friend bought it in 1907. It would not be surprising that Frank would style his new California development after such a magnificent model.

Villa Narcissa is only a short uphill stroll from the Cottage, and was an extension of the family quarters. Frank was content to relax on the ocean view terrace. *"Six hundred feet above the ocean we have a villa, a pure Italian house flanked by groves and gardens and facing a large brick terrace furnished as an outdoor living-room. I cannot believe there is a better stimulus to the imagination anywhere than the view afforded on that terrace. Far below, the Pacific roars against a cliff. My friend Julian Street will have it that the Pacific's emerald surface is our lawn and twenty-five miles out - half-way to our horizon - the hills of Catalina Island are shrunken nicely to the proportions of a hedge."*

Frank and Narcissa Vanderlip circa 1930 Villa Narcissa Terrace

Villa Narcissa entry, toward ocean from allee 2012

Now painted a bright coral color, the Villa still sits quietly on the hillside, surround by gardens that are the Olmsted's legacy. It is still owned by some of Frank's descendants, who welcome guests on the terrace as hospitably their grandfather did one hundred years ago.

The Gatehouse

Portuguese Bend Gatehouse 2012

No area of grand homes is complete without a grand entrance. At the entry point to Portuguese Bend, Frank built the Gatehouse in 1925, modeled after a chapel used by Michelangelo, just outside of Rome, while he painted the Sistine Chapel. At first, it was used to greet prospective land buyers for the one hundred acre lots Frank planned to sell in the area. The high, open-beamed ceiling welcomed guests into a cool, stuccoed interior for a snack and a drink before they toured the area by car or horseback. After falling into disrepair in the 1970s, the Gatehouse has been restored as a private home that will ultimately become a museum for works by the local group of well-known *plein air* painters.

Villa Francesca

Wherever Frank went, Harry Benedict was certain to be nearby. He and his wife Frances, and their two sons, lived "across the road and a large lawn," from Beech-wood. By 1930, Frank was spending more and more time in Palos Verdes, and Harry Benedict moved his wife and the boys

Villa Francesca 2012

there too. He planned a grand estate on a hilltop with a spectacular view, to be known as Villa Francesca. The first construction was his own gatehouse, along with a row of garages and two workers' apartments. The Benedict family moved into the gatehouse, planning to stay there until their large home was to be built.

The Grand Estates

Two other investors in Frank's Palos Verdes syndicate planned huge, elegant Italian homes. His sister Ruth and her husband, Frank's longtime friend Ed Harden, told Frank they would put money into his venture, but in return, they "must have," the forty-eight cliffside acres between the two Portuguese Bend points. Ruth got a good bargain. It was one of the most scenic pieces of property on the entire hill. Ruth and Ed Harden's gatehouse, just across the road from Frank's, went up in 1926, along with the standard row of garages and workers' apartments, plus walkways and scenic benches to enjoy the spectacular views.

Ruth and Ed Harden's Gatehouse, built 1926, Portuguese Bend 2012

Their large home was rumored to be planned with fifty-four bedrooms. Grading for it began in 1929, with neat rows of orchards already planted. While waiting for it to be completed, Ruth and Ed Harden stayed in the gatehouse when they were in California.

Portuguese Point graded for Harden mansion 1931
Harden Gatehouse on left, Portuguese Bend Gatehouse directly across road,
Villa Francesca on upper right

The second syndicate partner to envision his own estate was Edward Levinson. He, too, put up garages and two workers' apartments in an Italian themed structure straight out of Guy Lowell's book. But, his wife was purely a big city girl, and he gave up his further construction. The property passed through various hands, and is now owned by several generations of an artistic family.

Edward Levinson apartments, built 1931, with stables and garages 2012

Villa Palos Verdes

Of course, the grandest home of all was to be Frank's. The boy whose childhood farm was repossessed wanted his country place to be the biggest and the best. It was to be large enough to rival San Simeon, the northern California hilltop mansion of William Randolph Hearst, another man with newspaper ink in his veins, but one Frank did not admire. As a model, Frank chose the Villa Guilia, built in Rome by Pope Julius III in 1551, which is now the Etruscan Museum.

Villa Giulia, built in 1551-1553 for Pope Julius III, Rome, Italy 2008

Frank's copy was to be a regal Italian estate, known as Villa Palos Verdes. There would be groves of fruit trees and formal gardens, a magnificent arched loggia, enough rooms for even an explorer get lost in, and every comfort one could ask for.

Plaster model and sketch for Villa Palos Verdes circa 1920

Several of the monumental buildings connected with Frank's business life included proud facades supported by heavy stone columns. The Treasury Building in Washington had thirty, and the new National City Bank Building had two rows of twelve, with two of the original sixteen moved to Beechwood to stand sentinel at the entrance gate. Many of the other banks in New York, as well as the Custom House, used columns to exude an air of strength and stability. Frank wanted columns at Villa Palos Verdes.

Long before ground was even broken or plans completed, eight Rosa Verona pillars, six to eight feet long, were hauled up the dirt road in anticipation of the construction. Enough red clay roof tile was delivered to cover, as Frank, Jr., says, "acres of roof."

If Narcissa thought the house that became Sleepy Hollow Country Club, across from Beechwood, in Scarsborough, was "too grandiose," no one records what she thought of this much larger plan.

Villa Palos Verdes was never built. The Stock Market Crash of 1929 intervened. It was a banking crisis Frank had designed the Federal Reserve System to prevent. The Crash also halted plans for similarly large estates planned by his sister Ruth and her husband Ed Harden, by investor Edward Levinson, and by Harry Benedict.

Most of Frank's Rosa Verona pillars were eventually erected in the garden at the Cottage by his son John and his wife. The "acres" of roof tile went on top of other buildings all over Palos Verdes. Other small architectural stone pieces planned for the Villa can be found in use on various Portuguese Bend properties, or forgotten under overgrowth that may be shoots of Narcissa's smuggled Argonne ivy.

Rosa Verona marble columns planned for Villa Palos Verdes in place at the Cottage 2012

The Farmstead

Nothing said "grand estate" in the 1920s like a stable of fine horses and a pack of hounds for fox hunting. Frank never liked the killing of animals, ever since his childhood farm days. He did love the pony his father brought home for him, and was comfortable around animals.

The stables, known as the Farmstead, were built in 1927. It was a beautiful, Italian complex of stables and apartments around a courtyard. Overnight guests could be accommodated in the rooms, and there were happy evenings with parties on the grounds.

Fox hunters ride down Villa Palos Verdes allee *1935*
Image taken from movie film

There are foxes in the Palos Verdes hills, but not many. If they were hunted with horses and dogs, there would soon have been none. While an unfortunate creature or two may have tangled with a group of riders, most of the excitement was from following a fox-scented trail spread by a huntsman.

When plans for the area were scaled back, the Farmstead was leased to a succession of trainers, some of Olympic quality. It was sold in the 1950s to the family that still operates it as the Portuguese Bend Riding Club.

Courtyard of Portuguese Bend Riding Club, formerly Frank Vanderlip's Farmstead 2013

A. E. Hanson - A Different Type Of Developer

Like E. G. Lewis, A. E. Hanson had a vision of how to turn empty Palos Verdes land into a community. Other than that, the only commonality between them was the fact that they both have become known to history by their first two initials.

A native of California, A. E. Hanson grew up in the orange groves then spreading across what is known as the Inland Empire, to the east of Los Angeles.

A. E. Hanson circa 1925

He first went to work in Canada, for a company developing apple orchards and building small towns. He learned land planning and landscape architecture. Eventually, he opened his own business to the "carriage trade" in Los Angeles. One of his clients was silent movie star Harold Lloyd, who spent $1.5 million over a five-year period on his garden at Greenacres, his Beverly Hills estate. As A. E. Hanson remembered, "That was 1929 gold dollars."

Harold Lloyd Estate garden, Beverly Hills, CA after 1933

A combination of Mediterranean and Spanish Revival styles, the *Los Angeles Times* called it "a gorgeous fairyland play-ground," and "a Modern Eden of groves and gardens." There was a nine-hole golf course, a canoe stream, a one hundred-foot waterfall, stables, gardens, an outdoor theater, and a dancing pavilion, plus a grand automobile entrance. It was exactly what Frank imagined for Palos Verdes.

A. E. Hanson must have been pleased when Frank requested to see the Greenacres gardens in January, 1930, and then hired the landscape designer, soon making him general manager for all of Frank's land. Once again, Frank changed the course of someone's life.

What had been known originally as the Vanderlip-Stillman Syndicate, the original purchasers of Palos Verdes, was now known as the Palos Verdes Corporation. It was comprised of the entire hill, minus the 3,200 acres that went into the Palos Verdes Project begun by E. G. Lewis.

There were three sources of income on this 12,000 acres that could be used to pay the tax bills. There were rents from about twenty-five Japanese farmers growing vegetables. There was acreage rented out to five ranchers, who grew barley for hay and grain, and who still kept some cattle grazing. And, there was a fairly small area leased out for strip mining of diatomaceous earth, which is the fossilized remains of diatoms, a type of algae used in filtration systems, toothpaste, cat litter, and a variety of other products. All three incomes together were not enough. The only return the original stockholders had ever received was from the sale to E. G. Lewis' project, and they did not contribute to the tax shortfall. Frank was paying the difference by himself.

The country was in the worst of the Great Depression. Sales of property for the type of community Frank envisioned were practically non-existent. A. E. Hanson told Frank all of this in the report he produced in the fall of 1931. Before Frank left for the East Coast in March, 1932, Frank told A. E. Hanson, *"Run the Corporation, but don't look to me for money. I am tired of bearing the other stockholders' burdens."*

After countless hours of driving over the entire area, known generally as the Ranch, A. E. Hanson devised a plan. He would first make the area as attractive to visitors as the famous 17-mile drive in Monterey, California. To do so, he needed a road, and he had to build it with no money.

In a move almost worthy of E. G. Lewis, A. E. Hanson convinced County Supervisor John Quinn to help get money from the State Emergency Relief Fund, which ultimately came from the federal government as part of President Herbert Hoover's plan to put

Americans back to work. A labor force of four hundred men worked for two years, much of the time with picks and shovels, finishing in 1935.

The result was Palos Verdes Drive. It circled the entire peninsula, and was marked with twenty-three milestones. An easily available map gave a description of what to expect on each mile of the circular journey along the northern edge and around the scenic coastline. A. E. Hanson was not shy in his printed descriptions.

> Palos Verdes Drive
> Twenty-three Miles of Unique Scenery
>
> Here one really senses the spaciousness of the sea. Here are unsurpassed views of coast, Channel and Island, the ship lane for freighters, liners and the Navy, the whole great harbor of Los Angeles at one's feet, all seen from one encircling drive. And on shore one passes for 23 miles through interesting unspoiled country and one of the most attractive and best protected home neighborhoods to be found in the United States . . .
> . . . the glory of this in Los Angeles is in the free expanse of ocean, the warm sunlight on blue bays, the unspoiled background of hills.

Part of route description included with tourist map 1935

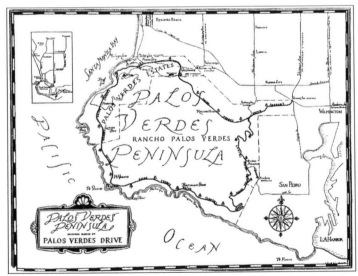

Map of Palos Verdes Drive showing scenic mile markers 1935

Frank and A. E. Hanson laid out an ambitious plan for Portuguese Bend, with a beautifully landscaped shopping area, but the Depression made it impractical to even consider beginning to build. Instead, they decided to concentrate on selling lots in a development on the northern side, to be named Rolling Hills.

It was to be an area of small "ranches", with white-sided homes, white rail fences, shingle or shake roofs, and plenty of horse barns. Originally, the plan was to sell lots of around fifty acres.

A. E. Hanson himself was the first inhabitant. During the fall of 1932, he moved his wife, four children and two housekeepers there from Beverly Hills for weekends and during the summer months. His home, an old place originally built as a small ranch house around 1890, was originally full of weeds and trash on the inside, and had to be literally hosed out. He reports that his wife "was entranced by the view, the location, and the climate." The children were thrilled to have a place to run, and were, he says, "in seventh heaven."

By the fall of 1935, however, only two other lots, of about ten acres each, were sold. One was to Elvon Musick, who was now the Palos Verdes Corporation attorney. Another was to one of his business associates. For a while, lots could be purchased for $185 an acre, but there were no takers. Before the end of the year, two more buyers actually committed to a purchase. The second of them only wanted one acre, enough to keep two horses and a cow.

Entrance to Rolling Hills from PV Dr. North, Los Angeles in background circa 1935

"We were running scared most of the time," A. E. Hanson said. The corporation did not have much money. "We were determined in spite of hell and high water, we would carry out our scheme." He offered lots of one to five acres instead of fifty. Land started to sell.

By 1937, there was a community with a post office. Rolling Hills incorporated as a city in 1957. In 2013, there are 684 homes, and a population of 1,860. Lots are at least an acre, and the average size is 2.7 acres. Many of the homes are originals from the 1950s and 1960s. Prices start around $1.7 million per acre. A. E. Hanson would be proud.

Palos Verdes In His Later Years

The year 1924 was a turning point in Frank's life. On the West Coast, the Palos Verdes Project's 3,200 acres were finally developing in a good way, in the hands of competent people. He was content to let them do their jobs, while he concentrated on his own personal piece of Portuguese Bend. At first, that meant construction of the Villa Palos Verdes. When that dream became impossible, he was still happy to be in California, sitting on his terrace, looking out to sea.

Villa Narcissa terrace looking toward ocean 2012

Reminiscing in 1935 about his acquisition, Frank said, "*The property still lies unharmed by architectural mistakes, in its original loveliness of winter verdure and summer browns. Hundreds of thousands have been expended in road-building and tree-planting . . . It seemed to me that with my experience with that mysterious force with which banking is concerned I might bring to the land, specifically to that 16,000 acres of fertile Palos Verdes ranchland with its equable climate and gorgeous scenery, all the benefits of our civilization filtered free of all the evils. I never worked out the details as to how that Utopia should be recruited. The vision was no more than a short dream.*"

The dream was interrupted by reality. As Frank and his men improved his remaining 12,804 acres, their property taxes went up. Because of financial conditions nationwide, lots were not selling fast enough to keep up with the assessor's bills. Palos Verdes was becoming an expensive experiment. As a banker, negative outlay did not sit well with Frank. Once there were roads in place, *"the property for a time seemed in my mind a great asset. In the years since, it has contributed in the neighborhood of a million dollars of taxes. We experienced a rise from $13,000 to $100,000 of annual taxation, and I have since wondered whether it was an asset or a liability to own such a tract of land."*

The Peninsula After Frank

Frank, Jr., served as president of Palos Verdes Corporation from 1937 until 1943, when the job and title passed to Harry Benedict. Frank's second son, Kelvin, took over in 1945, until he gave the position back to Frank, Jr., in 1950, to devote himself purely to the Portuguese Bend area.

Kelvin's own vision was to turn the Portuguese Bend area into a beach club and enclave of small houses. It was a fine idea, and off to a good start. He worked to develop other areas of the peninsula and championed the building of Wayfarer's Chapel. Just after his death at the age of 46, the county decided to cut a roadway over the hill and down to the beach. The excavation started an inexorable landslide in 1956 that is still moving some homes and the coastal road slowly toward the ocean.

Frank, Jr., was president of the Palos Verdes Corporation in 1953, when the land under the company's control was down to 7,000 acres. Great Lakes Carbon Corporation wanted to buy 165 acres to expand their diatomaceous mining. The family was understandably tired of the huge responsibility and financial drain. Frank, Jr., told Great Lakes Carbon they could only have the land they wanted if they bought all of the Palos Verdes Corporation stock, which Great Lakes Carbon did.

That land was sold off, lot by lot, and eventually divided into the cities of Rolling Hills Estates and Rancho Palos Verdes. Including Palos Verdes Estates and Rolling Hills, four separate cities in two zip codes have been created from Frank's original purchase. The entire area has a rural atmosphere with winding roads and only selected commercial centers, as Frank desired, even though the home lots are much smaller and closer together than he first planned. In 2013, there are 65,000 people living in what is collectively known as the Palos Verdes Peninsula, where only cattle roamed one hundred years before.

Ruth Harden's cliff top estate is preserved as an open, beautiful place. Forty-six of her original forty-eight acres, including Portuguese Point, eventually became Abalone Shoreline Park, now part of the city of Rancho Palos Verdes.

By 2013, of the original 16,004 acres, only 11.69 acres remain under the family ownership of Kelvin Vanderlip's four children.

Harry Benedict, Narcissa Vanderlip, Frank Vanderlip, Jr., at Villa Narcissa circa 1960

In spite of the financial headaches and the complexity of the development projects, Frank loved Palos Verdes for the rest of his life, staying often in his Cottage. He was proud of what he accomplished. Speaking of the Palos Verdes Estates area, he said, "*We did sell thirty-two hundred acres off the ends of the ranch, and under the skillful direction of the Olmsted Brothers, those acres have been developed into one of the choicest collections of modest homes that I know of anywhere in the world.*"

Expanding his thoughts to the entire peninsula, he added, "*But, paraphrasing Omar Khayyam and his wine, I often wondered what the realtors buy, one-half so precious as the goods they sell.*"

Frank Vanderlip In 1924

Certain situations in Washington in 1924 clashed with Frank's belief in the right of everyone to know what was actually happening in government and publicly owned companies. Powerful interests disagreed with his philosophy. It was a dangerous mixture. At a time in life when most men contentedly retire to a golf course, Frank's ideals severed a number of his friendships and most of his business ties. He was about to go into battle, for the sake of his own reputation.

If ever a man needed a hobby, now was that time. Exactly how Frank chose the one he did, he does not say. Perhaps, one day, the idea simply flew into his yard on its own. No matter what got him started, Palos Verdes residents even now have strongly opposite opinions on the wisdom of Frank's choice.

Frank Vanderlip walks along bluff above Inspiration Point, Portuguese Bend circa 1935
Image taken from 1935 promotional film

o o o

The Duck Pond

Peacock in a backyard pepper tree, Palos Verdes, California 2006

○ ○ ○

The Duck Pond

Portuguese Bend was a quiet place in 1924, sometimes too quiet. Even with the construction going on in Palos Verdes Estates, where Frank Vanderlip lived in California, there were few people, fewer cars, no gasoline-powered farm machinery or gardener's tools.

One day, Frank casually mentioned this fact to a friend. It was a good example of the law of unintended consequences, and it was the last day of silence in Palos Verdes.

Friends With Wings

Frank grew up with cows, pigs, and turkeys. His opinion of cows and pigs was not high. But, he developed a great love for birds.

Whenever he was in California, he had time for a real hobby. Being Frank, he wanted to do more than tend a canary in a small cage.

Just across the road from the Cottage, and just below the Villa, Frank built himself a duck pond. Not content to wait for whatever wild birds might discover his oasis, he imported a variety of ducks.

Duck pond with island, bird hospital, mule team, Portuguese Bend circa 1920s

Frank Vanderlip and rare heron Portuguese Bend 1931

Next came an aviary big enough for his flock, which grew to include 111 varieties of birds, from tiny finches to at least one four-foot tall heron. "It got to be quite an undertaking," Frank Jr. says.

Any animal lover knows that each species has particular needs, from temperature controls to favorite foods. Frank's solution was his own bird expert, Mr. Woodley. He was, Frank Jr. calls him, "a terribly nice little man." He and his wife stayed in one of the apartments in the Casetta until a small house was built for them. In their kitchen, they had two iceboxes, as refrigerators were accurately called. One was for their own food, the other was for the hamburger and fruit that were needed to feed the menagerie. Next to the duck pond, Frank added his own bird hospital to care for rescued creatures.

As the bird population increased, so did the size of the aviary. To the right of the duck pond, Frank put in a long walkway, with tall cages on either side, made of wooden supports and chicken wire. A manmade stream ran along the edge, beautifully landscaped, with water falling gently from pool to pool, and a small fountain in the center of one of them. It would have been a pleasant, calming place to spend an afternoon, visiting the flock, enjoying the ocean breeze, and looking out to Santa Catalina Island on the horizon.

Remains of duck pond stream bed 2013

Stairs from Cottage to duck pond 2013

The Great Peafowl Mystery

Everyone loves a good mystery, and Frank left one in Palos Verdes that is still debated almost one hundred years later.

When Frank complained to a friend that Palos Verdes was too quiet, the friend's solution was to gift Frank, and the entire peninsula, with two cages of peafowl. This much is certain fact. The two metal cages in which they came still sit beside the duck pond, and hundreds of peafowl roam freely on the hill, screeching their raucous cries all night, cracking roof tiles with their barely

Cages by pond, used in 1920s to import peafowl 2012

controlled landings, leaving daily messes on driveways, and gracing the area with their gorgeous plumage and adorable baby chicks.

All other details of their arrival can be divided into two sets of either fact or myth, Baldwin or Wrigley, depending on who one chooses to believe. Both stories trace back to Frank's descendants and their families. Both contain elements that cannot possibly be true.

Frank, Jr.'s Story

Frank, Jr.'s story dates to his 1976 recorded interview. "I guess it was about 1924 that my father complained to Lucky Baldwin that this place was too quiet, and Mr. Baldwin said, 'I think I know how to cure that, and I'll send you some peacocks.' . . . He sent us two males and four females."

This seems, on the face of it, to be a clear, concise, accurate story, direct from Frank's son, who was seventeen in 1924, certainly old enough to know what was happening, although he may have been on the East Coast at the time the peafowl actually arrived. There is just one problem.

Peacock on original cage 2013

Lucky Baldwin was a colorful, wealthy man who made his millions from his good luck in the silver mining business, which gave him his nickname. He was married four times, sued by four other women for breach of promise of marriage, and shot and wounded by the sister of a woman suing him for seduction. A fan of horseracing, he was an owner and breeder of fine racehorses, and the founder of the Santa Anita Race Track. Just for fun, he kept peafowl on his estate, now the Los Angeles County Arboretum and Botanic Garden, where the birds can still be seen roaming freely.

Elias J "Lucky" Baldwin date unknown

Unfortunately for the veracity of Frank, Jr.'s story, Lucky Baldwin died in 1909, four years before Frank even bought Palos Verdes.

John's Story

Anita Baldwin, peacock dress 1920s

Frank's youngest son, John, gives a different version of the story. If the peafowl did really arrive in Palos Verdes in 1924, John would have been only nine years old, and spent the school year at Beechwood. He did spend summers at the Cottage, and worked at the duck pond, even lining up as a young boy with the regular laborers each week for his pay.

A 1988 interview with the Palos Verdes Review magazine says, "John remembers that all the Portuguese Bend peacocks started from just nine birds that Anita Baldwin brought from the Lucky Baldwin estate in Arcadia as a birthday present for his father."

A Third Story

If only the two sons' stories existed, it would be easy enough to reconcile them, concluding that the regularly colored peafowl, totaling either six or nine in number, came from the Lucky Baldwin estate, through his daughter Anita Baldwin.

However, in 2000, the city of Rancho Palos Verdes commissioned a study titled "Peafowl Population Assessment," because so many residents were complaining about the numbers of peafowl fouling their property. They hired a prominent poultry specialist. Wanting a historical basis for her report, she logically called John Vanderlip, Frank's only son still alive at that time. To add confusion to history, his wife Suzanne answered the phone.

Quoting from the city's report detailing Suzanne Vanderlip's conversation with the professor, "Mr. Vanderlip made trips to Santa Catalina and the Wrigley family. Wrigley's daughter became quite fond of Frank. On one of his birthdays, she gifted him with 16 peafowl. So, the source of the birds was not from the East, neither eastern Los Angeles County (Arcadia), nor the eastern United States. Rather the peafowl came from the West, across the sea from Santa Catalina."

There is a problem with this story, also. Frank's peacocks arrived in Palos Verdes in 1924, at least according to Frank, Jr., who was the only person to give details who was old enough at the time to have some veracity. The Wrigleys did not have their famous aviary even started until 1927, and there were no peafowl on Santa Catalina Island before their aviary. Suzanne Vanderlip's version cannot be correct.

The Peafowl Truth

There is no original documentation of the birds' origin from Frank's own time. None of the Baldwin archives holds a clue, and there is no record from the time period on Santa Catalina Island. Even the most educated guess can only be just that - a guess.

Lucky Baldwin imported his peafowl from India in 1880. Those who survive to adulthood, at least in Palos Verdes, where they must fend off skunks, cats, and hawks, reproduce at a rate of two to four chicks per year. Ten years after the first birds arrived at the Baldwins, there were fifty wandering freely on the estate. Anita Baldwin loved them all. Apparently, the easiest way to get fired from her employment was to say or do anything that could be seen as a dislike for her birds. She even entered a float in the 1914 Pasadena Rose Parade with a giant peacock made of flowers as the centerpiece. Anita Baldwin would not have gifted even one of her precious flock to just anybody, but, if she did know Frank and his aviary, she would have known she was sending the peafowl to a good home.

Anita Baldwin's Rose Parade float with peacock, Pasadena 1914

On that basis, the best answer seems to be that the Palos Verdes peafowl originated from the Baldwin estate in Arcadia, gifted to Frank by Lucky Baldwin's daughter, Anita.

There were probably six original birds, as Frank, Jr., says, rather than John's estimated nine, with a male and two females arriving in each cage. Anita Baldwin would never have crammed eight peafowl into each of the 5x9 foot cages.

Two other peafowl joined the flock. "Pa bought a pair of pure white Indian peacocks," Frank, Jr. says. Technically, Frank bought a pea hen and a peacock. The plan was to breed them and have a flock of new little white pea chicks. But, Frank, Jr. says, "She bred with everything. The first and second generation of these cross-breeds looked like mongrels. You'd see a green peacock with a couple of white feathers off in some direction, or a white peacock with green or blue feathers . . . We saw the cross breeds for not more than ten years, and now (1976) they have settled down so that every year we have three or four pure white throwbacks and the rest are the complete throwback to the original Indian peacock." By 2013, the only clue to the white ones' existence is in the striking black and white wing feathers on a few of the males.

Wherever they came from, Frank's peafowl had a special home, in a fifty square-foot cage that was twenty feet high and enclosed with chicken wire. The cage was more for their own protection than to keep them confined. "The hawks particularly like peacocks," Frank, Jr. says. "When the third generation began growing up, a hole was cut quite high up on one side where the peacocks could get in and out. The hole was not more than two or three feet square. Hens would fly out with their young in daytime, and bring them back at night."

Frank Vanderlip, one of his peacocks, and Mr. Woodley, Portuguese Bend circa 1920s

Just to further confuse the Palos Verdes peafowl lineage, mention should be made that one of Palos Verdes Estates' former mayors also imported a few of the birds somewhere between 1960 and 1965. Therefore, any resident on the West side of the Peninsula, looking for someone to blame as they scrub their driveway, yet again, can point a finger at Fred Roessler, if they do not want to blame Frank.

Enjoying The Flock

Peafowl were not the only birds in Frank's aviary. There were finches and lovebirds, parrots, myna birds, macaws, and of course there were also ducks. The total number of birds seems to have been somewhere around five hundred. They gave Frank great joy, as can be seen in gentle photos of him interacting with some of his feathered creatures.

One of Frank's relatives from his home town of Aurora, Illinois, Mrs. William C. Evans, drove to California about this time with her husband, and arrived, unannounced, at the Gatehouse to Portuguese Bend on a "brilliant Sunday morning." The couple asked for, and were granted, permission to visit Frank's bird house, "the apple of Mr. Vanderlip's eye, - a wonderful place housing every sort of bird which could live in that climate."

Much to their surprise, "walking across one of the beautiful lawns came Frank himself, as simple, as nice and as pleasant as he had always proved to be and just as he was when visiting briefly in Aurora." Just as he was happy to share his cypress *allee* with local Japanese families posing for their family portraits, sharing his aviary with family from the Midwest was a pleasure for Frank.

Frank Vanderlip, Mr. Woodley, and two birds on his lawn, Portuguese Bend circa 1925

The Avian Legacy

One minor effect of the Stock Market Crash of 1929 was that the aviary became, according to Frank, Jr., "impossible to continue." Maintaining such a facility was not an inexpensive operation. The birds were crated up, and, "Mr. William Wrigley, Jr., very graciously accepted them as a gift," and added them to his own aviary. "But I would go back to that collection many years after it had been given to him, and certain of the parrots and macaws would recognize me and scream at me."

Live bird in birdbath, the Cottage circa 1930   Duck statue in birdbath, Duck Pond 2013
Roses growing up glass wall   Overgrowth of Narcissa's Argonne Ivy

Other than a few birds that were domesticated, the only ones not sent to Santa Catalina Island were the peafowl. They were simply let out of their cage, free to roam, and still propagate almost a century later. Their loud calls, sounding much like someone desperately calling out, "Help!" can sound particularly unnerving on a dark grey night when ocean fog rolls silently across the Palos Verdes hills.

Frank Vanderlip at his aviary, Portuguese Bend 1925

○ ○ ○

Washington
Part II

Frank Vanderlip at Senate Committee Hearing, Wahington, D. C. February 1924

o o o

Washington - Part II

How far will a man go to do what he feels is right? Will he jeopardize his reputation, or his fortune, or his family, or even his life? For Frank Vanderlip in 1924, the answer was all of the above.

President Harding Promises A "Return To Normalcy"

Warren G. Harding, a newspaper owner from Ohio, was elected to the presidency in 1920, with sixty percent of the popular vote, the largest ever up to that time. He came into office on a wave of good will, after a campaign appealing to women, who were casting their first votes, and after reaching out to African-Americans. The country looked forward to a full time president, after Woodrow Wilson's incapacitated last months in the White House. Many people were ready to turn away from concerns in Europe and get back to leading normal lives. Warren Harding believed government should be managed like a business.

President Warren G. Harding 1920

Unfortunately for the country, when Warren Harding came to Washington, so, also, did a large number of his friends. They were known as the Ohio Gang, with headquarters in what became known as the Little Green House at 1625 K Street. Among them was his campaign manager, Harry M. Daugherty, who was appointed Attorney General as a reward for getting President Harding elected. Although the new president wanted to have "the best minds" in his cabinet, there were rumors about members of the Ohio Gang involved in political and financial scandals long before investigations were opened.

"Skullduggery In High Places"

One of the worst instances of corruption was the only one discovered before President Harding's death. He appointed his friend Charles R. Forbes as Director of the Veterans' Bureau. Charles Forbes promptly used his position to sell off stockpiled hospital supplies left over from World War I at a fraction of their cost, pocketing something for himself on each transaction. He gave his own friends inside information on bidding for government contracts, and took control of construction and supplies for the new veterans' hospitals for the 300,000 returning wounded soldiers, moves that raised the cost per bed from $3,000 to $4,000.

1625 K Street, Washington D.C. circa 1920

Warren Harding's own doctor brought Charles Forbes' kickbacks and bribes to the President's attention in 1923, and the President promptly appointed a general to take over the Bureau, declaring that, "Someday the people will understand all that some of my erstwhile friends have done for me." Charles Forbes was finally brought to trial in 1926 and given two years in jail, a sentence of which he served only half behind bars.

As head of the U. S. Shipping Board, the President appointed his donor and general campaign manager Albert D. Lasker, even though he had no experience at all with shipping companies. Albert Lasker sold off excess World War I steel cargo ships, worth $200 per ton, for prices as low as $30 per ton, making a profit for himself along the way. He resigned in July, 1923, as the facts became public knowledge.

Prohibition laws went into effect in January, 1920. With general liquor sales illegal, the Prohibition Commissioner was a powerful man. Roy Asa Haynes, a newspaper editor from Warren Harding's home state, was given the job. Although he had close ties to the Anti-Saloon League, he apparently had no qualms about making money for himself and his friends off of liquor.

Pharmacies were granted exceptions to sell alcohol for medicinal purposes, as long as they had special permits, which had to be signed by Commissioner Haynes. He set up a system for issuing the permits, running through the K Street house, that gave payoffs to various people all along the bootlegging distribution system. In the first year alone, bootleggers made an estimated $100 million dollar profit. The K Street gang made nothing off of the actual liquor, but plenty off of the kickbacks. A Federal agent named Gaston Means kept track of all the proceedings in basement file cabinets at the Little Green House.

Eventually, word had to leak out, with so much money piling up. The man chosen to take the blame, Jess Smith, conveniently shot himself. Not so conveniently, he chose to do it in Attorney General Harry Daugherty's D.C. room. Roy Haynes remained as Prohibition Commissioner until Jess Smith's ex-wife, angry at not getting what she thought was her fair share, spoke up to a Senate investigating committee. Roy Haynes was forced to resign in March, 1924.

All of this money illegally changing hands should have come to the notice of the Department of Justice. It did, but not in the way any law abiding citizen would wish. The Ohio Gang on K Street included Attorney General Harry Daugherty.

His head of the Bureau of Investigation was William J. Burns, who Julian Street described at the time as, "a man of doubtful reputation." As hints of the massive corruption spread, William Burns had no qualms protecting his boss by ordering unauthorized searches and seizures of Justice Department enemies. Even congressmen and senators were wiretapped, and discovered their files searched and copied.

Roy Asa Haynes   William J. Burns Harry M. Daugherty
Harding adminstration members of Little Green House 1920s

Harry Daugherty himself had impeachment charges brought against him for protecting from prosecution for fraud those companies in which he owned stock. A 1924 Senate investigation found that he approved systematic graft for government appointments, as well as prison pardons and freedom from prosecution, particularly for bootleggers. He was tried twice for corruption, with two hung juries as the result. He managed to hold onto his job into the Coolidge administration, when he resigned in March, 1924, amid bribery allegations.

Teapot Dome

Even for those who know nothing else about the Harding administration, the words Teapot Dome are still as connected with scandal as is the term Watergate.

One of Warren Harding's executive orders created a Naval petroleum reserve, to safeguard a supply of oil for use by the U. S. Navy. Both the Secretaries of Navy and Interior believed they should have control over management of these resources. Interior won.

Teapot Dome Rock at oil field, WY 1922

Albert B. Fall was a senator from New Mexico plagued with a large personal debt, but blessed with enough friends in the Ohio Gang to become Secretary of the Interior. When it came time to give out contracts for new oil drilling leases in the petroleum reserves at Teapot Dome, Wyoming and Elk Hills, California, Albert Fall apparently though he would solve his financial problems.

Without putting out bids, he gave the leases to his friends Edward Doheny, of Pan-American Petroleum and Transport Company, and Harry F. Sinclair, of Mammoth Oil Corporation. That, in itself, was not illegal under the laws of the time. But, Albert Fall took large amounts of cash, labeled personal loans, from both men. This was not legal.

The Wall Street Journal reported on the contracts in April, 1922. By early 1924, Congressional hearings were looking into a variety of charges stemming from $100,000 in cash that Albert Fall had not managed to hide, given to him by Harry Sinclair. He would eventually be the first former cabinet officer sentenced to prison, where he served one year, apparently having accepted a total of about $400,000.

In a world where legalities often do not make sense, although Albert Fall was convicted of accepting bribes and illegal no-interest personal loans, the two bribers, Harry Sinclair and Edward Doheny, were acquitted. Harry Sinclair did serve six months for contempt of court. Edward Doheny's corporation foreclosed on Albert Fall's New Mexico home, for unpaid loans that were actually the bribe money.

Harry F. Sinclair   Edward L. Doheny   Albert B. Fall
Men implicated in Teapot Dome scandal 1920s

What Did The President Know?

There was never any evidence that President Harding ever profited from any of his cronies' activities. He did play poker in the White House twice a week, often with members of the Ohio Gang. In spite of Prohibition, Teddy Roosevelt's daughter Alice Longworth said that "bottles containing every imaginable brand of whiskey stood about," all delivered from the K Street house. Mrs. Harding herself often mixed the drinks.

As various revelations came to light, the president's popularity started to dwindle. He, of course, claimed to know nothing about the illegalities, but seemed unable to put a stop to them. "I have no trouble with my enemies," he told a journalist, "but my damn friends, they're the ones that keep me walking the floor nights!"

The president decided that a cross-country trip would be good for public relations, and probably hoped that just getting out of the Washington gossip mill would be good for his declining health. After a train trip all the way to Alaska, with many stops along the way to deliver speeches to large crowds, Warren Harding's heart gave out, and he died in a San Francisco hotel on August 2, 1923. Vice President Calvin Coolidge became president. Mrs. Harding burned most of her husband's personal and official papers.

Headline August 3, 1923

Frank Vanderlip Decides To Step In

Frank Vanderlip, who worried about the state of the economy and the country, who kept up with politics through newspapers and through a wide circle of influential friends, and who, according to Julian Street, "has never bought one drop of bootleg liquor," would have been horrified to see such men in the government.

Since leaving the National City Bank, Frank had been searching for something that would make him feel as useful as when he ran the largest bank in the country. He published his opinions on restoring the European economy, rebuilt the city of Sparta, and set Palos Verdes on the road to a beautifully developing community. Now, he decided to help *"clean a very dirty house."*

Unfortunately, before getting out the broom, he should have been certain that what he wanted to clean was really dirty. A newspaperman's first duty, just like a detective's, is to get all the facts.

Frank was scheduled to give a speech to the local Rotary, at Briarcliff Manor in Ossining, on Lincoln's birthday, February 12, 1924. He telephoned a friend at the *New York Tribune* and said that he was planning to make an interesting speech. He suggested that the *Tribune* might want to send a reporter to get a scoop. If Frank could have seen into a crystal ball, he might have called in sick from Beechwood, instead of delivering his speech.

The Speech That Changed His Life

Frank gave hundreds of speeches during his lifetime. This one was titled "Courage and Leadership." He was accustomed to speaking without a script, often from simply notes. Harry Benedict later said of him that he could speak, extemporaneously, in perfectly composed paragraphs. When a Senate investigating committee, a few days later, seemed incredulous that there was no prepared copy, Frank merely shrugged and said, "*I had only a few notes.*" As it turned out, there was a *New York Tribune* reporter in the room, who wrote down most of what Frank said.

"*A certain Marion newspaper,*" Frank told his Rotary Club audience, "*sold for $550,000, when it was well known to every one that it was not worth half that sum.*" Given only those facts, this hardly seems like shocking news.

But, the paper in question was anything but ordinary. Its previous owner was none other than recently deceased President Warren Harding, leader of a government being tainted with any number of corruption scandals.

Nebraska State Journal *headline February 14, 1924*

As reported through Associated Press, Frank said, "*Two young men of no financial standing purchased it. Everybody in Washington, including the newspaper correspondents, knew this, but no one wants to look under the edge of a shroud.*"

"*Where did the money come from? Where did it go? These are matters of public interest. The last administration stands challenged. We cannot wait*" *for Congress or the courts, especially when we remember that Mr. Daugherty is attorney general."*

To the listeners, and to readers of newspapers around the country the following day, Frank was suggesting that President Harding was paid much more than his newspaper was worth, pocketing a considerable sum, from unknown sources, in return for unknown services.

Frank then went even further. He "whirled into the Teapot Dome scandal." He suggested that several of the members of the Senate investigating committee were "undesirable investigators of any moral question," and that Albert Fall was not being thoroughly questioned because he was ready to talk and, *"what he would have said would have gone into high places."*

There were other scandals even worse than Teapot Dome, he said, including at the Veteran's Bureau and on the Shipping Board, which, *"if not dishonest, were incredibly stupid."* He called on President Coolidge for the resignation of the Secretary of the Navy, *"and every other official besmirched in the public mind."*

The news "traveled like wildfire thru the Senate cloak room and throughout official Washington," Associated Press reported. The Senate committee investigating Albert Fall and Teapot Dome decided that they needed to talk to Frank immediately.

> An air of almost feverish tension pervaded the senate chamber.
> Senators gathered in groups on the floor, in the cloak rooms and in the marble room, discussing the latest shift in the storm of charges and suspicions enveloping the capital. Until they saw the actual dispatches on the Vanderlip speech they were too astounded to comprehend that a man of Mr. Vanderlip's recognized standing had publicly challenged an investigation into the financial affairs of Warren G. Harding.

Aware of the furor the next morning, Frank talked to reporters. *"My purpose,"* he said, *"in bringing it to public notice is to encourage an investigation of gossip concerning a dead president, gossip which is outrageous, if untrue.*

"I have made no formal request to President Coolidge for an investigation. He might say that it is not his business and it may not be but it seems to me that a newspaper could best conduct the inquiry - if the publishers abandon their policy of silence toward the gossip which they have heard. I have no unusual sources of news."

Frank went on to say that he had *"profound faith in the honesty and courage of President Coolidge and his ability to clean a very dirty house,"* and that he had high regard for Senator Thomas J. Walsh, a member of the investigating committee, not meaning to include him with *"several of his associates who were undesirable investigators of any moral inquiry."*

The Marion Star Fights Back

In Ohio, Roy D. Moore and Louis H. Brush, the two men who Frank had labeled *"young men of no financial standing,"* immediately denied any connection between their purchase of the *Marion Star* and the Teapot Dome scandal.

THE PURCHASE OF MARION, OHIO, STAR AND PRICE PAID

Joint Buyer of Mr. Harding's Paper Asserts Price Was $380,- 000, Not the $550,000 Financier Mentioned—Sharp Denials.

The Troy Times *headline February 14, 1924*

"I hesitate," Roy Moore said, "to dignify Mr. Vanderlip's Ossining speech, which apparently tries to implicate the sale of the *Marion Star* in the Teapot Dome scandal, with denial . . . The control of the *Star* was bought by Mr. Louis H. Brush and myself as individuals, the Harding estate still holding a large amount of stock in the company. We regard it as worth all we paid for it, which figure, incidentally, has never been available for Mr. Vanderlip's investigation.

"Had Mr. Vanderlip taken the trouble to consult the records in the probate court of Marion County and ascertain the facts he would not have made himself so utterly ridiculous. If all the Teapot Dome scandal is based on information so ridiculously and unnecessarily false as Mr. Vanderlip's Ossining speech it should be very encouraging to the American republic."

Then, Roy Moore issued his most damning insult:

> "If Mr. Vanderlip were a newspaper man he would edit his copy and watch his facts more closely."

A Senate Subpoena

In Washington, committee chairman Senator Irvine Lenroot and Senator Thomas Walsh issued a subpoena for Frank to appear at ten o'clock the following morning, and tell what he knew about the *Marion Star*, specifically, its relationship to the Teapot Dome scandal they were investigating. As a good citizen would, Frank appeared in Washington the next day, February 14, ready to testify. When he arrived at the Capital, he was told he would not be called until the next day.

Frank Vanderlip enters Capitol to testify, Washington D. C. February 14 1923

On February 15, Frank faced the Senate committee, identifying himself for the record as *"a retired businessman and banker."* His first statement was that he had been misquoted in some of the papers.

"Substantially, I said there were rumors coming from Washington which went far beyond gossip. You heard it everywhere, about this story. I believed that out of respect to President Harding's memory this scandal, for I believe it scandal, should be coldly looked at."

Senate Oil Committee hearing testimony, Washington D. C. February 1924

Senator Lenroot asked Frank why, if he had heard rumors, he did not simply get in touch with the investigating committee. Frank answered that it was a committee looking into scandals connected to public land, and he did not think it had the power to look into the purchase of a newspaper.

"You felt that, as a matter of public duty, it was up to you to broadcast these mere rumors about the country?" Senator Lenroot asked.

"*Yes, I thought it a patriotic duty,*" Frank answered.

"Do you think truth follows as fast as a slander?"

"*The truth will kill a slander,*" Frank responded.

The Senator's questions, according to Associate Press, "became emphatic and were asked in a loud and almost menacing tone."

"Do you think it is proper for a man of your standing to assist in the circulation of such rumors?"

Frank answered that he did think so, and that by bringing slanders against the dead president to the public's attention, the slanders could be investigated and the president cleared.

"Do you think that the proper method to kill rumors?"

Having had experience with rumors all of his life, Frank said, he knew there was a substantial difference between rumors and gossip.

"You would have the committee believe that your only purpose in making these statements was to clear the name of President Harding?" Senator Lenroot asked.

"*Certainly, what other purpose could I have had?*"

The questioning turned to Frank's assertion that the committee did not want Albert Fall to testify because he would tell too much. He was asked if he knew that Albert Fall had refused, on the grounds of self-incrimination. Frank said he did not know this.

"Do you mean to say that you didn't see that in the newspapers?"

Frank answered that there had been endless articles and that he probably did not read all of them.

"Do you mean to say that you would make a statement like that without ascertaining the facts, on the basis of mere idle rumors?"

"I thought it was a fair inference to draw."

Senator Lenroot asked if Frank thought he had performed a public service by making a statement not founded on fact.

There was a burst of laughter when Frank answered that, if it were possible to bring in all of the people who have a bad opinion of the Senate, it would not be possible to adopt much new legislation.

A new inquisitor took up the questioning. Senator Alva Adams rephrased Frank's statement that it was respect for the memory of a dead man (President Harding) that had caused Frank to bring up the newspaper sale, and asked whether any such purpose inspired Frank in regard to his statements about the senators on the committee.

"No, I think this is a very live committee," Frank answered.

"How many people spoke concerning these rumors about the *Marion Star*?"

"Oh, possibly a dozen. "

"Were they responsible persons?"

"Yes, they were people who usually know what's going on. The stories were not only told in Washington. I heard them in New York and every place I went."

Frank Vanderlip testifies
Photo in Senate committee hearing
On banking reform
Washington D. C. May 31, 1935

Senator Adams asked Frank to distinguish between gossip and rumors.

Frank answered that while gossip was *"mere tittle-tattle,"* rumor was much more substantial and might have a basis in fact. He then refused several times to name any of the dozen people who had supplied him with the rumors, saying, *"I do not care to do so."*

"Was there a rumor current that you had a grudge against President Harding?

"*Nothing could be further from the truth.*" Frank said he was a lifelong Republican. "*I admired him. I have reverence for his memory.*"

Senator Adams referred to Frank's disparaging remarks about some of the senators on the committee. "Was that with the intention of helping their reputations?"

"*They have made their reputations,*" Frank countered. "*I haven't.*"

Senator Walsh, noting that the value of the committee depended on the confidence of the country, asked if Frank thought his Briarcliff speech had destroyed that confidence.

"*Hardly that. What I said to a little group of neighbors can't destroy the country's confidence in the committee.*"

"But it has become known over the whole country."

"*I think it's for the welfare of the country that it did.*"

"You made the speech deliberately?" Senator Lenroot asked.

"*Yes.*"

"You wanted publicity?"

"*I got it,*" Frank answered, to the sound of laughter in the room.

"Did you try to find out any of the facts respecting this rumor?"

"*No.*"

"Did you talk with any one who purported to know any facts?"

"*I never found any one who purported to know any facts. Facts were needed and I believe that facts will kill the scandal.*"

"Did you tell the people that you addressed that you didn't believe these rumors?"

"No."

"You didn't express any confidence in Harding's integrity?"

"No."

Senator Holm O. Bursum asked Frank what connection there was between the *Marion Star* and the oil scandal being investigated. Frank answered that he had never heard of any connection until he read the insinuations in the paper after his speech.

According to the Associated Press:

> Mr. Vanderlip was visibly agitated. His hands twitched nervously and beads of perspiration rolled off his forehead. His voice almost broke on several occasions and his face assumed almost a pallor. A more distressed witness could hardly be imagined. The committee pounded him from all sides, and no sooner did Mr. Vanderlip attempt to straighten out one thing than he was assailed from another side about another matter.

"You felt justified," Senator Bursum pressed, "in broadcasting this statement to the world on the strength of the fact that twelve persons out of more than 100 million knew of it."

"One rarely interviews 100 million people. I said the rumor was widely circulated because these men were of widely different walks of life and, if they knew, many others must have known of it."

"Do you think a rumor started by twelve men is a widely circulated rumor?"

Frank answered that yes, under the circumstances, it was. Senator Bursum asked about circulating scandal. Frank replied that he had circulated no scandal, and that this was the Senator's expression.

The attorney representing the two buyers of the *Marion Star* was then allowed to ask questions. He wanted to know what measures Frank had taken to insure the truth of the reports about the paper before making his speech. Frank said he had done no investigation.

"Did you try to ascertain the financial standing of the two men who bought the paper?"

"I refuse to answer that question, because I already have said repeatedly that I made no inquiries of any kind."

"Don't you think it would have been the courteous thing, the fair thing, the kind thing, to have communicated with some one connected with the *Star* before you made this statement?"

Frank did not answer.

"Don't you know it is one of the cunning ways to libel a man to publish outrageous things about him and say they are rumors?" Senator Key Pittman asked.

"That can be handled by suits for libel." Unfortunately for Frank, these were prophetic words.

After a few more questions:

Senator Pittman ended his questioning by excoriating Vanderlip for having made himself the instrument through which the story of the *Star* sale was spread. He used the words "violent" and "awful" in denouncing Mr. Vanderlip.

The New York banker quailed under this attack and made the following final statement: "I know nothing about the facts. I have no connection with the facts. All I heard was rumor."

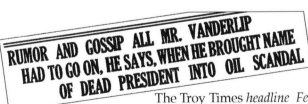

RUMOR AND GOSSIP ALL MR. VANDERLIP HAD TO GO ON, HE SAYS, WHEN HE BROUGHT NAME OF DEAD PRESIDENT INTO OIL SCANDAL

The Troy Times *headline February 15, 1924*

After an hour and forty-five minutes, Frank's inquisition was over. One of the *Star's* new owners testified next, explaining in great detail, with corroborating proof, exactly where they got the actual $380,000 purchase price, where it went, and why they were good, qualified buyers and not, as Frank claimed, insubstantial people.

He added that Frank's reports of scandal had done them "great harm," and that he wanted to clear up the details of the transaction.

"Our negotiations with President Harding for the purchase of the *Star* were made possible by my very intimate personal acquaintance with Mr. Harding over a period of twenty-five years. During this time, we were practically constant advisers with each other in connection with our newspaper plans and problems . . . he emphatically stated that he would not sell his newspaper to any one if we did not buy it."

By the time Frank left the Capitol, it was clear to everyone he had made a gigantic mistake when he involved himself and the *Marion Star* in any of the real corruption scandals.

Frank Vanderlip leaving Capitol after testimony Feb. 16, 1924
Derogatory newspaper cartoon depicting donkey ears

The Aftermath

In the following days, Frank's reputation was both lambasted and defended. Even his defenders agreed that the charges against the Star's owners were false, they simply tried to put a positive spin on Frank's motives. One of the worst printed attacks came from a newspaper in upper New York State, the *Lyons Republican*.

Vanderlip A Coward

A brave man may slander the living but only a coward will slander the dead. Frank A. Vanderlip now stands before the civilized world as a coward and a cad . . .

A man who will thus slander a dead president of the United States upon nothing more substantial than idle gossip proves himself devoid of all decency, honor and integrity. A man who will without any definite knowledge willfully and maliciously circulate a slander is as mean and despicable as the man who originates. The punishment for such a crime ought to be the death penalty. Such a man is no better than a murderer.

The purchasers of the paper were prominent newspapermen who owned several other daily papers. Therefore the conduct of Mr. Vanderlip under all the circumstances has earned for him the contempt of men and the derision of women.

We have characterized Mr. Vanderlip as a coward, on the theory that any man who will slander the dead who cannot reply to his accusations is the meanest kind of a coward. When a man slanders a dead president of the United States, when he admits that he has no facts upon which to base his statement, he may be also classified as a traitor to his country . . .

When we think of Mr. Vanderlip's cowardly conduct we are reminded of the fact that once upon a time an ass kicked a lion, but the lion was dead.

No one reports how the publicity must have affected Frank. He had, indeed, been a friend of President Harding's, even hosting an event for him at Beechwood when Warren Harding was still governor of Ohio. For a man who prided himself on always trying to do what was right, it must have been quite a blow to have the country see him make a false accusation, especially when his mistake was plastered over headlines across America.

Other papers were kinder. The *Torrance Herald*, close to Frank's Palos Verdes property in California, tried to defend the area's grandest citizen.

> Frank Vanderlip's insinuation . . . did one good thing. An ugly rumor which apparently had gained considerable headway throughout the East was shown up in its true light as mere gossip. The name of Harding remains unsullied. The American people have always rightly considered the high office of the presidency to be above graft. The responsibility of the office is and always has been purifying . . .

> . . . It would be a sad day when that confidence of a people were shattered.
>
> It is probably a good thing that Vanderlip gave voice to the rumor. His testimony before the committee will stop the rumor's progress.
>
> Whatever else one may think of Warren G. Harding, few will believe that he used his high office as a means of acquiring ill gotten wealth.

One week after the first news stories, Roy Moore and Louis Brush each filed a lawsuit in federal court for $600,000 in damages against Frank. There were three charges - "that the plaintiffs were charged by Vanderlip with being financially irresponsible, insolvent and not entitled to credit; that the retired banker caused his speech to be reported in the New York Tribune; and that he approved a report of the speech submitted to him by the Associate Press, thus authorizing publication of the report."

The lawsuit apparently did not concern Frank much. He hired as his attorneys a former ambassador to Great Britain and a former Secretary of War, but had not even bothered to talk to them by the end of March.

The lawyers went to work on his behalf. By April 10, they filed a 1,200 page answer to the charges. In it, Frank stated that rumors of irregularities had been in circulation for some time before his speech. He denied "that he ever made either defamatory statements concerning the new owners of the *Star*, or that the market value of the newspaper's stock had been reduced as a result of the utterance or publication of any of his statements." He also denied knowing whether the newspaper stock had lost value or whether the plaintiffs had been damaged by his speech, and said that he had not "authorized the *New York Tribune* to publish a fair report" of his words.

His answer laid the blame for "added and general circulation and publicity to the alleged and pretended slander" to the *Star's* publication of a false report of the speech. It quoted in full "an editorial from the *Star*, accusing him of bringing President Harding's name into the oil discussion, and it alleged that thus the *Star* publishers 'themselves gave added and general circulation to the current rumor'."

A Crusade

Instead of retreating into seclusion to lick his wounds, Frank was energized by the whole debacle. He decided to organize what he called a Citizens Federal Research Bureau, with an executive committee of prominent men, to conduct their own corruption investigations and report directly to the American people.

He soon realized this would be an unwieldy and slow-moving group, and chose instead to work with two eager young Harvard men. One of them was John Pearmain, son of a Harvard graduate and Boston stock broker. He was, according to Julian Street, "a good man and the finest sort of fellow," who had been at the Briarcliff speech, was apparently inspired by what he heard, and probably hoped that associating with Frank would be good for his career.

A few days later, finding it impossible to interest the press in his work, Frank moved himself and his small staff to Washington, offering his services to the Senate committee, telling Senator Wheeler, "*I want to serve you in your work of investigation, in any way I can, spending my money as you may direct to assist the investigation, and even being your office boy if I can help in that way.*" To many of his business associates, it was another example of Benjamin Strong's belief that "Vanderlip gets very much excited with his experiences, always, and loses his perspective."

Friends worried about his safety, given the reputation of the Bureau of Investigation's William Burns. Frank must have been worried, also, because he tried to take out an accidental death policy for one million dollars, which was refused, something bound to make anyone even more concerned. When Frank realized, one day, that he was being followed, he "went up to the man who was following him and asked him if he cared to know where he was going. The man made some feeble excuse and went away," Julian Street says.

Resignations

A blow came that was much harder on Frank than the lawsuits that soon followed. American Can Company, who counted Frank as a member of its board, asked for his retirement. So did eleven others. A letter from E. P. Swenson, who had served as a vice-president of National City Bank with Frank, and who was president of the Freeport, Texas company, asked for Frank's resignation, saying the company was "not in sympathy with your attitude in public matters."

Frank's reply, given out to the newspapers on April 2, 1924, tells exactly where his own sympathies lay.

"My one regret in the matter is that men with whom I have long been associated in business are now so blind to the present situation in the government at Washington. Had you and your associates the slightest conception of the truth in regard to the corruption which has been current you could not, without the most complete sacrifice of honor, do anything but applaud honest effort to uproot that corruption.

"There have been times, notably 1919, when my judgment regarding the debacle in Europe was at odds once with that of many of my associates, but events confirmed my prophecies with terrible reality.

"Now again, I find Wall Street at variance with my views, but I vouchsafe another predication. If there is not full exposure of the corruption that has honeycombed some of the departments and several of the bureaus of the federal government, business will be at the mercy of the corrupt courts, corrupt prosecuting attorneys and breaking officials will ultimately suffer far more than it ever did through this exposure.

"The great danger to business and government alike lies in suppressing the facts."

With that notification, Frank resigned from all of his directorships, including United States Rubber, International Mercantile

Marine, and a number of railroads. His days of crossing the country in the luxury of private rail cars were at an end. So were many of his business friendships, and their connections to the latest investment tips.

Friends In Old Places

Frank was lucky. Although his peers disagreed, he had strong support among those who had known him well for many years.

Writer Julian Street, whose son would marry Frank's daughter Narcissa three years later, became "more and more Mr. Vanderlip's friend and admirer." He was with Frank in Washington during the Senate investigations. In a letter to his aunt, he voiced his feelings, which he must have also shared with others.

"He has two motives: First, as a public spirited citizen he is determined to render a great and necessary service to the country. Second, he desires to regain the esteem of his fellow citizens which in the past he has always had, and of which he has been justifiably proud. And I want to add this: that important as the second motive is to him, the first motive outweighs the second in his mind. His spirit is that of a crusader . . .

"He is doing a heroic thing for which he is, as yet, getting little thanks from the nation, simply because the nation does not yet understand what he is trying to do for it, and how much what he is doing needs to be done. . . .

"During the war the people were surfeited with sensation. Their nerves were continually on edge; their sense of proportion became distorted with the result that things which before the war would have deeply moved them now hardly catch their interest. In order to attract their attention you must shock them, and since the war that has become hard to do. Mr. Vanderlip did, however, shock them with his 'indiscretion', and I am now convinced that he thereby performed a great public service . . .

"It is true that Mr. Vanderlip has diabetes, but it is equally true that under this new magical insulin treatment he is as vigorous and clearheaded as he was when president of the National City Bank. He can do more work than any of his assistants; he wears them out . . . If his mental equipment is impaired, as his enemies would have us believe, I can only wish that mine was impaired in the same way . . .

"At huge expense and at some risk to his life, he is trying to render a great service to you and to me and to all other Americans."

Another old friend, a few years later, published an article with her own opinion of Frank and his anti-corruption crusade. Caroline Stolp Johnson, the wife of Frank's first mentor, Joseph French Johnson, gave a warm account of an evening spent with Frank beside the fireplace at Beechwood, talking of "old friends, old times and new." Their conversation was "only interrupted by the prattle and play of a charming little granddaughter."

> "The world is unhappy, feverish, poisoned by fear and distrust. Yet even so, it will stand at attention to salute honorable success wrought out of hard conditions. God help sorely beset America if our citizens lack nerve to speak the truth, to defend friends and to try to right wrongs as soon as they are seen!"

The Lasting Effects

Almost a year later, on January 15, 1925, newspapers announced the end of Roy Moore and Louis Brush's lawsuits against Frank. The settlement would be out of court, for an undisclosed sum. Frank would not be found guilty of anything in a court of law. The court of public opinion would remain harder to convince.

For a man who thrived on having a prominent place in economic affairs and public life, 1924 was the end of his career. Frank continued to write and travel, and even appear before another Senate committee, but there would be few headlines, interviews with reporters on the state of the country and the world, or news photographers wanting his picture.

No one goes through that sort of public scrutiny and drama without having some residual effects. Although Julian Street claims that Frank was energized by the fight, which he must have been, the physical toll on him can easily be seen in his 1925 portrait.

Frank A. Vanderlip 1925

When the stock market took its disastrous plunge in 1929, Frank paid a huge price for his anti-corruption stance. His Wall Street connections shut him out of the loop of inside information when he resigned from all the boards of directors. Although a number of his former business peers seem to have been able to pull their money out of the market ahead of the crash, Frank lost a considerable amount. His financial situation never recovered.

Why Did He Do It?

Why would a man like Frank Vanderlip, with an upstanding reputation, work ethic and moral character, make such a gigantic factual and public relations blunder? Did he make an honest mistake, or was he, as he claimed, simply trying to bring a rumor out into the open to be investigated?

He had been out of the excitement of action on the national stage for four years, and, to some extent, probably out of the loop on all the inside news. He loved his country deeply, and was horrified to learn of the type of corruption in government that he would never have considered or allowed to take place in his bank.

One of the men present for the speech, John D. Pearmain, met Frank for the first time at the meeting. "I asked him whether he thought Harding or Wilson had either of them been personally corrupt and he answered instantly and vigorously, "*Not at all, but I feel certain that thorough investigation would reveal a lamentable amount of corruption in their administrations'*." John Pearmain said that Frank stated in the speech, "*The* Marion Star *rumor ought to be investigated in order to clear Harding's name.*"

The best that can be said in Frank's defense is that he honestly thought he was doing the right thing in bringing the story as he knew it out into the light for scrutiny. In the wake of all the other corruption that was being uncovered, it was an understandable, but erroneous, assumption. This theory is backed up by John Pearmain's discussion with Frank just after the speech.

The worst that can be said is that Frank made the horrible mistake of not checking his facts and his sources before bringing negative publicity to himself and to a dead president, and that he did believe, when he spoke, that there were shady dealings in the *Marion Star* transaction. Seen in this way, Frank compounded his error the next morning, when talking to the reporters, by trying to explain his way out of the situation rather than simply admitting his mistake and apologizing to Warren Harding's memory and to the new owners of the newspaper. CEOs up to the present time, when facing reporters with note pads or digital recorders, would sympathize with Frank's predicament.

Perhaps the simplest explanation of his actions comes from Frank himself. In 1935, he wrote his autobiography, "*From Farmboy To Financier.*" The very last paragraph of the last chapter addresses his concerns for the future and gives an insight into a guiding principle of his entire life.

> "*The older I get the more strongly I am persuaded that what we are lacking in our nation and in the world is not economic leadership so much as moral, spiritual leadership. Our greatest need is a philosophy of morality so widely indoctrinated that no man could rise to power among us who was not dominated by that morality.*"

Frank Vanderlip, Genoa, Italy May 6, 1922
Posing in morning suit for news photographer at European Economic Conference

○ ○ ○

Home

Narcissa and Frank Vanderlip look out to sea from their terrace circa 1935
Villa Narcissa, Palos Verdes, California

○ ○ ○

Home

T he yacht *Henrietta* cruised smoothly along the Palos Verdes coastline one March Sunday in 1926. Frank Vanderlip was studying his land.

On board were Frank and Narcissa Vanderlip, their daughter Narcissa, Harry Benedict, and Palos Verdes Project and Syndicate associates and long-time friends Elvon Musick, Jay Lawyer, his son Don K. Lawyer, their wives, and an assortment of other local leaders.

It was a beautiful day. The guests could see most of the coastline of the Peninsula, with gentle waves breaking along the cliffs, and soft folds of the terraces as they angled up to the top of the hill. They gave special attention to the spot in Portuguese Bend where the new Vanderlip home was scheduled to begin construction in the fall, at a cost of $250,000. After owning the hill for 13 years, Frank was building a grand residence that would redefine the meaning of retirement.

View from ocean looking north, Portuguese and Inspiration Points, Palos Verdes 1926
Villa Narcissa, right of center, Harden Gatehouse, top end of Portuguese Point

Just the week before, Frank, former president of the largest bank in the country, had accepted the presidency of the San Pedro Chamber of Commerce. According to the local Torrance newspaper, he "announced his desire to put his shoulder to the wheel as an ordinary California citizen".

The following Thursday, he spoke to the local Torrance Rotary Club. It was the same organization he addressed two years earlier in Briarwood, New York, when he made the speech that irrevocably altered his business life. This time, he talked about making Torrance a great industrial center, and urged a "constantly increasing community spirit as the magnet to new residents".

He declared himself thankful that the test holes in Palos Verdes for oil came up dry. "*The discovery of oil on that property might have burdened me with a large fortune, but it would have destroyed one of the most beautiful spots in the United States.*" Frank sounded very much like a man at peace with himself and his newfound, diminished role in the world.

Three years later, Frank may have wished those wells had spouted gushers of oil.

Oil wells in Torrance, California, Palos Verdes hill in background circa 1920s

The "Unpleasantness of Wall Street" - 1929

The world knows what happened on Black Tuesday, October 28, 1929. On Wall Street, the stock market started a slide that lost over $30 billion dollars in two days. This came after the warning of a mini-crash in March. At that time, National City Bank's newest president, Charles E. Mitchell, had announced a $25 million credit aimed at stopping the slide. His action helped stabilize the market from March until October.

It must have been frustrating to a financial mind like Frank's to sit on the sidelines while all of Wall Street and the banking world were caught in such a crisis. He always felt most alive when he was in the middle of solving a monetary meltdown.

Even though he was somewhat ousted from the halls of financial power, Frank Vanderlip was never a stupid, or uneducated man, when it came to banking. He did not engage in the sort of speculative market gambling that caused so many investors, large and small, to buy stocks on margin, with as little as ten percent of their own money down. He would have seen the signs, and would not have been caught with large amounts of cash or collateral in a volatile market. When brokers were leaping out of office windows in despair, Frank would never have needed to be one of them.

But even prudent men were affected. If most of the people in the country have lost their life savings, they will not be buying new cars from the Auburn Motor Company, where Frank sat on the board of directors. They will not be taking unnecessary train trips or buying unnecessary items shipped to them over rail lines in which Frank was invested. They will not be purchasing land for homes in Palos Verdes.

Frank did not go broke in 1929. His house and school at Beechwood continued functioning as before, with all the employees necessary to make it so. His acreage in Palos Verdes was still well tended. He still cut a dignified appearance in his finely tailored suits, and still wrote articles for respected journals.

What did change was his income from investments compared to his outgo. As he spent money to improve Palos Verdes, the taxes went up exorbitantly. There was simply not as much discretionary money as before to spend on luxuries like a huge mansion. Nor, if there had been funds available, would it have been wise, with the rest of the country falling into a depression that lasted over ten years, until World War II brought life to the economy.

Decorative stone pieces 2013
Originally for Villa Palos Verdes

The building of the Villa Palos Verdes was to have been begun in 1926. Construction had been pushed back until January 1930, when it would have started if the "unpleasantness of Wall Street hadn't happened," according to Frank, Jr. "Acres" of roof tile were already delivered, tons of decorative stone pieces were piled up for use, and a long cypress *allee* was already growing nicely. All would sit silently in place for decades, before most was hauled away for other uses.

At the bottom of Portuguese Bend, where Palos Verdes Drive runs along the cliff, Harry Benedict finished his Villa Francesca gatehouse in the first months of 1930. While both he and Frank's sister Ruth, along with her husband Ed Harden, had planned large mansions, they all abandoned these plans after the Crash.

Somewhere after 1931, even Frank's beloved aviary was deemed too expensive to maintain. The birds were carefully caged up and shipped off to the Wrigley collection on Catalina Island. Their long row of chicken wire cages sat in place for years, before being dismantled in the 1980s.

Sidewalk remnants from bird cages 2013
Looking south to ocean, Portuguese Bend

Frank gave A. E. Hansen approval to develop Rolling Hills from the thousand acres Frank considered to be the "agriculturally worst land" they owned on the peninsula, as long as Frank did not have to lay out any money.

Invested in the World

Frank never gave up on his belief in America's place in the world, especially after the destruction he saw in Europe in 1919. He supported the economic plans set out in the Treaty of Versailles, even though he took issue with some of the provisions. He felt the League of Nations would be beneficial, although he thought it should not inhibit *"national honors or the moral stability of the people."*

He believed disarmament would be good not only to stop senseless destruction and loss of life, but to bring financial stability, when funds being spent on war supplies could be turned to better uses.

When a major economic conference took place in Genoa, Italy, in 1921, Frank sailed to Europe once more to attend as a freelance journalist, without the backing of any financial institution or American governmental department. He no longer was president of a prestigious bank, but the conference seemed, for a time, to be swayed by his ideas, before stronger personalities intervened.

On the same trip, he re-visited a number of European countries, with a goal of studying the financial situation and searching for solutions to Europe's problems. Several of his former colleagues suggested simply ignoring him as the best way to counteract his proposals.

Vanderlip family sails for Europe July, 1921
Narcissa, Frank, Narcissa, Charlotte, Virginia

After the stock market crash in 1929, Frank had plenty to say on the subject, not always in step with other bankers. The depression began, he said, because *"capital kept too much and labor did not have enough to buy its share of things."* If he had not already been forced from the boards of directors of a number of companies, that particular simple statement certainly would have had the same effect.

The national debt under President Hoover had grown from sixteen to forty percent of the Gross National Product, due to the depression. It was not the fault of Frank's longtime friend, Republican Herbert Hoover, but Frank decided to support the policies of Democrat Franklin Roosevelt, who ran for president in 1933. Roosevelt's plan, the New Deal, emphasized relief, recovery and reform.

Frank also backed President Roosevelt's plan to abandon the gold standard, still a controversial topic. Rallying his fighting spirit for a new cause, Frank headed up the Committee for the Nation. It called for the creation of a Federal Monetary Authority, to keep prices stable by controlling foreign exchange, offering national gold stocks and Treasury bills, and regulating the discount rate. While Frank gave a number of talks on the subject and wrote articles and another book, *"Tomorrow's Money - A Financial Program for America"*, the world was controlled by new men with new ideas.

Inventor William Bendix and Frank Vanderlip, Chicago 1934
Union League Club "Gold Policy" dinner

A Quieter Life - 1930s

Life does, however, go on. There were no more parties at Beechwood for 1,000 guests, but there were quieter evenings with friends, in New York and Palos Verdes.

Frank Vanderlip escorts guests to terrace, Villa Narcissa, image from film 1935

Frank and Narcissa Vanderlip dressed for a formal evening out, Beechwood circa 1935

Some time in the early 1930s, taxes also started rising on the land in Spokane, Washington, and Los Molinos, California, with no compensating income. Frank got rid of it all.

He walked with a cane, from affects of his diabetes, but still stood proud and straight, and his mind was as sharp and interested as ever. In 1933, he became one of two editors of the *Economic Forum*, a magazine advocating "stable money," or a price level rule for monetary policy. The same year, he became chairman of a group known as the Committee for the Nation, which wanted to abandon the gold standard and stop the devaluation of the dollar.

Still thinking like a banker, and pondering the financial future of the country, Frank wrote *Tomorrow's Money* in 1934. In it, he promoted a plan for investment banks to be barred from managing investment companies, as a way to dampen the sort of easy margin loans that brought on Black Tuesday. Once again, his suggestions would not have endeared him to a number of prominent bankers. It was part of the debate leading to the Revenue Act of 1936, regulating the activities of mutual funds and giving protection to investors.

There was time now for reflection on a life lived large. The result, in 1935, was Frank's autobiography, *From Farmboy to Financier*. Here, he set down his own story, in his own way, with portions about his youth and early life he had been doling out to reporters for so long that they were almost a recitation, and can be found almost word for word in newspaper interviews given twenty years earlier. Other sections were as reflective as can be expected of a man looking back at a long lifetime, wanting to have his full say.

Ghosts of 1924

The government, also, wanted to hear his story. Not the tale of his life, but his possible knowledge of some still unresolved government issues. This time, the Senate committee was investigating even further back than the Harding administration. Once again, Frank mounted the Capitol steps to face photographers and interrogators.

Senator Gerald Nye headed the Special Committee on Investigation of the Munitions Industry, looking into U. S. financial and banking interests before and during World War I. The Senator wanted to know about the munitions industry in general, illegal bidding for government shipbuilding contracts, why the U. S. entered the war, and who profited from it. Between September 1934 and February 1936, the Committee called 200 witnesses during 93 hearings.

The first week in January 1936, Frank appeared before the committee, along with J. P. Morgan, Jr., and Thomas Lamont. J. P. Morgan. Jr., explained why his bank gave massive loans to Britain, in spite of the State Department's stated neutrality toward the European war in 1914. He said his bank, and finally the country, were not driven to help the Allies "by any individual or individuals or any class, but came in because Germany had made it impossible for the U. S. to refrain any longer." He spoke quickly, to avoid being cut off with questioning. "There are some things it is better to die for than to live without, and a nation's self-respect and independence are two of them."

Nye Commission hearings Jan. 8, 1936
Thomas Lamont & J. P. Morgan listen
While Frank Vanderlip testifies

Frank testified next, telling how the National City Bank came to make loans to Mr. Stillman's beloved France. He admitted the bank had offered loans to France in October 1914, after President Wilson appealed to the country to remain neutral the previous August. Frank said the bank did so because of sympathy for the Allies.

The Nye Hearings, as they were known, sparked the Neutrality Acts of the 1930s, designed to keep the U. S. out of any further foreign wars. No newspaper reports on the state of neutrality between longtime bankers and sometime antagonists J. P. Morgan, Jr., and Frank A. Vanderlip.

Saying Goodbye

Frank Vanderlip left Palos Verdes for the last time at the beginning of June 1937, after a four-month visit. A week after his return to Beechwood, he checked into New York Hospital, on June 16, with "intestinal complications".

The man who took pride in his strength and vigor was very sick. In spite of his diabetes, and a bout of typhoid in his later years, writers still described him as "strong", and "blessed with a magnificent physique".

Two weeks later, his strength gave out. Frank A. Vanderlip died on June 29, 1937, while still in the hospital. At his bedside were his wife Narcissa, daughter Virginia, and sons Kelvin and Frank, Jr.

The New York Times headline June 30, 1937

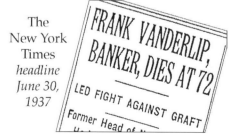

FRANK VANDERLIP, BANKER, DIES AT 72

LED FIGHT AGAINST GRAFT

Former Head of ...

According to at least one source, medicines available later in the century would have saved him, but the truth of that statement will never be known nor, in the end, did it matter at the time.

Frank's death made headlines throughout the country. There were recaps of his life story, praise from many quarters, listings of his business associations and international honors. None of those accomplishments meant as much to his family and those close to him as the loss of the most important force in all of their lives.

The funeral service was held at Beechwood on July 1, with his remains taken afterward for cremation. Frank's ashes were interred at the local Sleep Hollow cemetery, in Westchester County, New York.

The Estate

As would be expected, Frank paid careful attention to the planning of his estate. It was not nearly as large as those of his Rockefeller neighbors, or his mentor James Stillman. Narcissa was his main heir, with trusts set up for his six children, and for the present and future grandchildren.

He trusted and assumed that they would be intelligent enough to handle their financial decisions, and gave the executors and trustees the ability to liquidate the trusts and give them the principal outright. "*I recognize clearly,*" he wrote, "*that there may be in the future changed conditions in regard to property rights, taxation and many other social, economic and political matters, which, if I could foresee, might lead me to make different disposition of my property.*" Frank knew how easily financial conditions in the world could change, and did not want his family put in an unchangeable situation.

There were no bequests to charity, because, Frank said in his will, he made such gifts during his lifetime. Counted among his many contributions to society would, if a list were made, include all of the young bank employees he taught and encouraged, as well as the students and teachers who benefited from Scarborough School, and the residents of property he developed throughout the country.

The Survivors

Narcissa continued to live at Beechwood, with occasional trips to Palos Verdes. She was president of the New York Infirmary for Women and Children for 37 years, and was active in many other charitable organizations. She died in 1966, at the age of 87, in Scarborough.

Palos Verdes has Narcissa to thank for the land donated to build Lloyd Wright's famous Wayfarer's Chapel, completed in 1951, with Narcissa proudly in the front row for the dedication of the Swedenborgian church. It still welcomes thousands of visitors and wedding parties each year. Narcissa

Narcissa Vanderlip circa 1960
Wayfarer's Chapel, Palos Verdes

was a strong supporter of her son Kelvin's promotion of Palos Verdes as the site for development of Marineland of the Pacific, which opened in 1954. It is now the location of a well-planned, luxury hotel.

Five of Frank and Narcissa's six children passed away by 1974. The youngest, John Vanderlip, lived in the Cottage until his death, at the age of 86, in 2001.

Harry Benedict, Frank's "right hand man" for twenty-one years, was widowed twice. Along with attorney Elvon Musick, who was involved in the early formation of Palos Verdes, Harry Benedict invested in Barker Brothers Furniture, and sat on their board of directors for many years, while also helping with the management of Vanderlip family property holdings in Palos Verdes. He continued to

Harry Benedict, Villa Francesca circa 1960s

live at Villa Francesca, with his third wife, until shortly before his death at age 87, in 1977.

Edward Walker Harden returned to the Philippine Islands for an anniversary visit forty years after his Spanish-American War adventure. He died in 1952, at the age of 84. His wife, Frank's sister Ruth, survived him for seven years, passing away in 1959. Their home in Westchester, N.Y, known as the Wilderness, now has its 152 acres divided into single family homes, with the owners all able to use the pool and gardens, while the mansion is their clubhouse. In Palos Verdes, the Harden Gatehouse is still a private home, on just under two acres. Their remaining land is a shoreline park, belonging to the city of Rancho Palos Verdes.

Edward Walker Harden 1939

Joseph French Johnson, Frank's earliest mentor, died twelve years before Frank, in 1925, at the age of 72.

Former Secretary of the Treasury Lyman J. Gage, Frank's second mentor, retired to San Diego, California, where he lived with his third wife, after being twice widowed. He passed away in 1927, at the age of 90.

The Legacy

In many ways, Frank Vanderlip lives on, and not only through his intelligent and artistic descendants, who are active in the arts, finance, technology, and ranching.

Starting with his days in the Aurora machine shop, Frank tried to improve himself, while looking for ways to help those around him. He gave constant financial support to his mother and sister, even long before it was easy for him to do so. Even when he was busy as president of the bank, he still took time and interest to offer a prize to the student at West Aurora High School judged most improved in English composition.

In Chicago, while still a young man learning the world of business, he forced corporations to report the facts of their operations to the public. His early methods of reporting the financial news brought changes to journalistic profession.

In Washington, he not only devised ways to make a war bond purchase seem like a patriotic responsibility, but he tried to be a conscientious employer of thousands of government workers.

At the National City Bank, his list of changes and improvements was legendary. He opened the first American overseas branch banks, actively recruited new business, set up an intern program that is still a high standard for any company to match, proved that a bank's image was not diminished by asking for customers, and advocated a general openness in the bank's dealings. He constantly looked for young recruits to bring into the banking business, as his mentors had helped him find his way to the top.

He located and encouraged a number of men of working class backgrounds who later became prominent, and even stopped, one day while motoring in the White Mountains with a friend, to talk to a poor, barefoot boy. He spent the rest of the day talking to his friend about how to help the boy have a chance to make his way up in the world.

On the world stage, his trip to Japan may not have been of earth shattering importance, but it was a step in bridging a cultural gap between two countries who had much in common, as Frank realized.

In Europe, both before and after World War I, Frank's under-standing of financial conditions was more accurate than he could have known. His ability to interview both kings and factory workers, and his talent for analyzing their concerns, was a rare combination of talents. His books on the subject still have lessons for modern times.

Residents of both coasts, in Sparta, New York, and Palos Verdes, California, thank him for the quality of their surroundings. In Palos Verdes, his vision of "*all the benefits of our civilization filtered free of all the evils*" may not have ever been possible, but the peninsula looks much as Frank imagined, with Mediterranean architecture and a peaceful ambience too often lacking near crowded cities like Los Angeles.

In gratitude for his vision, the city of Rancho Palos Verdes dedicated a small park to Frank, by the edge of the cliff, facing directly toward Catalina Island. Residents often use its benches for quiet contemplation, for a peaceful moment, and even for writing poetry.

Frank A. Vanderlip, Sr., Park, Palos Verdes 2013

His involvement in the founding of the Federal Reserve was not an impulsive act, nor was it something he was directed to do by other bankers. It was the culmination of years spent thinking about the theories of economics, and their applications in the real world of banking business.

His most famous legacy, the Federal Reserve System, is still hotly debated by some. What exists today is not exactly the program Frank envisioned, and he would be the first to join in any intelligent debate over what direction modern banking should take. He was never anyone's "yes man", and he was never afraid of change. Frank would be horrified at the later 20th and early 21st century financial scandals and meltdowns. It would not be surprising to hear him come up with innovative and controversial solutions.

His sense of what was right and good for the country, and his dedication to public knowledge of public affairs, cannot be faulted, even by those who still disagree with the direction of his ideas.

In the end, when analyzing the man that was Frank Vanderlip, one wonders what it was that brought a small town farm boy to the notice of so many intelligent men, who elevated him to such positions of prominence.

Writers who knew him commented on his charm, easy manner, and excitement over any of his projects. His own writing shows his intelligence, dry humor, and strong sense of whatever was the right thing to do in any situation.

But the answer given by Joseph French Johnson is probably the best summation of Frank's life.

"First - he always loved work. He always seemed glad to have something to do and was more interested in his work than he was in his pay envelope.

"Second - he never waited to be told. In his first Chicago job he began to help in making reports before anybody thought of asking him to do so.

"Third - by his study and reading he was always fitting himself for opportunities. And when Dame Opportunity appeared on the horizon Vanderlip always met her more than half way.

"Fourth - that something which he got from his Dutch ancestors, that quality which we call character and personality. No one can describe it accurately, yet all of Vanderlip's friends, if they tried to describe his character, would certainly use such expressions as 'generous, thoughtful of others, open-minded, strong-willed, unpretentious, just and big-hearted.' "

"There we have the secrets . . . summarized in these qualities: a love of work, initiative, constant preparation, and personality founded upon solid character. Nothing new about them, nothing startling - just plain facts that all young men and women in business would do well to keep before them. They are like beacon-fires, pointing the way."

Frank Arthur Vanderlip   November 17, 1864 - June 29, 1937

Looking Forward

Frank would want to have the last words. They are about his belief in the inherent goodness of America, and they are one last vision of his concerns and hopes for the future of the country. They are also words to help explain and understand his perspective on his long, varied, colorful, rewarding life.

"Of course I am proud that I was able to do that, but I have never ceased to wonder whether I was able to do it because I was Vanderlip, or because I was an American.

"And now in conclusion I want to say one solemn word in regard to the supreme lesson which I have drawn from my observation . . . Wherever there has been moderately good government, there has quickly followed astounding progress. The inherent capacity of people under modern conditions to improve their surroundings, given the boon of honest, wise and just government, is marvelous; but whatever a government lacks in honesty, wisdom and judgment this is quickly reflected in a plight that seemingly no amount of fine individual characteristics can overcome.

"No matter in what direction we look, we find some men in governmental positions who seem more moved by personal ambition than by an unselfish desire wisely to serve. No matter what desperate national circumstances may exist, we see that great national needs fail sometimes to bring out from national leaders the unselfish service that their people should have.

"I have said that it appears that half the woes of the world were occasioned by economic ignorance, and it seems as if most of the other half could be traced to selfish political ambition. And so this is the lesson that has dominated all that I have learned. It is that the crime of all crimes, most far-reaching in its effect, the crime which involves harm to more innocent people than any other in the whole category of human frailty is the crime of abusing the privilege to serve.

"And so it all goes back to a sound citizenship, to a comprehension by all of us of our individual responsibility for good government, to the active acceptance of individual responsibility by every man who lays any claim to the rank of good citizenship."   ○ ○ ○

In His Own Words

On politics, reporting, and finances -

"Long ago I discovered that black is not black; never."

On conservatives in financial circles -

"A conservative is a man who thinks nothing new ought ever to be adopted for the first time."

On working to provide a fine environment for children -

"But the truth is that by the time I really could play with them, most of them had gone right ahead and grown up."

On workers having knowledge of their own investment programs -

"The wage earner ought to know the value of stocks himself. He knows the prices of flour, meat and shoes. Frequently he can tell you about the batting records of ball players. If he can master the mathematical details of pitchers, catchers and race horses, he can comprehend the complexities of the stock market."

On the responsibilities of a corporation -

"A great corporation carrying on a public service is not a private thing; it affects too many lives."

On the basic principle of balance of trade -

"No matter how rich a nation may be within itself, if it is deficient in some essential that must be imported, it must have some commodity of equal value that the world wants and will pay for."

On maintaining peace and freedom in the world -

"A normal man needs three meals a day. That need is immediate and he cannot wait for an adjustment which will come 'in the long run.' The human stomach cannot wait."

On relations between labor and management -

"Cutting a cow's throat while you milk her interferes with that maternal quietude of mind which is conducive to a generous down-giving of milk."

On freedom of information -

"The great danger to business and government alike lies in suppressing the facts."

On the value of work and responsibility -

"In this changing world too much ease does not necessarily make for lasting comfort, for contentment or well-being."

On a fair distribution of wealth -

"I am convinced that we will not reach that happy state either by resisting all change or by believing that wealth can be redistributed so that every one can draw material abundance from an inexhaustible government treasury."

On what the country owes to each person -

"I profoundly believe that society does not owe every man a living, but only a fair chance to contribute to the welfare of society sufficient effort to warrant his drawing back from society the elements of an abundant life."

On America's place in the world -

"If we concentrated our wealth and our efforts on America alone and were utterly careless of the fate of the rest of the world, I believe that we would lose our soul."

o   o   o

Out-Takes

In the course of research, there are bound to be stories that have no logical place in a narrative. Below are a few too good to leave out.

Canada

There is a peaceful, tree-lined street in the quiet town of Niagara-On-The-Lake, Ontario, Canada. It is about ten miles north of Niagara Falls, where the river empties into Lake Ontario. On the street, there is a neat house covered in clean, white siding, trimmed with dark shutters, and capped with a proud pair of chimneys. It is known as the Vanderlip House, although no one by that name has lived there in almost two hundred years.

The first of Frank Vanderlip's direct ancestors to come to America was William, who arrived in Pennsylvania from Holland around 1756, with his brother Edward and his grown son Frederick. There is no mention of any women coming with them. If not, William must have found a wife after he arrived, for he had two more boys and two girls. The oldest of them, John, born in 1758, was Frank's great, great grandfather.

The three immigrant men sailed on a British-sponsored ship, under British protection. Like many of the Pennsylvania settlers, they swore allegiance to Britain before they set foot on what was then British territory. They could not have known the consequences of what seemed to be an act of gratitude to the British for giving them a new start in a new land.

When Revolutionary sentiment stirred in the 1770s, many of the Pennsylvania Dutch settlers, known as Pennamites, refused to break their oaths to the British. The results were disastrous. They were attacked repeatedly by Vermont settlers, known as Yankees. Atrocities occurred on both sides. Eventually, many of the Pennamites, including the Vanderlip family, fled to the safety of friendly Indian tribes in 1777, then on to Fort Niagara, in Canada, where they settled in 1784. In the confusion of the escape from Pennsylvania, Edward's wife and two-year-old son Hiram were lost in a swamp. Edward, thinking they were both dead, after fending off several Indian attacks, went on with his brother and family to Canada. The wife managed to survive long enough to get her son to safety and then died. Hiram and his father Edward would not reunite for twenty-eight years. Edward remarried in Canada and had eight more children.

William and his son Frederick both rode with British loyalist militia known as Butler's Rangers around 1780. The requirements to join were simple. A man must bring his own arms, and be able to "shoot well, to march well, and to endure privation and fatigue." Frederick, apparently underage at the time, was mustered out after a year. William served three years, and died in 1785. All of William's surviving children, including the two girls, were each given two hundred acres of land in the area by the British government, somewhere around Niagara.

One of history's many confusions is a family propensity to recycle the same first names, often without a qualifying middle name to help sort out the many Williams and Edwards. This is one of those cases, as the early Vanderlip clan seemed to favor those two names, with more than one indistinguishable set of cousins.

Judging from their ages, it was probably William's younger brother, Edward, who came from Holland, who purchased a house in Niagara-On-The Lake in 1808, and owned it until 1818. Nothing else is known about him, except that he died in 1830. He seems, however, to have been a man of great physical and mental strength.

There was a second Edward, the son of William's son William. This Edward, born in 1793, was 19 when he fought on the Canadian side in the War of 1812. He would have been only 15 when the home was purchased in 1808, rather young to buy a house. He rose to prominence in the area, becoming a militia captain, the owner of a large and prosperous tract of land, and a member of the Brantford township council. If it was this Edward's home, there would be reason to still remember the property as Vanderlip House two hundred years later.

Besides simply being a bit of Vanderlip family history, an interesting part of the tale is the style of construction. A comparison of Beechwood, the Cottage, and the Canadian Vanderlip House speaks for itself.

Beechwood
Scarborough, N. Y.
Before Vanderlip addition
photo 1907

The Cottage
Palos Verdes,
California
photo 2012

Vanderlip House
Niagara-On-The-Lake
Ontario, Canada
photo 2012

Frank Vanderlip's two homes and his ancestor's Canadian house

William Vanderlip's son John, later described as a "sturdy woodsman", moved from Canada to Vermont and took the Freeman's Oath in 1792. He and his son Stephen then went on to Waverly, N. Y. in 1805, moving the rest of the family there two years later. Their house became an inn, interestingly also known for years as Vanderlip House.

A Famous Suit

This story could not be told any better than it appeared in the Aurora Beacon-News on August 16, 1907.

VANDERLIP OUT IN PURE WHITE

FORMER AURORA MACHINIST
MAKES BIG SENSATION

It is a far cry from overalls in a machine shop in Aurora to immaculate white evening clothes in a fashionable hotel at Long Beach, N. Y., but Frank A. Vanderlip has successfully looped the gap.

Saturday night all had to sit up and take notice when he strode into the dining room at the hotel garbed in evening clothes of pure white serge . . .

. . . The trousers were the regulation dress trousers, the waistcoat the regulation V shaped evening waistcoat. The front view of the coat was much the same as the regular dresscoat, but instead of having long flowing tails it hugged the waist tightly and came to a point just a few inches below the waistline.

The collar and the facing of the lapels were white silk. The effect was carried out by white soft leather shoes and a white silk bow tie.

Mr. Vanderlip's white evening clothes held all eyes and were on all tongues and imbittered all feminine hearts.

Frank's outfit was apparently not photographed for posterity, but it must have been so dazzling that no one bothered to report on what Narcissa was wearing.

Pipe Damage

Frank took up the habit of smoking cigars, after being left a number of fine ones in the will of a man he admired. Some time later, he apparently switched to a pipe. As a charitable gift in 1915, Frank donated $30,000 worth of radium to help a convict in Sing Sing prison, whose life was threatened by a cancer on his lip, caused by "smoking a short stemmed pipe."

The prisoner's life was saved. Frank, reassured that his own pipe smoking did not have to be deadly, arranged for the unused radium to be kept for the free use of other inmates when necessary.

The Scroll

When Frank Vanderlip was a raw new recruit to his position as vice president of National City Bank in 1902, he accompanied Mr. Stillman to a hotel one day, to extend a dinner invitation to a gentleman visiting from overseas. The man was such an important personage that Mr. Stillman uncharacteristically kept readjusting his cravat as they waited while their cards were sent up.

Frank describes the scene. *"Then we were ushered into the presence of Viscount Shibusawa and found him to be as roly-poly as a friendly, gilded statue of Buddha; in a richly made kimono of silk embroidered with golden threads, he sat with a fat leg tucked under him in an easy-chair. The fatty eyelids that he lifted to meet our gaze had been cast down as he read from an enormous scroll covered with the black brush-strokes of Japanese characters. The unread portion was still tightly rolled upon a polished stick but the yards of paper through which he already had tracked his way made a rustling pile upon the floor about his chair, and it was truly fascinating to find this big man of another world in the very act of absorbing information."*

When the introductions were made through a translator, the Viscount surprisingly fixed his gaze on Frank, and spoke with excitement. *"The Japanese characters on the scroll in his hands, he explained, were the translation of some articles about the American commercial invasions of Europe written by Frank A. Vanderlip."*

After a further polite exchange and the offering of the dinner invitation, Frank and Mr. Stillman returned to the bank, without Mr. Stillman even mentioning the scroll. A few days later, one of the other vice presidents came to Frank's desk to say the bank would like to publish Frank's articles in a booklet. Nothing about Viscount Shibusawa was mentioned, but Frank knew the "suggestion" came down from Mr. Stillman.

Frank took his trip to Japan eighteen years later, after Mr. Stillman's death. If the older man's spirit could have gone along, he would have looked on with pride and envy. Frank's host was the very same Viscount Yeiji Shibusawa, the greatest banker in Japan.

Viscount Yeiji Shibusawa
1908

The Mystery Of The Overcoat

Secretary of the Treasury Lyman J. Gage was one of Frank's oldest friends. Frank called him a *"loyal friend, a wise instructor and a noble example, to whom I owe the thing of greatest value in my career, Opportunity."* In his photographs, he is a serious, no-nonsense money manager. While he may have been all of this, he did have a lighter side. It shows in his following letter to Frank. The greeting also illustrates how rare the use of Frank's first name normally was.

Point Loma, California, October 2nd, 1923

Dear Frank: -

I call you 'Frank' to show you that I wish to be kindly and considerate in the *painful* matter whereof I am obliged to write. It is a sad tale of an overcoat, and there is money in it, but I will not expose you to the public, as I have known you too long to do that.

But let me begin. When I visited you at Palos Verdes some weeks ago, it never entered my head that you would 'short change' me on overcoats. Perhaps you did not intend it. It does not look as if you did because the overcoat which was worked off on me had in it, it now seems, quite a decent pair of gloves and a small purse containing a five dollar bill and some small change, and you are too good a business man to throw those items in, if it was of set purpose you made the swap of overcoats with me. Besides, there was very small value in *my* overcoat, which was retained at Palos Verdes, and a superior value in the one which in my innocence I brought away.

Some time has elapsed since this occurrence took place, but there is an old adage that 'murder will out'. It is now out!

For weeks, after discovering in one of the pockets of what I supposed was my overcoat, the purse and contents in question, I have been with consistent honesty trying to find the owner thereof. My theory was that some one had on some occasion borrowed the coat from me and unconsciously left the purse in it. All my efforts in that direction, however, were futile.

But yesterday, Mrs. Ballou was at our house and I asked her if she had lost a purse. To this she answered no and put out several interrogatories and finally took into her hands the coat in question and triumphantly exclaimed: "This is not *your* coat - here is a tag stitched under the collar - it reads F. A. Vanderlip and it was made in London." Thus the whole mystery was cleared up and I am revealing it to you. See?

Understand, I am not accusing anybody. Nor am I complaining about the situation. The coat is a better one than mine - a good deal better one. Why should I worry? Besides, as I said, there is cash money in it.

Nevertheless, you ought to know what I know, and so I'm telling you. If you were ashamed that I was wearing too cheap a coat and resorted to this method of exchange as a delicate artifice, that's one thing; but if, as is probably the case, you then knew nothing of it, why that's different. Now what? Can I get my old coat back? Where is it? How can the re-exchange be accomplished?

Are you soon to return to California? I will do anything you suggest, even to returning you the money.

Awaiting your advice, and enjoying in the meantime the feeling of having money in my pocket and a good overcoat on my back, I am, as ever, with full confidence in your good intentions.   Your friend, Lyman J. Gage

A Final Victory

Frank Vanderlip predicted the second World War, as far back as 1919. He did not live to see its horrors.

Frank preached that, in times of crisis, people would starve if supplies could not actually arrive where they were needed. For this reason, he saw the American International Corporation, which he helped develop *"the most important business thing I have ever done."* When the U. S. went into the first World War, AIC quickly built merchant ships for the government's Emergency Fleet Corporation, to deliver American-made goods to a desperate Europe. Even though the war was over before the ships were ready, the lessons learned about naval construction were put to good use during the next great conflict.

The World War II Liberty Ships are famous. There were 2,710 of them built, all exactly alike, so they could be mass-produced from the same parts. They were 442 feet long, and 57 feet wide. They could carry 2,840 Jeeps, or 440 tanks, or 230 million rounds of rifle ammunition.

To honor patriots, the first one was named the Patrick Henry. Next were names of the signers of the Declaration of Independence. Each ship cost $2 million to build. Any group raising that amount in Liberty Bonds could suggest a name for a ship, within certain parameters. The name had to be a prominent, but deceased, American.

Liberty Ship Frank A. Vanderlip 1944

Liberty Ship number 1821 was launched as the Frank A. Vanderlip, in 1943. Before being completed, the ship was turned over to Great Britain in the Lend Lease program, and renamed the Sambuff, as all such loaned ships were given names beginning with Sam. Frank would have been happy his ship was helping the British, but probably not so thrilled to see his name removed from her bow.

Turned back over to the U. S. in 1944, the Frank A. Vanderlip sailed under her original name for four years, until being laid up at Wilmington, North Carolina in 1948. The Frank A. Vanderlip was scrapped in New Jersey in 1967, thirty years after Frank's death.

A Liberty Ship was a fitting monument for a man who did not want to see a war. But, when his country did get into two wars during his lifetime, he devised new ways to raise funds - $200 million in bonds for the Spanish-American War, and an amazing $4 billion in Thrift Stamps during World War I.

The Frank A. Vanderlip was a sturdy, no-nonsense ship, designed to do its job well, not a slim, flashy racing schooner. While Frank enjoyed his famously elegant homes and lifestyle, he never, as he himself pointed out, was part of a culture buying yachts or racehorses, preferring to spend his time on work, his family, and the school he proudly built at Beechwood.

Improvement through construction seems to have been in Frank's DNA. No project was too large, from the new bank at 55 Wall Street, to his redesign of Beechwood and its grounds, to a brand new port city in Texas, to the rebuilding of the entire town of Sparta, to his grand vision for Palos Verdes. He would have wanted to be a part of the mass building of thousands of Liberty Ships.

Frank's journeys to Europe were all by ship, much more luxurious than any could be on the Frank A. Vanderlip, but through the same Atlantic waters. He believed it was America's duty to help Europe during and after World War I by delivering not only weapons, but all the supplies necessary to feed the starving, demoralized survivors he saw after the conflict's end. He would have been pleased to see his ship laden with such supplies.

When the 1924 Harding administration scandals raised their ugly heads, Frank stood up against secrecy in government. Although his stance cost him dearly, he believed it was his duty as a citizen.

Seeing his name proudly emblazoned on the bow of a ship sailing with the American Navy would have been a proud vindication for a banker who, in many ways, made changes in America that have lasting effects all the way to the present day.

Stone with Frank Vanderlip's initials 2012
Carved for use at Villa Palos Verdes circa 1920s

o   o   o

Awards and Memberships

International Awards of Frank A. Vanderlip

France - Chevalier of the Legion of Honor
Belgium - Commander of the Order of Leopold
Greece - Royal Order of George I
Montenegro - Order of Danilo I

Club Memberships of Frank A. Vanderlip

<u>New York, N. Y</u>

Economic Club
Metropolitan Club
Bankers Club
India House
City Club
Union League Club

<u>Washington, D. C.</u>

Cosmos Club
Metropolitan Club
Commercial Club

<u>Scarborough, N. Y.</u>

Sleepy Hollow Country Club

<u>Chicago</u>

Union League Club
Press Club

Partial List of Directorships of Frank A. Vanderlip

American International Corporation
Carnegie Foundation for the Advancement of Teaching - Trustee
Riggs National Corporation
Union Pacific Railroad
National City Bank of New York
Continental Can Company
Freeport - Texas Company
United States Rubber Company
International Marine Company
International Mercantile Marine Company
United States Realty and Improvement Company
Aviation Corporation

o o o

Illustration Credits

Farm To Factory

Chicago

Washington - Part I

The War Years, Continued
p. 192   Both, Op. Cit., LOC

The Shield

p. 193   Courtesy Museum of the City of New York
p. 196   Courtesy Library of Congress George Grantham Bain Collection
p. 197   Collection of Vicki Mack

Russia
p. 199   Courtesy Nevsky-Prospekt.com
p. 201   Photo by John Nelson
p. 202   Courtesy Nevsky-Prospekt.com
p. 203   Upper, Courtesy Nevsky-Prospekt.com
p. 203   Lower, Photo by Grigori Petrowitsch Goldstein
p. 204   Courtesy Alan Mason Chesney Medical Archives of the Johns Hopkins
         Medical Institutions, Vashti Bartlett Collection
p. 205   Left, Painting by Ivan Vladimirov
p. 205   Middle, Photo by Fridtjof Nansen
p. 205   Right, Op. Cit., LOC
p. 206   "Railway Trip Across Russia"

Europe
p. 209   Collection of Stephen Benedict
p. 211   Collection of Vicki Mack
p. 212   Upper, Photographer unknown
p. 212   Lower, Photographer unknown
p. 213   Op. Cit., LOC
p. 214   Op. Cit., LOC
p. 215   Left, Photographer unknown
p. 215   Middle, Op. Cit., LOC
p. 215   Right, Photographer unknown
p. 216   Collection of David Kase
p. 217   Op. Cit., LOC
p. 218   Both, Collection of David Kase
p. 219   Courtesy of Military Intelligence Division, General Staff, U. S. Army
p. 220   Op. Cit., LOC
p. 222   Collection of David Kase
p. 223   Upper Left and Right, Photographer unknown
p. 223   Lower right, Photographer unknown
p. 224   Op. Cit., LOC
p. 225   Both, Photographer unknown
p. 226   Both, Collection of Vicki Mack
p. 227   Courtesy National Library of France
p. 228   Photo by Vicki Mack
p. 230   Collection of Vicki Mack

Palos Verdes - Part II, Continued

The Duck Pond

The Duck Pond, Continued

Washington - Part II

Home

Out-Takes

o o o

Bibliography

The following listings are main sources of information. Most are contemporary to the time, a number are first-hand accounts.

Benedict, Harry, Unpublished Autobiography, 1969.

Booth, Charles Edwin, "*The Vanderlip, Van Derlip, Vander Lippe Family In America*" (Published Privately 1914).

Cleveland, Harold van B., and Thomas F. Huertas, "*Citibank 1812-1970*" (Cambridge, Massachusetts: Harvard University Press 1985).

Gage, Lyman J., "*Memoirs of Lyman J. Gage*" (New York: House of Field, Inc. 1937).

Hanson, A. E., "*Rolling Hills - The Early Years*" (Pasadena, California: City of Rolling Hills 1978).

Roberts, Priscilla, "Frank A. Vanderlip And The National City Bank During The First World War", *Essays in Economic and Business History*, Vol. 20, p. 145-166 (Mt. Pleasant, Michigan: Economic and Business History Society 2002).

Stephenson, Nathaniel Wright, "*Nelson W. Aldrich - A Leader in American Politics*" (New York: Charles Scribners' Sons 1930).

Vale, Gilbert, "*Fanaticism; Its Source and Influence: Illustrated by the Simple Narrative of Isabella, in the Case of Matthias, Mr. and Mrs. B. Folger, Mr. Pierson, Mr. Mills, Catherine, Isabella, &c. a Reply to W. L. Stone, with Descriptive Portraits of All the Part*" (New York: G. Vale 1835).

Vanderlip, Frank A., "*The American 'Commercial Invasion' of Europe*" (New York: Republished by National City Bank of New York from Scribners' Magazine 1902).

Vanderlip, Frank A., "*From Farmboy To Financier*" (New York: D. Appleton-Century Company, Inc. 1935).

Vanderlip, Frank A., Letters from Frank A. Vanderlip to James A. Stillman, 1919.

Vanderlip, Frank A., *"Tomorrow's Money - A Financial Program for America"* (New York; Reynal and Hitchcock 1934).

Vanderlip, Frank A., Unpublished Japan trip diary 1920.

Vanderlip, Frank A., *"What Happened To Europe"* (New York: The MacMillan Company 1919).

Vanderlip, Frank A., *What Next In Europe"* (New York: Harcourt, Brace and Company, Inc. 1922)

Winkler, John K., *"The First Billion - The Stillmans and the National City Bank"* (New York: The Vanguard Press 1934)

Periodicals include the following:

New York Times, Los Angeles Times, Spokane Spokesman, Scribner's Magazine, Moody's Magazine, Mid-Wee Pictorial, Aurora Beacon-News, Chicago Tribune, McClure's Magazine, Palos Verdes Bulletin, Torrance Herald, Sunset Magazine, Kendall County Record, New York Tribune, The Economist, New York Spectator, Spokane Daily Chronicle, Lyons Republican.

○ ○ ○

Eucalyptus trees in the fog, Palos Verdes Drive North 2001
Planted during Frank Vanderlip era development of Palos Verdes, California

Timeline

Year	Events In Frank A. Vanderlip's Life
1864	Born in Aurora, Illinois
1878	Father dies on farm in Oswego, Illinois
1880	Family loses farm, moves to Aurora
1885	Editor, *Aurora Evening Post*
1886	Moves to Chicago, Investor's Agency
1889	Reporter, *Chicago Tribune*
1892	Financial Editor, *Chicago Tribune*
1893	
1894	Editor, *The Economist*
1896	
1897	Moves to Washington, D. C., Assistant Secretary of the Treasury
1898	
1902	Moves to New York, Vice President, National City Bank of New York
1903	Married Mabel Narcissa Cox
1905	Purchases Beechwood
1907	
1909	President, National City Bank of New York
1910	Jekyll Island Federal Reserve Planning Session
1913	Purchased Palos Verdes, California
1914	
1917	Spends one year in Washington, D. C.
1918	Bank Chairman James J. Stillman dies
1919	Trip to Europe; Leaves bank
1920	Rebuilds Sparta, New York; trip to Japan
1923	Begins developing Palos Verdes
1924	Testifies during Teapot Dome scandals
1937	Dies in New York

Timeline

World Events Affecting Frank A. Vanderlip	Presidents
Civil War; President Lincoln re-elected	Abraham Lincoln 1861-65
	Rutherford Hayes 1877-81
Thomas Edison patents electric incandescent lamp	James Garfield 1881
· · · · · · · · · · · · · · · · ·	· · · · · · · · · · · ·
	Chester Arthur 1881-85
Haymarket Riots, Chicago	Grover Cleveland 1885-89
	Benjamin Harrison 1889-93
Columbian Expostion, Chicago; Stock market panic	Grover Cleveland 1893-1897
William Jennings Bryan "Cross of Gold" speech	
· · · · · · · · · · · · · · · · ·	· · · · · · · · · · · ·
	William McKinley 1897-1901
Spanish-American War	
	Theodore Roosevelt 1901-09
Bank Crisis of 1907	
· · · · · · · · · · · · · · · · ·	· · · · · · · · · · · ·
	William Taft 1909-1913
Federal Reserve founded	Woodrow Wilson 1913-21
World War I begins in Europe	
· · · · · · · · · · · · · · · · ·	· · · · · · · · · · · ·
U. S. enters World War I; Russian Revolution begins	
· · · · · · · · · · · · · · · · ·	· · · · · · · · · · · ·
	Warren Harding 1921-23
Teapot Dome scandal begins	Calvin Coolidge 1923-1929
	Herbert Hoover 1929-1933
	Franklin Roosevelt 1933-45

About The Author

Vicki Mack is a photographer and author, and a graduate of the University of Missouri School of Journalism.

She has photographed six presidents of the United States, three governors of California, and thousands of happily married wedding couples.

Her previously published books include "The Groom's Guide - Almost Everything A Man Needs To Know," and "Up Around The Bend - Stories and Legends In Palos Verdes' Portuguese Bend," which she co-authored with Don Christy.

Vicki lives in one of the historic Spanish-style homes built in Palos Verdes during Frank Vanderlip's development of the area, with her David, and a backyard frequently filled with peafowl.

o   o   o